CW00558735

D

SCOTTISH GAELIC TEXTS

VOLUME EIGHTEEN

TUATH IS TIGHEARNA

TENANTS AND LANDLORDS

THE SCOTTISH GAELIC TEXTS SOCIETY

OFFICE BEARERS: Session 1994 – 95

MAR CHUIMHNEACHAN AIR

Eric Cregeen agus Eachann Ceanadach

CERTIFICATE OF MEMBERSHIP

of the

Highland Land Law Reform Association

(Hector McDonald was the Editor's great-grandfather.)

TUATH IS TIGHEARNA

TENANTS AND LANDLORDS

An Anthology of Gaelic Poetry of Social and Political
Protest from the Clearances to the Land Agitation
(1800–1890)

edited by

Donald E. Meek
MA, PhD, FRHistS
Professor of Celtic, University of Aberdeen

Published by Scottish Academic Press

for the

SCOTTISH GAELIC TEXTS SOCIETY

Published in 1995
by Scottish Academic Press Ltd.
56 Hanover Street, Edinburgh EH2 2DX
on behalf of The Scottish Gaelic Texts Society

ISBN 0 7073 0752 X

ACKNOWLEDGEMENTS

The Society gratefully acknowledges grants from the following
towards the costs of publication of this volume:

The Western Isles Islands Council
The University of Edinburgh
The University of Glasgow

Chuidich Comhairle nan Leabhraichean
am foillsichear le cosgaisean an leabhair seo.

Printed in Great Britain by
Martins the Printers Ltd, Berwick upon Tweed

CONTENTS

INDEX OF FIRST LINES

INDEX OF GAELIC TITLES

INDEX OF TITLES OF TRANSLATIONS

PREFACE

THIS book has been many years in the making. The possibility of such a volume first occurred to me in the mid-1970s, when, at the invitation of Professor Derick S. Thomson, I was preparing my edition of the songs of Màiri Mhòr nan Oran (Meek 1977b). Scanning the files of late nineteenth-century Highland newspapers, I became aware that, in addition to songs recorded from oral transmission and those already in print, a number of relevant poems had been preserved in the newspaper columns. I reasoned that, on the basis of these sources, it might be valuable to compile an anthology of Gaelic poetry of social and political protest.

Initial scanning of the sources in the mid-1970s was followed by visits, as time would allow, to newspaper offices and libraries, chiefly the *Oban Times* Office, John Street, Oban, and occasionally Inverness Public Library and the Mitchell Library, Glasgow. I wish to thank the staff of these institutions for their helpfulness, but special acknowledgement is due to Mrs E. MacKillop of the *Oban Times* for accommodating my frequent visits.

I owe more than I can adequately express to my immediate family. My wife, Dr Rachel Meek, has acted as my voluntary research assistant, indexing and transcribing some of the texts, compiling the General Index and cross-checking the entire Glossary. My daughters, Rhoda and Anna, have exercised great patience. On several occasions (some as recent as 1994), they have excused me, when, during a 'holiday', I have disappeared to consult newspaper files which have been suspiciously close at hand. As the book has been compiled in my 'spare' time, in the midst of many competing demands and without any formal academic support, my family has, inevitably, borne the brunt of my commitment to the project, particularly during weekends.

1

Beyond my family, my first debt is to Mr Hugh Barron, Honorary Secretary of the Gaelic Society of Inverness, who transcribed the texts of three songs and provided valuable references. The Gaelic Society of Inverness has also allowed me to re-use material published initially in Meek 1977c.

Other friends and institutions have generously provided texts recently recorded from oral transmission. One poem (Poem 40) has been furnished by Mrs Mary Allan, a native of Kilmuir, Skye, and I am deeply indebted to her and to her family for their generous co-operation. Mrs Jo MacLean (née MacDonald) has kindly allowed me to use texts which she herself collected from oral transmission in Skye (or from Skye sources) in the early 1970s. Mr Allan Campbell, Director of Commun na Gàidhlig and formerly a producer with BBC Radio Highland, has permitted me to publish the text of a song (Poem 20) which he recorded in Glendale. He has also kindly read the text and notes of Poems 20, 21 and 22. Mr Donald M. MacCuaig, Bowmore, sent texts of Poem 7, and shed light on Islay place-names. The School of Scottish Studies has permitted the use of texts and parts of texts first published in *Tocher*; Dr Margaret Mackay, Director of the School, has allowed me to incorporate material from the important versions of Poems 11 and 30 furnished by the late Hector Kennedy, Heylipol, Tiree.

I am grateful to those who have listened to my lectures and have provided an opportunity for publication. In particular, the Scottish Oral History Group invited a lecture on this theme as part of a memorable conference, 'Go Listen to the Crofters', held in Inverness in October 1986 to celebrate the Centenary of the Crofters' Holdings (Scotland) Act. My lecture was later published as 'The Role of Song in the Highland Land Agitation' (Meek 1990), some of which has been re-used in this volume.

Mr Murdo MacDonald, Archivist, Argyll and Bute District Council, gave useful references relating to mainland Argyll, and Dr David Bebbington of the Department of History, University of Stirling, has helped me to understand some of the complexities of government administration in the 1880s, especially with reference to the career of Jesse Collings. Mr Hugh Cheape, Assistant Keeper, National Museums of Scotland, Edinburgh, spontaneously provided the text of his forthcoming article on Poem 1, and elucidated points in the poem. In the wider field, the foundational research of Dr James Hunter offered the first historical framework for understanding this greatly neglected body of Gaelic evidence. The later, meticulous work of Dr I.M.M. MacPhail provided invaluable detail about particular localities, and has facilitated the contextualising of several poems. Further specific debts are acknowledged in the Notes to the poems.

I am grateful to the Scottish Gaelic Texts Society for the invitation to contribute this volume to its main series. Professor Derick S. Thomson, President of the Society, gave advice on the presentation and production of the material. Mr James Gleasure, Honorary Secretary of the Society, supervised the production of the volume, and helped to apply some gentle pressure to the beleaguered editor. The Readers appointed by the Society, Mr Kenneth D. Mac-Donald (Glasgow) and Dr John MacInnes (Edinburgh), read an earlier draft of this book, and I thank them for help on specific points. Mr MacDonald's detailed comments and suggestions have been of great value, both in eradicating errors and in enhancing the interpretation of texts.

My final debt is perhaps the greatest. I was introduced to the living tradition of Gaelic song and its role within the Gaelic community in the early 1970s, when I was invited to accompany the late Eric Cregeen, of the School of Scottish Studies, on his field-trips in my native island of Tiree. As my friend and later my colleague at the University of Edinburgh, Eric taught me to appreciate the historical value of song – 'true' song, as one of Tiree's song-bearers, Hector Kennedy, would have called it. It was through Hector's singing in 1971 that I first became fully aware of the remarkable resources still available within the active tradition of Highland communites. I therefore dedicate the volume to the memory of Eric and Hector, who represent, respectively, the collectors and tradition-bearers of the Highlands and Islands. In so doing, I trust that it is a 'true' book, fairly reflecting the range of perceptions of those poets who lived through the turmoils of the nineteenth century.

Donald E. Meek
King's College, Old Aberdeen
January 1995

BIBLIOGRAPHY

Manuscripts
Minutes of the Argyllshire Constabulary Committee (Argyll and Bute District Council Archives, Lochgilphead).
Mulbuie Land League Minute Book. Minute Book of the Mulbuie Branch of the Highland Land Law Reform Association. (For a photocopy of the volume I am deeply grateful to the late Dr Marinell Ash.)
National Library of Scotland MS 14986. J. Murdoch, 'The Queen of the Hebrides'.
Scottish Record Office GD 1/36. Sheriff Ivory Papers.
Scottish Record Office. High Court Records.

Newspapers
The Northern Chronicle. Inverness.
The Oban Times. Oban.
The Scottish Highlander. Inverness.
The West Highland Free Press. Breakish, Skye.

Books, journals and articles
Barron, H. (1976): 'Verse, Fragments and Words from Various Districts', in *TGSI*, 48: 339-70.
Barron, H. (n.d.): 'Some Notes on the Gillespies: An Inverness-shire Sheep Farming Family', in *Sàr Ghaidheal: Essays in Memory of Rory Mackay*, 17-33. Inverness.
Cameron, A. (1986): *Go Listen to the Crofters.* Stornoway.
Cameron, H. (ed.) (1932): *Na Bàird Thirisdeach.* Glasgow.
Campbell, J. L. (ed.) (1958): *Gaelic Words and Expressions from South Uist and Eriskay*, compiled by the Rev. Father Allan MacDonald. Dublin.
Cheape, H. (1995): 'Song on the Lowland Shepherds: Popular Reactions to the Highland Clearances', in *Scottish Economic and Social History*, 15: 85-100.
(A') Chòisir Chiùil (no date): *The St Columba Collection of Gaelic Songs.* Parts I-III. Paisley.
Collings, J., and Green, J. L. (1920): *Life of the Right Hon. Jesse Collings.* London.
Cregeen, E., and MacKenzie, D. (1978): *Tiree Bards and their Bardachd.* Coll.
D. C. M. [Donald C. MacPherson] (1877): 'Oran nan Ciobairean Gallda; agus mar a thàinig na caoirich cheann-riabhach do'n Ghaidhealtachd', *An Gàidheal*, 6: 203-6.
Devine, T. M. (1988): *The Great Highland Famine.* Edinburgh.

Devine, T. M. (1989): 'The Emergence of the New Elite in the Western Highlands and Islands, 1800-60', Chapter Six in T. M. Devine (ed.), *Improvement and Enlightenment: Proceedings of the Scottish Historical Studies Seminar, University of Strathclyde.* Edinburgh.

Devine, T. M. (1994): *Clanship to Crofters' War: The Social Transformation of the Scottish Highlands.* Manchester.

Dùghalach, A. (1829): *Orain, Marbhrannan agus Duanagan Gaidhealach* le Ailein Dughalach, Filidh Mhic-Ic-Alastair. Inverness.

Ewing, W. (ed.) (1914): *Annals of the Free Church of Scotland,* I, II. Edinburgh.

Gibson, R. (1986): *Crofter Power in Easter Ross: the Land League at Work 1884-88.* Highland Heritage Educational Trust.

Gillies, H. C. (ed.) (1880 edn): *The Gaelic Songs of the Late Dr MacLachlan, Rahoy.* Glasgow.

Grannd, S. (1990): 'Three Songs of the Land Agitation Period from South Argyll', in *SGS,* XVI (1990): 55-65.

Grant, J. S. (1992): *A Shilling for your Scowl: The History of a Scottish Legal Mafia.* Stornoway.

Grimble, I. (1962): *The Trial of Patrick Sellar.* Edinburgh.

Hunter, J. (1974): 'The Politics of Highland Land Reform' in *SHR,* 53: 45-68.

Hunter, J. (1976): *The Making of the Crofting Community.* Edinburgh.

Hunter, J. (1986): *For the People's Cause.* Edinburgh.

Hunter, J. (1995): *On the Other Side of Sorrow: Nature and People in the Scottish Highlands.* Edinburgh.

Knudsen, Th. (1969): *Calum Ruadh, Bard of Skye: Seminar at the School of Scottish Studies, June 13th 1968.* Dansk Folkemindesamling (Danish Folklore Archives: DFS Information 69/1). Copenhagen.

Livingston, W. (1882): *Duain agus Orain le Uilleam Mac Dhunleibhe, am Bard Ileach.* Glasgow.

MacAmhlaigh, D. (1980): ' "Aramach am Beàrnaraigh"...1874', in D. MacAmhlaigh (deas.), *Oighreachd agus Gabhaltas,* 1-11. Aberdeen.

MacArthur, E. M. (1990): *Iona: The Living Memory of a Crofting Community 1750-1914.* Edinburgh.

MacCallum, D. (1912): 'The Bards of the Movement', in J. Cameron, *The Old and the New Highlands and Hebrides,* 144-55. Kirkcaldy.

MacDhòmhnaill, I. (1980): 'Blàr a' Chumhaing agus Cor nan Croitearan 1882-1883', in D. MacAmhlaigh (deas.), *Oighreachd agus Gabhaltas,* 12-22. Aberdeen.

MacDonald, A. and MacDonald A. (eds) (1911): *The MacDonald Collection of Gaelic Poetry.* Inverness.

Macinnes, A. I. (1994): 'Landownership, Land Use and Elite Enterprise in Scottish Gaeldom: from Clanship to Clearance in Argyllshire, 1688-1858', in T. Devine (ed.), *Scottish Elites,* 1-35. Edinburgh.

Mackay, M. (1979): 'Hector Kennedy', in *Tocher*, 32: 69-106.
MacKenzie, A. (1966 edn): *The History of the Highland Clearances.* Inverness.
McKichan, F. (1977): *The Highland Clearances.* Harlow.
MacLean, D. (1915): *Typographia Scoto-Gadelica.* Edinburgh.
MacLean, D. (ed.) (1913): *The Spiritual Songs of Dugald Buchanan.* Edinburgh.
Maclean, of Dochgarroch, L. (1980): *The Raising of the 79th Highlanders.* Coll.
McLean, M. (1991):*The People of Glengarry: Highlanders in Transition 1745-1820.* Montreal.
MacLean, S. (1985): *Ris a' Bhruthaich: The Criticism and Prose Writings of Sorley MacLean*, ed. W. Gillies. Stornoway.
MacLeod, Murdo (1962): *Bàrdachd Mhurchaidh a' Cheisdeir.* Edinburgh.
MacLeòid, I. N. (deas.) (1916): *Bàrdachd Leódhais.* Glasgow.
MacLeòid, I. N. (1980): 'Reud na Pàirce, no Creach Mhór nam Fiadh, 1887', in D. MacAmhlaigh (deas.), *Oighreachd agus Gabhaltas*, 32-43. Aberdeen.
MacLeòid, N. (1975 edn): *Clàrsach an Doire.* Glasgow.
Mac-na-Ceàrdadh, G. (deas.) (1879): *An t-Oranaiche.* Glasgow.
MacPhàil, C. C. (1947): *Am Filidh Latharnach.* Stirling.
MacPhail, I. M. M. (1979): 'The Highland Elections of 1884-1886', in *TGSI*, 50: 368-402.
MacPhail, I. M. M. (1985): 'Gunboats to the Hebrides', in *TGSI*, 53: 531-67.
MacPhail, I. M. M. (1989): *The Crofters' War.* Stornoway.
Meek, D. E. (1977a): 'The Prophet of Waternish', in the *West Highland Free Press*, 8 July 1977.
Meek, D. E. (ed.) (1977b): *Màiri Mhór nan Oran: Taghadh d'a h-Orain le Eachdraidh a Beatha agus Notaichean.* Glasgow.
Meek, D. E. (1977c): 'The Gaelic Poets of the Land Agitation', in *TGSI*, 49: 309-76.
Meek, D. E. (1980): 'Aimhreit an Fhearainn an Tiriodh', in D. MacAmhlaigh (deas.), *Oighreachd agus Gabhaltas*, 23-31. Aberdeen.
Meek, D. E. (1987): ' "The Land Question Answered from the Bible": The Land Issue and the Development of a Highland Theology of Liberation', in *SGM*, 103, No. 2: 84-89.
Meek, D. E. (1988): 'Evangelicalism and Emigration: Aspects of the Role of Dissenting Evangelicalism and its Preachers in Highland Emigration especially to Canada c. 1800-c. 1850', in G. MacLennan (ed.), *Proceedings of the First North American Congress of Celtic Studies held in Ottawa 26-30 March 1986*, 15-35. Ottawa.
Meek, D. E. (1990): 'The Role of Song in the Highland Land Agitation', in *SGS*, 16: 1-53.

Meek, D. E. (1991): 'Dugald Sinclair: The Life and Work of a Highland Itinerant Missionary', in *SS*, 30: 59-91.

Meek, D. E. (1995): 'The Catholic Knight of Crofting: Sir Donald Horne MacFarlane, M.P. for Argyll, 1885-86, 1892-95', in *TGSI*, 58.

Meikle, H. W. (1912): *Scotland and the French Revolution*. Glasgow.

Moody, T. W., and Martin, F. X. (eds.) (1984): *The Course of Irish History*. Cork.

Munro, J., and Munro, R. W. (eds) (1986): *The Acts of the Lords of the Isles 1336-1493*. Edinburgh.

Napier Commission Report (1884): *Report and Evidence of the Commissioners of Inquiry into the Conditions of the Crofters and Cottars of the Highlands and Islands of Scotland*. 5 vols. London.

Newton, N. S. (1988): *Islay*. Newton Abbot.

Nic-a-Phearsoin, Màiri (1891): *Dàin agus Orain Ghàidhlig*. Inbhirnis.

Nicolson, A. (1882 edn): *A Collection of Gaelic Proverbs and Familiar Phrases*. Edinburgh.

Nicolson, A. (1994 edn): *History of Skye*. Skye.

Orr, W. (1982): *Deer Forests, Landlords and Crofters*. Edinburgh.

Palmer, A. (1986 edn): *The Penguin Dictionary of Modern History 1789-1945*. Harmondsworth.

Palmer, R. (1974): *A Touch on the Times: Songs of Social Change 1790-1914*. Harmondsworth.

Ramsay, F. (ed.) (1969): *John Ramsay of Kildalton*. Toronto.

Richards, E. (1982): *A History of the Highland Clearances: Volume 1: Agrarian Transformation and the Evictions 1746-1886*. London.

Richards, E. (1985): *A History of the Highland Clearances: Volume 2: Emigration, Protest, Reasons*. London.

Ritchie, L. A. (1985): 'The Floating Church of Loch Sunart', in *RSCHS*, 22: 159-73.

RSCHS: Records of the Scottish Church History Society.

Scott, H., et al. (ed.) (1866-): *Fasti Ecclesiae Scoticanae*. 10 vols. Edinburgh.

SGM: The Scottish Geographical Magazine.

SGS: Scottish Gaelic Studies.

SHR: The Scottish Historical Review.

Sinclair, A. MacLean (ed.) (1890): *The Glenbard Collection*. Charlottetown.

Sinclair, A. MacLean (ed.) (1900): *Na Bàird Leathanach: The MacLean Bards: Volume II*. Charlottetown.

SS: Scottish Studies.

Stenton, M., and Lees, S. (1978): *Who's Who of British Members of Parliament: A Biographical Dictionary of the House of Commons, Volume 2, 1886-1918*. Sussex.

Storrie, M. C. (1981): *Islay: Biography of an Island*. Islay.

TGSI: The Transactions of the Gaelic Society of Inverness.

Thomson, D. S. (1968): 'The Harlaw Brosnachadh: An early fifteenth-century curio', in *Celtic Studies: Essays in Memory of Angus Matheson*, ed. James Carney and David Greene, 147-69. London.

Thomson, D. S. (1974): *An Introduction to Gaelic Poetry*. London.

Thornber, I. (1985): 'Some Morvern Songwriters of the Nineteenth Century', in *TGSI*, 53: 1-90.

Tocher: School of Scottish Studies, Edinburgh.

Trial (1874): *Report of the Trial of the so-called Bernera Rioters at Stornoway on the 17th and 18th July 1874*. Edinburgh.

Vicinus, M. (1974): *The Industrial Muse: A Study of Nineteenth-century Working-class Literature*. London.

Watson, W. J. (1937): *Scottish Verse from the Book of the Dean of Lismore*. Edinburgh.

Who Was Who (1967 edn): *Who Was Who I, 1897-1915*. London.

Woodward, E. L. (1939 edn): *The Age of Reform 1815-1870*. Oxford.

INTRODUCTION

The sample of Gaelic verse in this volume covers most of the nineteenth century, from the period of the Clearances (up to 1870) to that of the Land War in the 1880s, when land agitation was at its height in the Highlands. As there are very few Gaelic commentaries which survive from this significant period in Highland history, such verse is of great value in allowing us to see how Gaelic poets, who were often the spokespersons of the crofting communities of the Highlands and Islands, reacted to events around them.

The majority of the poets covered in this volume were themselves crofters or cottars, or belonged to that class. Most were affected by the various processes of social dislocation which afflicted the Highlands, and, later in the century, some were participants in the fight for Highland land rights. Such people had first-hand experience of the scenes they describe. A few poets, like Dr John Mac-Lachlan of Rahoy, were members of the professional classes, but they were closely identified with the communities which bore the brunt of 'improvement' and tenurial reorganisation.

Yet, in spite of the potential value of this body of verse in illuminating the perceptions of those who experienced the nineteenth-century Clearances and the Land Agitation, it has been little used by modern historians. There seems to be some reluctance on the part of certain historians to allow the Gaelic evidence to speak for itself, even when part of that evidence is available in translation. Such tardiness is not, of course, helped by the inaccessibility of much of the material. This book is, in fact, the first printed anthology devoted specifically to Gaelic poems of social and political protest. After the passage of more than a century, Gaels themselves are only now beginning to appreciate the importance of what survives of this sizeable and significant body of verse.

Survival of the Texts

Contemporaries were in no doubt about the importance of
Gaelic song and verse in the context of the Clearances and
the Land Agitation. This is demonstrated by the manner of
the poems' transmission and survival. Most poems were
composed for singing and for transmission throughout their
own localities – and sometimes farther afield – by oral
means. Several poems in this collection have been derived
directly from recent oral tradition, among them ' "Venus"
nan Gàidheal' ('The "Venus" of the Gaels') (Poem 7),
composed in 1862; 'Cumha a' Bhàillidh Mhòir' ('Lament
for the Factor Mòr') (Poem 10) composed in 1872; 'Thàinig
Sgeula gu ar Baile' ('Word Came to our Township') (Poem
20), probably composed in 1883; and 'Is muladach mi 'n-
diugh 's mi 'g èirigh' ('Sad am I as I rise today') (Poem 40),
composed in early 1887. In these cases the texts have been
preserved in the traditional Highland data-base – the
memory – for upwards of a century. The excellent condition
of these texts bears witness that they were highly esteemed
in their time, and subsequently transmitted with great care.
In some instances, the traditional data-base has preserved
verses which were somehow overlooked when certain
individual poems eventually found their way into the
printed collections after 1900 (see Poem 30). When such
verses are taken to the bar of historical evidence, they are
often found to be accurate in relation to the events
described in them.

The significance of the poems can be measured not only
by their endurance within oral transmission, but also by the
space given to them in nineteenth-century newspapers.
Newspapers which were sympathetic to, or advocates of,
the crofters' cause regularly carried specimens of Land
Agitation verse in the 1870s and especially the 1880s. These
papers included the *Highlander*, the *Oban Times*, and the
Scottish Highlander. Indeed the *Oban Times* is a primary
source for poetry of this kind, which it obtained from a wide

catchment area, extending from Lewis to the southern
Hebrides and embracing the western Highland mainland
and areas where Highlanders had settled in Scotland and
beyond. Poets were no doubt well aware of the value of the
new patronage provided by crofter-friendly newspapers,
whose editors (pre-eminently Duncan Cameron of the
Oban Times) were very much alive to the power of poetry
in assisting the campaign.

There was room in the papers for all kinds of verse. Some
poems were formal, carefully crafted pieces; others were
perfunctory; and still others were entertaining squibs. A
chuckle of impish delight can be detected in the words of
'D. McN.' when asking the advice of Counndullie Morison
with regard to his satirical off-the-cuff poem on Sheriff
Ivory's adventures in Glendale in 1886: 'The foregoing
verses I have just scribbled down. Do you consider them
deserving of a corner in the "Oban Times"? Ought such a
personal effusion be published? Sheriff Ivory deserves to
have his name handed down to all generations in rhyme'
(*Tocher*, 17 (1975): 24). The *Oban Times* certainly agreed,
and the poem (Poem 36) duly appeared under the pen-
name 'Calum Posta'. In fact, Gaelic poems with up-to-the-
minute comment on current issues were 'hot news'. When
John MacRae recited his poem on the Crofters' Bill (Poem
33) in Lochcarron Schoolhouse on 11th March 1886, it was
published in the *Oban Times* nine days later. It is worth
noting also that newspapers which were not crofter-friendly
joined the others in giving the poets a platform, sometimes
to discredit an otherwise lauded friend of the crofters, or to
do down the crofters themselves; thus the *Northern
Chronicle* published Alexander MacLean's poem on the
Glendale Martyrs (Poem 22) because, said the paper, it
represented the crofters' views 'only too truly in shutting
out the landlords' side of the question'. In all of this, the
newspapers were recognising the time-honoured role of
poets as commentators on events of relevance to their own
communities.

Newspapers also published older poems from the period of the Clearances. These earlier items were usually presented as free-standing pieces, but occasionally they might form part of a speech by a crofting leader. A speech given by the Rev. Donald MacCallum in December 1884 and reproduced in the *Oban Times* in January 1885 included part of a song on the Arichonan eviction of 1848 (Poem 5). For this reason, the nineteenth-century press is a very valuable, and under-used, archive of Gaelic poetry, preserving much that otherwise would have been lost. Even when texts are known in other sources after 1900, the newspapers can furnish forgotten verses or amplify the current oral record. The oral and printed records are thus, to some degree, complementary; the *Oban Times* contains what is probably a full text of Poem 21, which had survived in oral transmission in an attenuated form until the early 1970s. The newshounds and newspaper editors, in their desire to present hot news, had become collectors of what we now appreciate as a significant treasury of Gaelic songs.

Displacing the Tradition

When the emotions generated by the Clearances and the Land Agitation died down at the end of the nineteenth century, the socio-political role of the poets declined in importance. Although individual poems and poets were remembered (see MacCallum 1912), the wider body of material was neglected. Songs identified with particular regions of the Highlands tended to find their place, if they found it at all, in post-1900 collections from the localities, such as *Na Bàird Thirisdeach* (Cameron 1932) or *Bàrdachd Leòdhais* (MacLeòid 1916). In the wider national context, the poets as a whole failed to find a niche. The poets who did survive as important figures in the wider Gaelic consciousness were William Livingston of Islay, John Smith of Lewis and Mary MacPherson of Skye, two of whom were fortunate enough to have the bulk of their poems preserved in individual collections (Livingston 1882;

Nic-a-Phearsoin 1891). The majority of the poets had to rest content with the transient patronage of the newspaper editors and the more lasting esteem of their local communities – and we therefore owe a major debt to these editors and to tradition-bearers.

Various reasons can be offered for the loss of the radical voice represented by the forgotten poets of the nineteenth century. First, their poetry was closely connected to particular events within that century, and it lost much of its immediate relevance after these events. In order to appreciate the poetry afresh, it is necessary to reconstruct, as accurately as possible, the social and historical contexts in which it originally flourished. The lack (hitherto) of an annotated anthology, providing substantial and accessible texts, has meant that the wider body of verse has been represented only in selective quotations, and its strength and texture have not been properly assessed. Second, Highland people all too easily forgot the struggles of the nineteenth century, especially when they moved to the Lowlands or bettered themselves in other ways; the Lowland ceilidh circuit and the neo-romantic collectors administered heavy doses of cultural anaesthesia which served to blot out the hardships of the past. Third, the printing presses, generally located in the Lowlands, were inclined to publish the works of the more romantic school of poets whose view of the Highlands was that of a 'land of lost content', an escape-route from the pressures of contemporary readjustment to urban life. The strongest poets of the Clearances and the Land Agitation addressed themselves to the harsh realities of existence, and not to the construction of a fey and couthy view of the Highlands.

Because of the dominance of the ceilidh culture and the romantic songsters (represented pre-eminently in the 'bens and glens' mentality of Neil MacLeod of Skye and Edinburgh: see MacLeod 1975), the 'alternative voice' of the nineteenth-century Highlands was effectively silenced to the public ear for the next hundred years. In addition, it is highly probable that a great deal of verse was destroyed during the social upheavals of the period, especially since there was no systematic attempt to collect and preserve it beyond the newspapers. As a result of both processes, the nineteenth century has lost much of its poetic credibility, and critics such as Professor Derick Thomson have characterised it as an 'age of flux and resignation and triviality', its banality relieved only by the poems of Livingston, Smith and MacPherson, who have, Thomson argues, 'a special individuality, strength and gravitas' (Thomson 1974: 233). The general weaknesses of the period have also been noted by Dr Sorley MacLean, whose ground-breaking essay, 'The Poetry of the Clearances', was, nevertheless, the first critical essay to identify that 'alternative voice' of resistance and struggle (MacLean 1985: 48-74).

The alleged weaknesses of the nineteenth century have not been restricted to themes. Professor Thomson has argued, with much justification, that style and form suffered, as English and Lowland influence was brought to bear on metre and structure. The principal exponent of the *dòighean Gallda* ('Lowland ways') was Neil MacLeod, whose regular rhythms and predictable vowel melody encapsulated the essence of 'a poetry basically lacking in surprise, shock, tension' (Thomson 1974: 232). This technique can be seen in MacLeod's poem, 'Na Croitearan Sgiathanach' ('The Skye Crofters') (Poem 16).

Redressing the Balance

The sample of poems in the present volume helps to redress the balance of our thinking with respect to the nineteenth century. It cannot be said that we will discover any further major poets beyond the 'great trio' – Livingston, Smith and MacPherson. Nevertheless, there are numerous individual poems which are filled with 'surprise, shock, tension' and, let it be said, with the power that it took to move men and women to action against social injustice. If regularity of vowel melody is a romantic cover-up for lack of personal conviction, the present selection contains poems in which the message takes precedence over the form, with a resulting ruggedness of style. But even more significantly, it is in these less ornate poems of the Clearances and the Land Agitation that we find the most noticeable use of traditional Gaelic genres of verse. Here we encounter the time-honoured genres of panegyric (eulogy and elegy) and satire, as well as other verse types, being put to use in the context of the last great heroic struggle of the Highland people.

Some of these poems are powerfully outspoken, with a deep undercurrent of anger, as if the poets, having already lost much, are prepared to lose all in a worthy cause; others are sorrowful and reflective; others again are celebratory, and a few are delightfully pawky and humorous. Occasionally, the moods are mixed in a heady cocktail of conflicting emotions. We will see, too, that alongside the stronger specimens, there are poems which are gentle and remarkably resigned to hard circumstances. A couple (see, for example, Poem 30) show the subtle influence of 'bens and glens' and tartanism and even 'Balmorality'. Yet, for all that, there is unquestionably an 'alternative voice' which deserves to be heard. Its cadences will be best appreciated by placing the poems in their historical and generic contexts. Perspectives and approaches will be seen to change as the nineteenth century progresses, and, as the events of the Land Agitation unfold, the poems will offer, at the very least, glimpses of individual viewpoints within the wider crofting community.

The Great Dispersal

The collection contains several poems which were composed in the years from 1800 to 1874, the latter being the date of the Bernera Riot and the beginning of the active phase of the Land Agitation. These 'early' poems thus belong, for the most part, to the period of the Clearances. The events and personalities of the Clearances – evictions, sheep-farmers, factors and landlords – shaped the consciousness of the campaigners for land law reform and motivated the crofters and cottars whose interests required to be protected. When touring the Highlands to investigate crofters' grievances in 1883, the Napier Commission gathered a large amount of evidence which referred in both general and specific terms to the circumstances of the preceding eighty years. In Tiree, for example, the Commissioners listened to chilling accounts of the role of John Campbell of Ardmore (Islay) and tenant of Ardfeenaig in the Ross of Mull (Napier Commission Report 1884: 2128-63). As the *Bàillidh Mòr* (Tiree) or *Factor Mòr* (Mull and Iona) ('Big Factor', i.e. Chamberlain) of the Argyll Estates, he was at the height of his powers during and after the Potato Famine of 1846-47. Large in build and blunt in his application of estate management, Campbell evoked conflicting expressions of loyalty or loathing from his tenants, as if he were a prototype of Jekyll and Hyde. Because of the impact of such men on the minds of later land agitators, some poems about landlords, factors and other estate officers have been included in the collection, and so too have poems which are concerned with the effect of estate policies on the land and its people.

The pre-1874 poems are valuable if only in dispelling the view that Highlanders reacted tamely, if at all, to the evictions and territorial engineering of the period. The poems chosen here show remarkable strength. No less than four of the main items (Poems 3, 4, 5, 6) hit out against landlords (Malcolm of Poltalloch, Riddell of Ardnamurchan [subject of two poems], MacLeod of Gesto) and two strike hard at factors (Poems 2, 10). All of these poems show anger, and most are powered by a deep desire for vengeance. It must be understood that poems of this kind were strong, verbal weapons by which the actions of the men commemorated in them were held up for public condemnation. In terms of traditional perspectives, they were 'wrongful rulers' whose tyranny ruined the land.

Two types of Gaelic verse are prominent in this period, namely satire and elegy, and these genres are sometimes mixed to powerful effect. In the category of satire we find *aoir*, traditional vituperation and condemnation, as in the poem by Allan MacDougall attacking the Lowland shepherds (Poem 1) and in the song (Poem 2) on Patrick Sellar and his associates, which, by portraying Sellar as a grotesque hybrid with animal characteristics, drives home the view that he does not belong to the human race. The song opens with the vision of a great fire in which Sellar's henchmen have been placed, and the image of fire is very noticeable in the satires of this period. It is implicit in the satire on Malcolm of Poltalloch (Poem 5), composed after the eviction at Arichonan in 1848. It is explicit in the satire on Kenneth MacLeod of Gesto in Skye (d. 1869) (Poem 6), and the ultimate fire of Hell is central to the swingeing satire on John Campbell, the Chamberlain of the Argyll Estates (d. 1872) (Poem 10). It seems likely that the use of this image was inspired by the alleged firing of houses by some estate officers at times of clearance; their own methods, by implication, have caught up with them.

The satires on Malcolm of Poltalloch, MacLeod of Gesto and Campbell of Ardmore show a different approach from that of the poem on Sellar. In these poems, vituperation is not evident; rather, the poet portrays the landlord or factor in circumstances which humiliate and destroy him, and by which a dire revenge is taken. The satire on Campbell of Ardmore is no less than an inversion of the normal conventions for the commemoration of the dead; it is a bitter satirical elegy, which turns conventional elegy on its head, and delights in the real death of the perceived villain. Precedent can readily be found for such drastic satire, which was apparently reserved for the worst of villains, and had its own set of conventions. It is exemplified more than three centuries earlier in the Book of the Dean of Lismore, where there is a satirical elegy on the bad Clanranald chieftain, Ailéin mac Ruaidhrí, who died about 1509 (Watson 1937: 134-9). Like Campbell of Ardmore, he is consigned straight to Hell.

The possibility that there was a well recognised genre of

satire for the denunciation of bad factors and landlords is further suggested by the poem 'Oran air Fear a bha a' Fuadachadh nan Gàidheal' ('Song on One who was Evicting Highlanders') (Poem 9). This shows features of all the poems that we have discussed, especially the derogatory imagery: the subject is to be buried in cow dung, nettles will grow on his grave, and people will clap their hands and rejoice at his funeral.

In the foregoing instances, satire refashions elegy in order to provide a strong denunciation of a factor or landlord. In other examples the blend is rather less stark. The content of an elegiac poem, lamenting the change in the countryside as a result of clearing, is sometimes modified so as to serve the poet's purposes in condemning the perpetrator(s). Allan MacDougall's 'Oran do na Cìobairibh Gallda' ('Song to the Lowland Shepherds') (Poem 1) laments the changes in social customs and rural practices which the poet regards as a consequence of the shepherds' arrival. The poet shows a physical detestation of the shepherds, whom he, rather naively, regards as the cause of the change. More focused and better targeted is Dr John MacLachlan's restrained and deeply moving poem 'A' Dìreadh a-mach ri Beinn Shianta' ('Climbing up towards Beinn Shiant') (Poem 3). It describes poignantly the desolation caused by the landlord's policies, but turns mid-way to condemn his rapacity and to remind him of the judgement to come. New Testament parallels form a backcloth; the landlord should learn from the rich man who built his barns with no heed to the afterlife, and the widow who gave her mite in quietness, in contrast to the self-interest of the wealthy. A rather similar mixture of elegy and plain speaking is found in the poem condemning Malcolm of Poltalloch, which is reminiscent of folk lament in its unadorned simplicity (Poem 5). The blending of elegy and satire is evident again in the poem on Riddell of Ardnamurchan, where the poet claims that he can no longer appreciate the simple beauties of nature because of the sweated labour required to meet the three-fold rise in his rent (Poem 4).

The poem on Malcolm employs a selective code of symbolism in portraying the change in the countryside; according to the poet, the songs of the milkmaid can no longer be heard, and 'yellow sheep' have displaced human life. Such symbolism, often following the trend set by poets such as Allan MacDougall (Poem 1) and adding Lowland shepherds and their dogs to the catalogue of objectionable intruders, came to be a dominant note in elegiac verse of this kind. Elegies devoted entirely to *caochladh* ('change' or 'death' caused by the loss of population) became common, and the theme remained prominent for most of the century. It can be seen in John MacLean's 'Manitoba' of 1878, which conveys the mood of sorrow occasioned by the departure of emigrants who had contributed greatly to the conviviality and life of their native community (Poem 11).

Sorrow, tinged with a deeper sense of anger, is also apparent in William Livingston's poem of the early 1860s, 'Fios chun a' Bhàird' ('A Message for the Poet') (Poem 8), where the main theme is the ecological transformation of Islay as a result of 'improvement', chiefly, it would seem, on the Kildalton estate. Luxuriant foliage and grass, providing lush pastures for cattle, contrast with the decline of the native population who have been displaced by sheep. Livingston uses symbolism to greater effect than most of the nineteenth-century poets, and he displays a wider range of symbols. There is an element of well-paced surprise in the final symbol in his poem – that of the speckled adder lying in coils on the floors of deserted houses where 'big men' were once reared. Livingston's restraint in using this symbol, rather than producing a tirade against landlords, adds to the poignancy of the poem and leaves us in no doubt that he regarded the displacement of the native population as the result of cunning and intrinsically wicked scheming, though he fails to name names and blames the innocent sheep for population displacement. The pre-clearance 'Eden' has been destroyed by those who have succumbed to the wiles of this intruder. The prophetic voice of the bard foretells the extinction of cultivation and the final, irreversible departure of the native Gaels from their land, their places being taken by the hated *Goill* (a word embracing 'foreigners', 'Lowlanders' or non-Gaels in general).

Elegy inspired by the departure of the native stock is again evident in '"Venus" nan Gàidheal' ('The "Venus" of the Gaels'), describing the voyage of an emigrant ship carrying Islay people from Port Ellen to Canada in 1862 (Poem 7). The most significant feature of this splendid poem is its hard-headed realism, which focuses on the storm encountered by the ship and the deaths of some of the passengers and the injuring of some of the crew. The composer, who was closely related to the emigrants, concludes the poem by deciding to follow them. He or she weighs up the various issues, and, having achieved a personal catharsis by facing the hardships of the emigrant voyage, finds new hope in the decision to cross the ocean to 'the land of the trees'. Not all Gaelic poets spent their time bemoaning their fate and condemning the supposed per-petrators of their misery.

It can be said fairly that the pre-1874 poems in this collection are characterised by realism rather than roman-ticism. Although it is clear that several of these operate in terms of particular codes (e.g. in the denunciation of landlords and factors), their power and sincerity are striking. Their focus, however, tends to be individualised and personalised: when the poets go on the offensive, specific targets – shepherds, landlords and factors – are attacked, but not the system of landholding which pre-vailed throughout the Highlands and was tolerated by the British government. Livingston comes closest to expressing the broader perspectives, but it was only after 1870, and especially after 1874, that the attack on the system, rather than its representatives, was launched in earnest by poets and people. Among the first to open fire on the broader front was Calum Campbell MacPhail of Muckairn, whose poem 'Bochdan na Rìoghachd' ('The Paupers of the

Mr. Donald Fraser, Inveralle next spoke and recommend
-ed unity and boldness in advocating our course.
Mr. John Maclean Drynie Parks, sang a Gaelic song
of his own composition in honour of "Dr Macdonald"
and on the motion of Mr. Mackenzie Secy. John Main
appointed poet to the Association, Subscriptions to
the amount of 57/- were collected. a Vote of thanks
to the Chairman, after which Mr. John McKenzie
Newton Kirkell closed the Meeting with 3 cheers.

Mr. John Maclean, the Association's bard, rendered
the following original Gaelic song:—

THOGAINN FONN NAN GAISGEACH.

Air fonn "Co-dhiu thogainn fonn mo leannain,"

Co-dhiu thogainn fonn nan gaisgeach,
Anns gach aite 'n olainn drama ;
Co-dhiu thogainn fonn nan gaisgeach.

'S e Doctair Domhnullach tha mi 'g raidhtinn,
Is mac croiteir o gun àichoadh ;
Thug o buaidh air Fear Nobhàr,
A Tigh na Parlamaid chum o mach o.

Ach gur e mo chelst an t-uasal
Sheas gu-dileas anns a' chruadal ;
Thug o nise uile buaidh orr',
'S tha o suas a dheoin no dh' aindeoin.

Bha na *raguichean* an comhnuidh,
A' sior ruith le an cuid boilich,
Ag innseadh air a' h-uile doigh,
Gun tugadh Nobhar og dhuinn ceartas.

Ach gur e mo chelst an t-armunn
A fhuair urram mor nan Gaidheal ;
Thug o buaidh air a namhaid,
'S bheir o bhan duinn mal an fhearainn.

Tha Doctair Domhnullach lan cruadail,
Dh' cirich Leodhas bho 'n Taobh Tuath leis,
Siorr'achd Rois nam fearaibh cruaidh ;
'S o n t-Eilein-Dubh chum suas a' bhratach.

'S ann a tha mo chelst air Ruairidh
A fhuair urram o 'n Taobh Tuath so,
'S tha o nis am measg nan uaislean,
Chum bhi cumail suas a' cheartais.

Bha 'n Domhn'lach Camaron air thus ann—
'S mor tha bhailtean air a churam—
Ma gheobh esan uile dhurachd,
Cha bhi curam oirnn a ceartas.

Doctair Clark, an sar dhuin-uasal,
'S mor bu mhisde sinne uainn o ;
Air Mac-na-Cearda thug o buaidh,
A's bheir o uainn am fuachd 's an t-acras.

Tha Jesse Collings air ar culaobh,
Gu ar scasamh aig na Cuirtean,
'S chan 'eil Baillidh fo 'n a' Chrun,
Bheir mal dubailt uainn an ath-bhliadhn'.

Na Cataich na'n do sheas cho cruaidh
'S bu choir dhaibh aig am a' chrundail,
Bhiodh aca Sutharlanach suairce
Chuireadh gruaim air Diuc 's air Marcus.

Mr. Donald Fraser, Tarradale next spook (*sic*)
and recommended amity and boldness in advocating our cause. Mr John MacLean Drynie
Park, sang a Gaelic song of his own composition
in honour of "Dr Macdonald" and on the motion
of Mr MacKenzie Secy, John was appointed <u>poet</u>
to the Association. Subscriptions to the amount
of 37/- were collected, a vote of thanks to the
Chairman, after which Mr. John McKenzie
Newton Kinkell closed the Meeting with prayer.

The text of John MacLean's song, extracted from
the 'Scottish Highlander' newspaper, then
follows. See Poem 29.

Extract (opposite) from the Minute Book of the
Mulbuie Branch of the Highland Land Law Reform
Association of Ross and Cromarty, recording the
appointment of John MacLean as 'poet to the
Association' on 18th December 1885.

Kingdom') (Poem 12), first published in the *Oban Times* in 1872, considers the effect of the Poor Law on the landlords' treatment of Highlanders.

The Struggle for the Land

After 1874 the poets' role as spokespersons on behalf of their communities became more prominent than it had been before that date, mainly because they had a strategic part to play in reinforcing the emerging struggle for land rights. Every nineteenth-century Highland community had its own poets, who were the heirs of the earlier classical bardic tradition, although their verse was shaped by influences from the non-classical tradition, including the form and music of 'folk songs' of vernacular provenance (such as waulking songs and love songs).

Some poets had a greater bardic persona than others: thus Mary MacPherson, 'Màiri Mhòr nan Oran', who had moved extensively in the wider Gaelic world of the Highlands and the Lowlands, where there were many colonies of emigrant Gaels, assumed a matriarchal role in her defence of the Highland people (Meek 1977b). A broader concern is also apparent in the work of Calum Campbell MacPhail of Muckairn, while John Smith of Lewis paints a larger canvas than any of his contemporaries. Other poets, notably the 'township bards' or 'community poets', had a primary allegiance to the struggle as it related to their own particular districts: examples of such poets include Alexander MacLean of Glendale, Skye, and John MacLean of Balemartin, Tiree; while another John MacLean, this time of Drynie Park, Mulbuie, in the Black Isle, became the 'official' poet of the local branch of the Land League in 1885. For Jura and Islay, the voice of protest was maintained by Neil MacPhee from Jura, whose songs have recently been discovered (Grannd 1990). Murdo MacLeod, the hymnwriter, was a strong and early supporter of crofter activism in Lewis.

Poets in certain districts had such a strong voice that they became conspicuous for their challenge to authority. When the Napier Commission took evidence at Bonar Bridge, the members conducted a cross-examination of a certain Alexander Ross, known as 'The Bard', from Achnahannet in Strathoykell near Carbisdale. They had obviously been informed that Ross had been composing verse critical of the lairds. He himself had been evicted from Rielonie of Culrain, part of the estate of Munro-Ferguson of Novar which had been bought by another proprietor (Napier Commission Report 1884, IV: 2577). Some poets, it is said, ran the risk of imprisonment because of the strong support that they gave to the Land League; an example of such a poet was Lachlan Livingstone of Mull, who lived latterly in Lismore, and who, tradition asserts, was threatened with imprisonment because of his political verse. (I owe this information to his great grand-daughter, Mrs Margaret Lobban, Edinburgh.) Alongside such poets, there were many others, operating in both Highland and Lowland communities of Gaels, who produced occasional songs on the Land Agitation but attained no major local or national recognition as supporters of the movement.

This last category included Neil MacLeod, a native of Glendale in Skye, who migrated to Edinburgh where his relatives established the company of tea merchants, MacLeod's Tea. MacLeod's poem on 'Na Croitearan Sgiathanach' ('The Skye Crofters') (Poem 16) is included in this collection as a specimen of highly stylised romantic verse. With its portrait of an earlier, recoverable Golden Age and its exhortation to avoid violence, the poem was probably intended as a well-flavoured tranquilliser at a time of high tension in Skye, particularly in Glendale itself. Its intrinsic idealism is a useful counterpoint to the more vigorous sentiments of those poets who were closer to the heart of the crofters' movement.

In addressing themselves to the Land Agitation, the poets employed both elegy and satire as did their pre-decessors before 1874, but they also used several other traditional genres. In fact, the period 1874-1890 is remarkable for the number of traditional genres which were refashioned to convey the moods and aspirations of the time. The principal genres, which we will consider in turn, included: (1) *Meòrachadh* ('Reflection') (2) *Deasbad* ('Debate') (3) *Brosnachadh* ('Incitement') (4) *Moladh* ('Praise') (5) *Aoir* ('Satire') and (6) *Marbhrann* or *Cumha* ('Elegy' or 'Lament'). It needs to be emphasised that these categories were not always kept distinct, and that a single poem could interweave several different strands. In addition, the poets were capable of using the time-honoured genres in daringly new ways. It is also noticeable that some genres are more prominent at particular times than at others, depending on the prevailing mood in the crofting areas.

(1) *Meòrachadh:* Verse of this kind, in which the poet reflects on a philosophical, historical or contemporary theme and works out its implications, is relatively sparse within the surviving corpus. It finds its fullest and most satisfying expression before 1880 in the verse of John Smith of Lewis, especially in 'Spiorad a' Charthannais' ('The Spirit of Kindliness') (Poem 14). In this poem, composed soon after the Bernera Riot of 1874, which resulted in the toppling of Donald Munro, the Chamberlain of Lewis, Smith attempts to analyse the reasons for the hostility and ill feeling which have appeared not only in Lewis but in the Highlands as a whole. He diagnoses the problem in broadly theological terms: the displacement of the Holy Spirit of kindliness is achieved by the rise of self-interested secularism. Worldly self-interest is reflected in the appearance of commercial landlordism, the callous ingratitude of the imperial war-mongers, the credal clashes of contemporary denominations, and the actions of Donald Munro. In form and style, Smith's poem owes much to evangelical experience, and resembles a hymn in its tune and cadences, but it can also be read as a modern, politically conscious reflection on the implications of the New Testament passage in 1 Corinthians 13. Smith's broad grasp of the

contemporary issues is again evident in his 'Oran Luchd an Spòrs' ('Song on Sportsmen') (Poem 15), where he assesses and denounces the new breed of landlords who have converted large tracts of the Highlands into sportsmen's playgrounds.

Sometimes poets reflected not only on the present but also on the past, including the history of the Highlands and of the Highland population. The period produced a number of ponderous poems on such themes. Not infrequently they tended towards an elegiac view of the past. Lighter specimens were also produced, as exemplified in 'Oran mu Chor nan Croitearan' ('Song on the Crofters' Plight') (Poem 26).

(2) *Deasbad:* Contemporary matters were debated by the poets, and an element of debate is evident in John Smith's work. However, some poets created verse in which protagonists with different views discussed current trends. The protagonists could be a crofter and landlord, as in Calum Campbell MacPhail's poem, 'Oran eadar Tuathanach is Uachdaran' ('Song between a Crofter (lit. Farmer) and a Landlord') (Poem 19). Published in the early 1880s, MacPhail's poem highlights the determination of Highland landlords to use gunboats and force to bring crofters to submission. He assessed the mood of the time correctly, as gunboats were dispatched to Skye, Tiree and Lewis, and crofters were imprisoned in the course of the decade. Poems of this kind had their roots in a traditional form of verse in which dialogue was prominent.

Poets could also offer candid assessments of developments which were of significance to the crofting community. In so doing they gave their poems a debating edge, aimed at providing a succinct, serviceable response which could be employed on behalf of the community. Thus John MacRae's poem 'Oran air Bill nan Croitearan' ('Song on the Crofters' Bill') (Poem 33) provides a forceful critique of the Crofters' Bill going through Parliament during the spring of 1886. In his view the Bill did not get to the heart of the matter: there was, he claimed, nothing in it by way of restoring the lost lands which had been swallowed up in deer farms. Contemporary crofters and especially cottars would have agreed with the view of some modern historians that the Bill, when it became the Crofters' Holdings (Scotland) Act, failed to transform many of the circumstances against which they fought. In islands like Tiree, the struggle continued after it became law, and agitators were arrested, and imprisoned, in 1886. John MacLean, the Balemartin Bard, offered a response on behalf of the community following their trial in Edinburgh. In his song, 'Oran nam Prìosanach' ('Song on the Prisoners') (Poem 35), he challenged the evidence which had been led by the prosecution.

(3) *Brosnachadh:* Gaelic poetry had a long tradition of verse which aimed to stir the ardour of warriors before battle. This genre is represented in the so-called 'Harlaw Brosnachadh' which may date to the Battle of Harlaw in 1411 (Thomson 1968). Poets and people considered the Land Agitation of the 1880s to be a battle or series of battles. Gaelic heroic tradition, steeped in the language of warfare, provided a rich store of metaphors which could be re-used at strategic times in the course of the struggle. Such strategic times are reflected in the poetic profile of the period, and produced small surges of verse of this kind. A strengthening of spirit is apparent after the Bernera Riot of 1874, and is reflected in John Smith's poetry and more specifically in Murdo MacLeod's poem on the event (Poem 13). It emerges again following the Battle of the Braes in 1882; a strong element of *brosnachadh* is found in Niall Ceannaiche's warning that battle will be given in earnest if an officer without royal warrant appears in the locality. His poem (Poem 17) is filled with the rhetoric of soldiering and military prowess, serving both as a deterrent to outside interference and as a bracing of local courage.

The most obvious use of *brosnachadh* in a modern context occurred in late 1885, when crofters were voting in the General Election of November-December, and the poets were urging them to support the new pro-crofter candidates. Màiri Mhòr had a particularly prominent role in such exhortation, but other poets were of a similar mind. Thus Murdo MacLeod of Bru, Barvas, exhorted the Lewis people to vote for Dr Roderick MacDonald, the crofters' candidate for Ross and Cromarty, and not to yield to the blandishments of Munro-Ferguson of Novar, who was really a landlord (Poem 28). A prominent symbol in several songs was the banner, raised on behalf of one or more of the crofter candidates, as in 'Bratach nan Croitearan' ('The Crofters' Banner') (Poem 27). Such poetry encouraged the people to discriminate between candidates and to have the courage of their convictions. It was an important contribution to the development of 'people power' and the democratisation of the Highlands.

(4) *Moladh:* The praise of heroes and leaders was always close to the heart of Gaelic poets, and emerges vigorously in the 1870s and 1880s. It is noticeable that the focus of attention moves away from the clan chiefs who were often the subject of traditional panegyric, and comes to rest on the people themselves and their leaders. The community replaces the clan as the fighting unit; the people of Bernera or Tiree or Glendale are the stalwarts who have routed, or will rout, the enemy on the battlefield. Their allies are other local communities who will come to their assistance, as mentioned in Alexander MacLean's poem on the Glendale expedition (Poem 20). Their leaders, local heroes like those in Niall Ceannaiche's poem (Poem 17), are frequently praised. At other times the political thinkers take centre stage – men like the Rev. Donald MacCallum (Poem 42) and Donald MacRae, 'Balallan', a leading figure in the Park Deer Raid of 1887, who is celebrated in a poem composed by an unidentified poet (Poem 44). Influential figures beyond the Highlands are occasionally praised; Henry George, the American political philosopher who visited Scotland in 1884, is the subject of one poem in this collection (Poem 25).

The poets' praise operates in various ways. Sometimes it forms part of a poem, or is implicit, rather than highly wrought, in a matter-of-fact presentation of completed events (as in Poem 20). It can also be anticipatory, desiring a good outcome, as in the poets' heartfelt approval of the establishment of the Napier Commission in 1883. The songs by Charles MacKinnon of Kilmuir, Skye, and John MacLean of Balemartin, Tiree, reflect the high expectations which the Commission generated in the crofting areas (Songs 23, 24). The reductions in rent following the first sittings of the Land Court in 1887 activated the praise of Màiri Mhòr nan Oran, whose 'Oran Beinn Lì' ('Song on Ben Lee') (Poem 37) celebrates the restoration of the grazing of that hill to the crofters of Braes, Skye.

Full-blown panegyric reached a crescendo following the General Election of 1885 and the election of five of the crofter candidates to represent the Highland people in Parliament. This is reflected in two songs in this collection. One is by John MacLean of Balemartin, Tiree, and celebrates the victory of Donald MacFarlane as M.P. for Argyll (Poem 30). MacLean's poem, a form of bardic toast to the conqueror, resounds with jubilation, and has a strongly aural and visual quality, as it describes the blazing bonfires on the hills – an appropriate symbol of affection and achievement. The warmth of the bonfires contrasts with the cold voyage to Mull to vote for MacFarlane. At the same time, the poet's portrayal of the Highlands suggests that he was not immune from the influence of Victorian stereotyping; tartan and high hills give his song a glow of romanticism which jostles uneasily with the military metaphors used to describe MacFarlane's victory. Mac-Farlane was evidently much liked by several poets who composed poems in his honour at the time of the 1885 election (see Meek 1995). Dissenting voices were few, although they did exist.

The other song of celebration is by John MacLean of Mulbuie in the Black Isle, with its resounding refrain, 'Co-dhiù thogainn fonn nan gaisgeach' ('Regardless I would sing the heroes' praise') (Poem 29). Here the focus is on Dr Roderick MacDonald, a native of Skye who was returned as

M.P. for Ross and Cromarty; it portrays MacDonald as a man of action, who will carry out his manifesto and relieve the district of the cold and hunger which it has had to endure through the ineffectiveness of previous representatives whose words could not be trusted. The poet shows an awareness of the wider 'battle' in the Highland constituencies, and gives space to all of the new pro-crofter M.P.s. He has a good word too for other allies of the crofters, such as Jesse Collings, a Liberal Unionist whose importance to Highland history (in precipitating Gladstone's third Ministry) has been largely overlooked by modern historians.

(5) *Aoir:* Satire or dispraise is the other side of the bardic coin, the opposite of praise. It had a prominent place in the poetic output before 1874, and it appears again after that date. As with panegyric, it can form part of a poem, as in Murdo MacLeod's powerful invective against Donald Munro (Poem 13), or it can fill a whole poem, like the Rev. Donald MacCallum's satire on 'Bodach Isgein' ('The Old Man of Eishken') (Poem 43). Generally, the genre is reserved for enemies of the crofters' cause, but it is occasionally used against pro-crofter candidates in the period of a General Election. Thus Donald MacFarlane was given a scorching send-off by one poet of Argyll origin (though probably resident beyond the county) after his defeat by Malcolm of Poltalloch, the poet's hero, at the General Election of July 1886 (Poem 32).

Satires can commemorate the discomfiture of individuals, as in the case of MacFarlane and also of MacTavish, the sheriff officer who came to Glendale to serve summonses and was set upon by the crofters (Poem 21). Most satires, however, anticipate such discomfiture, and aim to achieve it. Indeed, the goal of a traditional satire was to incapacitate the perpetrator of the action deemed unworthy by the poet. Satire could also be employed to remove unwelcome intruders (e.g. rats). This role is exemplified splendidly in Calum Campbell MacPhail's remarkable poem of the early 1880s, 'Aoir na Bàirlinn'

('Satire on the Eviction Notice') (Poem 18); in which he denounces the Notice in the hope that it will be stopped in its tracks and become powerless. The poem moves on to include features of elegy in its description of those cast adrift by the actions of the Notice, and it turns finally to *brosnachadh* as it encourages Highland societies to support those affected by it.

The most consistent application of satire in the 1880s was stimulated by the actions of Sheriff William Ivory, the Sheriff of Inverness-shire, who achieved notoriety in Skye in the period from 1882 to 1886. The main aim would surely have been to stop Ivory's actions by holding them up to public censure and ridicule. His efforts to collect arrears of rates in Skye in late 1886 resulted in a torrent of condemnation by the poets, who held him responsible (not always correctly) for all that happened.

Several types of approach are shown by this 'Ivory Cycle'. The poem with the sharpest barb was composed by Màiri Mhòr (Poem 38). In general technique, it is very close to that on the death of the Bàillidh Mòr in 1872 (Poem 10), and takes the form of a mock elegy for Ivory, composed when it was heard that he had been – allegedly – drowned in a moorland pool. The satire focuses on the rejoicing which is occasioned far and wide by this happy event. Ivory's funeral is a time for conviviality and celebration, as in the case of the Bàillidh Mòr.

Other satires are not so strongly spiked, and some even show light touches of humour. 'Calum Posta's' poem on Ivory's campaign in Glendale is delightfully ironic, as it mocks the perceptions of crofters held by those in authority and by the landlord class (Poem 36). In so doing it moves off the attack on Ivory with which it opens. More sharply focused is the song by 'Eisdealach' (Poem 39), in which he draws attention to the process of poinding which was carried out, it is said, by Ivory, although one of his sheriff officers, Alexander MacDonald, was responsible for the notorious poinding of the child at Peinness. The poet laughs as he lists the goods and chattels gathered by Ivory, including chamber pots which are pulled out of dark corners and 'put to use' by him! In its comments on the sad state of the Highlands, which allows such things to happen, the poem has an elegiac strand in its structure.

The arrival of marines, soldiers and policemen in districts beyond Skye similarly provoked the protests and acerbic wit of local poets. Colin MacDonald of Tiree's poem, 'Oran nan Saighdearan' ('Song on the Soldiers') (Poem 34), comments on the attitudes of the marines who arrived in the island in July 1886.

(6) *Marbhrann* or *cumha:* Elegies serve more than one function in the context of the agitation of the 1870s and 1880s. We have already noted their role in portraying the adverse changes taking place in the demographic patterns of the Highlands, especially before 1874, and the present anthology contains one specimen of an elegy on the later plight of the Highlands (Poem 26). At least three further uses of elegy are apparent in the surviving body of verse. The genre can be used to commemorate the defeat of a crofting leader, such as Donald MacFarlane, who failed to win re-election as the M.P. for Argyll in the General Election of July 1886, and whose departure was lamented (just as his arrival had been celebrated) by John MacLean of Tiree (Poem 31). Elegy is also employed by Alexander MacLean of Glendale as he records the sorrow of the community at the imprisonment of the three Glendale Martyrs in the Calton Jail in Edinburgh in 1883 (Poem 22).

Elegiac mode was used by prisoners who were sent to the Calton, and two examples of verse of this kind have survived. The earlier example (Poem 40), composed when crofters from Herbusta were arrested and imprisoned early in 1887, is, however, an elegy only in terms of its refrain. The verses quickly turn to humour, as the poet makes fun of the changed circumstances in which he and his companions find themselves. The same good humour is shown in the second poem of this kind (Poem 41), composed by a crofter who was imprisoned in the Calton as a result of the Caolvin eviction case in Easdale. He laments his plight, but his main sorrows are occasioned by separation from his sweetheart – and his lack of tobacco!

For those outside the prison, who later received and transmitted these songs, the message would have been clear: the poets regarded their own circumstances as relatively insignificant compared with the success of the wider struggle to which they were committed. From being a vehicle for the expression of defeat and irreparable loss, as it so obviously was before 1870, elegy had been transformed to become a means of expressing perseverance and resistance to personal discomfort in the interests of the community itself.

The transformation of the elegy was symbolic of the manner in which new hope had brightened the prospects of the Highland people after 1870. This improvement might not have been achieved without the contribution of the poets whose songs form the core of the present anthology.

Poets' Perspectives

Although the poets use a variety of song types, and show a fair degree of individuality in the treatment of their themes, there are certain perspectives which most hold in common and which determine their approach to the social upheavals of the nineteenth century.

The poets' aims can be focused in one word – 'community'. In resorting to song, the primary motivation of the majority of poets was the preservation of the traditional Gaelic community in its local or wider Highland forms. Their perceptions of that community derived from the normal practices maintained across the centuries, and were based on such considerations as kinship, co-operation and collective defence. Maintenance of the community, as they knew it, was possible only when its ethical and social values were preserved. Violation of these values was part and parcel of the intrusion of external agencies, and had to be resisted.

The poets therefore react strongly against the manner in

which the traditional *mores* of their communities are breached by Lowland shepherds (Poem 1), the firing of houses (Poem 2), the intrusion of officials (Poems 20, 21), the arrival of gunboats (Poem 19), and the removal of the people (Poem 5), sometimes by force or by a failure of the traditional system of mutual support which linked tenant to landlord. John Smith of Lewis (Poem 14) identified the cement of the community as the intrinsically spiritual quality of 'kindliness', or consideration, and he saw the development of commercial landlordism as essentially antipathetic to traditional values. Economic determinism was, in his opinion, at variance with the preservation of a society based on mutual support.

No other poet of the time crystallised the issues with such clarity, but similar perspectives underlie several of the songs. Some poets (including Smith himself, Neil MacLeod and, to some extent, John MacLean, the Balemartin Bard) go so far as to portray life in the pre-Clearance Highlands as a Golden Age of kindly co-operation and harmony, contrasting with the restrictions imposed by modern landlordism. This may be more than a romantic invention; in origin, it may reflect a general awareness of the arrival of the *nouveau riche*, non-Gaelic landlords who had bought a very considerable number of Highland estates by 1850, and who undoubtedly introduced regimes which were much more closely aligned to economically motivated pragmatism (Devine 1989; 1994). A number of poems (see Poems 4, 14, 15, 16, 35) derive their power from the contrast perceived by the poets between the 'old elite' and the 'new elite', especially in their attitude to the people.

Nevertheless, the poets have little to say about the harsh realities of Highland life prior to 1850; the 'old elite' are better than the 'new elite'; the 'great Highland famine' (Devine 1988) following the potato blight of 1846 is seldom, if ever, mentioned. One might conclude that Highland society, inured to hardship, could come to terms with natural disasters much more easily than with the intrusion of a new economic order, which, in the poets' eyes, was being imposed from outside. If the poets do, indeed, intend to portray the virtues of the pre-Clearance Highlands, we must be aware that the historical boundary lies around 1770, and that the view from the second half of the nineteenth century may be somewhat hazy, perhaps conveniently so, despite the longevity of traditional memory.

Believing that there was once a better time, the poets approach the defence and liberation of the beleaguered community from their stance within the traditional body of understanding relating to communal survival. This advocated armed resistance to intrusion. The nineteenth-century symptoms, if not the cause, of such intrusion were visible on the hillsides, and their consequences were obvious in terms of heroic society. Sheep and (later) deer, by taking the place of people, could not contribute to the active life of the community, nor could they strengthen its capacity to resist invasion.

Several poets extend this argument from their own localities to the wider Scottish, and British imperial, context, since many Highlanders served in British regiments after 1745. The defence capability of the entire nation, they contend, is threatened by the arrival of sheep, by eviction and emigration (Poems 8, 12). Such defence calls for heroism and for the best actions of what is still seen as a warrior society. It is significant that references to the 'Forty-five' are sometimes made (as in Poem 17), since these help to reinforce the popular recollection of the once-great fighting force of the Gaelic people. Yet, if that force is to be mobilised again on the home front, it is only in the context of occasional pitched battles in the localities, and the poets do not encourage any sustained military campaign against the landlords or the leaders of the imperial war-machine; rather, some suggest that the French should come across to attack the landlords (Poems 1, 5), and others imply that, on the wider front, Highlanders themselves should fight, not for the Highlands, but for Scotland, Britain, or the Empire.

There is a strong element of irony in such a perception of the community's response to oppression. The broader, more subtle processes of attrition are seldom perceived. Death in a foreign field is preferable to eviction or clearance at home. The latter, rather than the former, is regarded as treachery. Injustice is, however, recognised. According to some poets, Highlanders are due proper recognition for their imperial services. Several contend that the Highlanders' bravery in previous British battles should be rewarded with the preservation of their traditional communities, and some protest at the ingratitude demonstrated through clearance and eviction (Poems 11, 12, 15, 16). Here the role of the old-style chief as the rewarder of his warband is transferred to the leaders of the British military machine, who, in truth, had little concern for the survival of Highland communities; as events made clear, they were as ready to send gunboats to the Hebrides as they were to bombard the Russians.

In perceiving individuals as integral parts of a national community with sympathetic leaders, rather than as disposable chattels at the mercy of social and political manipulators, the poets were controlled by the values of traditional kin-based society, and generally failed to recognise that, by participating in imperial conflicts, their people were not only being exploited, but were also (potentially or in reality) oppressing other people in like manner. With the exception of John Smith (Poem 14), the poets did not question the motives or morality of the British Empire and its global adventurism; it was seen by most as a 'noble cause'.

Motives for condemning clearance and for encouraging agitation were therefore based on what Highlanders suffered in their own home communities, and perspectives were usually localised. The poets raised public indignation by stressing primarily the exploitation of the Highland people by landlords and factors, rather than the broader ideologies of economy or empire. The enforced removal or maltreatment of Highlanders was an outrage which elicited a powerful response, often in the form of satire. Conversely, the defeat of a factor or landlord in a 'battle' with the community assumed an enormous symbolic value. The Bernera dispute and its outcome (Poems 13, 14) were celebrated as a victory of major proportions, and, indeed, their significance in promoting a spirit of active resistance beyond Lewis can scarcely be doubted. This was an example of right – with some degree of physical force – triumphing over fiscal might. As the struggle became better focused and 'battles' were won on home ground in the 1880s, hankerings for imperial recognition and reward appear to have become less compelling in the poets' minds.

Poets possessed the power to exalt their own people's achievements and to magnify the significance of events like the Bernera fracas. They were also custodians of the time-honoured heroic codes and images which made new developments acceptable, or unacceptable, by presenting them in terms which would be familiar to their audiences. They were thus key figures both in the preservation of old values and in opening the door to modern political perspectives and democratic methods. For instance, the franchise, extended to crofters in 1884, was portrayed by the poets as a weapon that was potentially no less effective than the sword. The ballot-box was a battle ground. Thus victorious pro-crofter sympathisers received the laudation due to heroes, and the crofter candidates of 1885 were portrayed as triumphant warriors of the traditional mould (Poems 29, 30).

In spite of their poetic warrior garb, it is noticeable that the new pro-crofter Members of Parliament were, in several cases, far removed from the crofting people and from Gaelic society. Dr Roderick MacDonald, the son of a Skye crofter, was closest to the social status of the voters. Men like Donald MacFarlane, who were the product of astute and profitable business ventures, cruised through the islands in their yachts, and represented a very different lifestyle, forged by those same commercial forces as were trans-forming the Highlands. Yet the poets sought to accommodate their new representatives within traditional perspectives, portraying them as crofter-friendly aristocratic warriors, 'people chiefs' rather than clan chiefs.

The majority of the new M.P.s retained their seats in several subsequent elections. Nevertheless, there were some sharp reminders that the crofting community alone could not determine the fate of even its finest heroes. In the case of Donald MacFarlane, the earlier support of John Mac-Lean, the Balemartin Bard, was insufficient to retain him as Argyll's M.P. in the election of July 1886. He was defeated by a landlord, Malcolm of Poltalloch, after a campaign which, in Argyll, was fought on the issue of MacFarlane's Roman Catholicism and support for Irish Home Rule. As the poem by the 'Lame Tailor' makes clear (Poem 32), broader, external issues could cause fragmentation in the Highland consensus, and no amount of 'hero-dressing' could prevent it.

Even so, the poets possessed some real political clout. The politicians were well aware of the poets' power in public relations and propaganda. Parliamentary candidates such as Charles Fraser-Mackintosh recognised the importance of the poets in creating a sympathetic image within the constituency, and, by taking poets such as Mary MacPherson with them on electioneering campaigns, they tried to enter into the self-understanding of their prospective constituencies. The power of poetry was no romantic delusion; it could help to make or break the prospective candidate. Absence of traditional poetic support at a critical juncture in a politician's career was, at the very least, a bad omen. It is probably significant that no poem in support of Donald Horne MacFarlane or Irish Home Rule was published in the *Oban Times* as part of the run-up to the election of July 1886. No poet in Argyll, it would seem, was brave enough to advocate MacFarlane as an Irish Home Ruler, rather than the champion of crofting.

Notwithstanding the uncertainties of political life, the emergence of the pro-crofter M.P.s demonstrated the extent of the revolution that was taking place in the Highlands. A 'brave new world' had arrived, and had found a small but significant place in Highland culture. The poets, who acted as the principal spokespersons of the Highland crofting communities, did not produce a new response to a new world; rather, they exercised discrimination, and welcomed the better features of the new era. They accommodated these features, as best they could, in terms of the old world, and gave the latter the pre-eminence. This is evident in their use of a heroic code of language drawn from the warrior era of the Highlands – an era which, in practical terms, had ended at Culloden, although the image and the illusion were retained in the British imperial context. Such conservatism was consistent with the poets' calling, which was not to innovate, or to fashion original policy, but to reinforce the existing community and to approve action leading to its survival and well-being.

Although most Gaelic poets considered in this volume were protectors of, and propagandists for, the traditional community, they cannot be seen as faultless participants in the battle for Highland land rights. Some were unable to disentangle the issues as clearly as we might wish; several (notably Neil MacLeod) sought refuge in romanticism, and a number exhibited a marked tendency to retrospection, offering the past as an antidote to the present. At times political argument was muffled by the rhetoric of traditional perspectives. A vision for the future was urgently needed. The real challenge for the successors of the militant crofters of the 1880s appears only in the final verse of the last poem (Poem 44) in this anthology, which anticipates further struggle for ownership of the land, as the battle had not yet ended:

> 'S on fhuair sinn nis ceann-feadhna,
> Cha stad sinn latha no oidhche,
> Gus am buannaich sinn an oighreachd
>   Gu h-aoibhneach 's gu h-urramach.
>
> (And since we have now found a leader,
> we will not cease by day or night,
> until we win possession of the estate
>   joyfully and honourably.)

EDITORIAL PRINCIPLES AND PERSPECTIVES

The anthology provides a sample of the poems and songs generated in response to social and political developments in the course of the nineteenth century. For reasons made clear in the Introduction, much of the original output is now lost, and the anthology therefore derives its material from a restricted data-base which is already unrepresentative of the period. Within these constraints, the anthology has two objectives.

The first is to represent the range of poetic responses to different events, persons and processes during the nineteenth century, from the arrival of sheep farmers in the Glengarry estates to the Park Deer Raid of 1887. The poems are therefore assembled in (broadly) chronological order, with three-quarters of the volume being devoted to the period from 1870 to 1890. This will enable the reader to see, through the eyes of the poets, some of the key events of the century as they unfold.

The second objective is to demonstrate, from the surviving material, the different types of song and verse which were deployed in responding to these events. The various categories of verse are discussed in the Introduction. Over-representation of particular genres (e.g. descriptive accounts of the changed rural environment) has been avoided. It is hoped that this will indicate the rich variety of approaches within the corpus, and enable other collectors and editors to identify the type and significance of any poems which may yet remain to be discovered.

These objectives have been attempted while recognising the need to acknowledge the geographical spread of social and political reaction in the Highlands and Islands. Incomplete though they are, surviving sources do succeed in preserving specimens of verse from a significant number of districts. Thus the geographical range of the volume extends from Lewis to Islay, with some concentration on Skye and Tiree, and it contains a fair number of poems from mainland localities, including Ardnamurchan, Easdale, Lochcarron, the Black Isle and Sutherland.

It is, however, noticeable that the surviving sources, especially the newspapers, tend to reflect their own immediate catchment areas, and some localities are better represented than others, depending on the interests of those who compiled the material. The *Oban Times*, for example, despite the breadth of its readership, had a primary loyalty to the Inner Hebrides (including Skye), and similar loyalties, political as well as territorial, have left their mark on the evidence of other newspapers.

Biases of other kinds are also evident. Inevitably, the sample as a whole tends to be crofter-friendly, and there are few instances of disputation or contention from within the crofter class. The views of landlords and factors, it would seem, were seldom articulated in Gaelic verse composed by members of their own social order. If such verse was composed, it is unlikely that it would have been preserved in any profusion within the normal, non-aristocratic channels of transmission.

More complex than the 'filtering out' of entire texts are those processes which have helped to shape the versions of the songs which have survived. Two developments need to be borne in mind in connection with our texts. The first is what may be called 'extended composition'. In response to the course of the event(s) which inspired the song, a poet could make adjustments to bring the text into line with later developments. Such reshaping could be relatively minimal, and would not normally extend beyond the period when the issue was 'live' within the community. It might involve no more than an updating of the text; thus, the reference made by John MacLean, the Balemartin Bard, to the prospects for Gladstone at the outset of 1886 in a song (Poem 30) which was composed mainly in December 1885.

The second process may involve more substantial alteration by the transmitters, rather than the composers, of the poems. A text could be extensively reshaped for reasons of decorum, as appears to have happened with Poem 28, the earliest text of which is substantially different from that published in an anthology of 1916. The 1916 text seems to reflect loss of verses containing criticism of ministers. More generally, references and arguments which may have been entirely apposite at the time of their composition may have been toned down or removed entirely by later 'transmissional editing'. Editors of newspapers sometimes omitted verses simply for reasons of space; but editors of certain anthologies, gathering material in the more sedate days of the twentieth century, apparently had some reservations about retaining derogatory allusions to landlords and clergy. Editing could also occur within the oral transmission of a poem; we need not assume that such transmission did not contribute to the reshaping of a song. Even when transmission is good, the failure of the earliest collectors to provide full texts must inevitably curtail our appreciation of some poems (see, for example, Poem 5). Only occasionally are we able to glimpse the processes lying behind our texts, and a modern editor is thus at the mercy of a range of transmissional pressures and prejudices which are now largely hidden from sight.

For these reasons it is particularly important to find the earliest versions of poems, and to check these versions, wherever possible, against other surviving evidence. Where discrepancies do appear between a poem and other sources, these may point to misinformation, transmissional dislocation, or later 'toning down' of the verse. On the other hand, such discrepancies may well have a significance beyond the merely editorial, perhaps reflecting a fundamental difference in perspective or interpretation. We should not assume that a poem is 'wrong' because it (or some part of it) conflicts with evidence of another kind. The latter evidence, too, could be subject to similar processes of adjustment. Even estate records are influenced, if not manipulated, by the perspectives of their compilers. In the texts presented here, there are very few difficulties with the 'facts'; the interpretation of these facts is what makes the poems distinctive and valuable.

We must therefore recognise the intrinsic value of our texts, but we must also acknowledge that there are large gaps in the record, and that we do not have a full view of perspectives throughout the Highlands and Islands. Although a good number of the songs and poems can be read (with some qualification) as the expression of viewpoints held generally within 'the crofting community', we must bear in mind that there were, in reality, several such communities, and that each community had its own set of social challenges or a different scale of priorities within the broader range of issues. Thus, one cannot conclude that a poem attacking a landlord in one community must have had its counterpart in another. The individualised nature of each response needs to be acknowledged within its own context, and set alongside other poems and records (where these are available) in order to judge the breadth of the application. Further research remains to be done in this complex field, and the present volume is no more than a first step in that direction. Readers who may wish to check the wider implications or applications of a poem would do well to consult I.M.M. MacPhail, *The Crofters' War* (MacPhail 1989), which is particularly sensitive to events and perceptions in different localities.

The incomplete nature of the surviving evidence makes it difficult to find individual poetic voices which are sustained throughout the period of the Clearances or the Land Agitation, with the result that changing (or static) perspectives cannot be easily identified. At the risk of being seen to favour my native island (Tiree), I have allowed the voice of John MacLean, the Balemartin Bard, to comment on several events, since he is (so far) the only township poet known to me whose relevant surviving output extends over a range of subjects from the late 1870s to the mid-1880s. Work is urgently required to recover what may yet remain of the verse of such poets as Alexander MacLean of

Glendale, whose output was clearly substantial in its time, but is now almost forgotten.

Some larger poetic voices have been curtailed, when they merit, or have already received, treatment in their own right: thus Mary MacPherson's songs have been represented by only two specimens, since she already has two published editions (and a revised version of Meek 1977b is in preparation). Where good modern editions of individual poems exist, these poems are not reproduced here, but the reader is directed to the edition in the introduction or the notes. An example of relevant songs in this category would be the poems of Neil MacPhee, edited by Dr Seumas Grannd (Grannd 1990).

The poems in this edition are presented as free-standing pieces. Explanatory notes follow each text. Where more than one version of a poem survives, or where part of a poem has been omitted, the decisions made in arriving at a representative text are indicated. A brief summary is given of the themes of any verses which have been omitted from the present edition. In addition to exposition of sources, dates of composition and exposition of contexts, line annotations are given, as required, for each poem. Tunes are identified where possible, but the tunes themselves are not written out. An extensive Glossary is provided, and considerable care has been taken to explain idioms and nuances which may no longer be readily accessible to a modern readership. Wider literary and historical perspectives are offered in two Biographical Indexes, the one of identifiable poets and the other of the main political figures featured in the poems.

Translations of all poems are given in the book. It is hoped that these will be of wide interest, especially to historians who would not otherwise have access to the material. In making the translations, my main concern has been to convey accurately the sense of the original texts, but I have also tried to reflect the style and structure of each item. Where rhyme and assonance have emerged without damaging the sense of the lines, I have utilised this as a means of providing a deeper 'feel' for the overall style of each piece (e.g. in Poems 12, 14, and 16), but, in general, I have resisted the temptation to sacrifice sense to form.

The orthography follows that recommended by the S.C.E. Examination Board, with some modifications which I have deemed essential to avoid ambiguity and needlessly ugly neo-spellings. Thus the apostrophe is used throughout to distinguish 'na, 'nam, 'nan etc. (preposition + possessive) from na, nan, nam etc. (forms of the article).

POEMS AND SONGS

1. Oran do na Cìobairibh Gallda

Ailean Dùghallach

Thàinig oirnn do dh'Albainn crois,
Tha daoine bochd' nochdte ris,
Gun bhiadh, gun aodach, gun chluain;
Tha 'n àird a tuath an dèidh a sgrios;   4
Chan fhaicear ach caoraich is uain,
Goill mun cuairt daibh air gach slios;
Tha gach fearann air dol fàs,
Na Gàidheil 's an ceann fo fhliodh.   8

Chan fhaicear crodh-laoigh air gleann,
No eich, ach gann, a' dol an èill;
'S ann don fhàisinneachd a bh' ann
Gun rachadh an crann bho fheum;   12
Chaidh na sealgairean fo gheall,
'S tha gach cuilbhear cam, gun ghleus;
Cha mharbhar maoisleach no meann,
'S dh'fhuadaich sgriachail Ghall na fèidh.   16

Chan eil àbhachd feadh nam beann,
Chaidh gìomanaich teann fo smachd;
Tha fear na cròice air chall,
Chaidh gach eilid is mang as;   20
Chan fhaighear ruadh-bhoc nan allt
Le cù seang ga chur gu srath;
An èirig gach cùis a bh' ann,
Feadaireachd nan Gall 's gach glaic.   24

47

Cha chluinnear geum ann am buailidh,
Chaidh an crodh guailfhionn à suim;
Chan èisdear luinneag no duanag,
Bleodhain mairt aig gruagaich dhuinn;   28
Bhon chaidh ar cuallach an tainead,
'S tric a tha pathadh gar claoidh;
'N àite gach càirdean a bh' againn,
Luinnseach ghlas am bun gach tuim.   32

Mar gun tuiteadh iad fon chraoibh,
Cnothan caoch dol aog sa bharrach;
'S ann mar siud a tha seann daoine,
'S clann bheag a h-aogais bainne;   36
Thilgeadh iad gu iomall cùirte
Bhon dùthchas a bh' aig an seanair;
B' fheàrr leinn gun tigeadh na Frangaich
A thoirt nan ceann de na Gallaibh.   40

Dh'fhalbh gach pòsadh – thrèig gach banais;
Sguir an luchd-ealaidh bhith seinn;
Chuala sibhse tric ga aithris
'Caidseirean a' teachd air clèibh';   44
'S ionnan siud 's mar thachair dhòmhsa –
Cha dèan iad m' fheòraich air fèill;
Far am b' àbhaist dhomh bhith mùirneach,
'S fheàrr leo cù ga chur ri sprèidh.   48

Gach aon fhear a fhuair làmh-an-uachdair,
Dh'fhògair iad uapa gach neach
A rachadh ri aghaidh cruadail,
Nan tigeadh an ruaig le neart;   52
Nan èireadh cogadh san rìoghachd,
Bhiodh na cìobairean 'nan airc;
'S e siud an sgeula bu bhinn linn,
Bhith gan cur gu dìth air fad.   56

Eiridh iad moch là Sàbaid,
'S tachraidh iad ri càch-a-chèil',
'S nuair a shìneas iad air stòiridh,
'S ann dhan còmhradh, tighinn air feur;   60

Gach fear a' faighneachd dha nàbaidh,
'Ciamar sin a dh'fhàg thu 'n treud?
Ciod i phrìs a rinn na muilt?
No 'n do chuir thu iad gu fèill?'   64

'Chan adhbhar talaich am bliadhn' e,
Rinn iad a sia-deug is còrr;
Ma tha thus' ag iarraidh fios air,
Cheannaich mi mhin leis a' chlòimh;   68
Dh'fhalbh na crogaichean air dàil,
'S ma ghleidheas mi 'n t-àlach òg,
Ged a gheibheadh trian dhiubh 'm bàs,
Nì mi 'm màl air na bhios beò.'   72

Nuair dhìreas fear dhiubh ri beinn,
An àm dha èirigh gu moch,
Bidh sgread Ghallda 'm beul a chlèibh,
'G èigheachd an dèidh a chuid chon;   76
Ceòl nach b' èibhinn linn, a sgairt;
Bracsaidh 'na shac air a chorp;
E suainte 'na bhreacan glas;
Uaimh-mheulan 'na fhalt 's 'na dhos.   80

Nuair thig e oirnn sa ghaoithidh,
'S mairg a bhios air taobh an fhasgaidh;
Chan fhaod fhàileadh a bhith caoin,
'S e giùlan nam maoidlean dhachaigh;   84
'S tric e ga fhoileadh sa ghaorr,
A-sìos bho chaol-druim gu chasan,
'S ge b' e rachadh leis a dh'òl,
'S fheudar dhaibh an sròn a chasadh.   88

Nuair shuidheas dithis no triùir
San taigh-òsda 'n cùis bhith rèidh,
Chìtear aig toiseach a' bhùird
Cìobair agus cù 'na dhèidh;   92
Bu chòir a thilgeadh an cùil,
'S glùn a chur am beul a chlèibh,
Iomain a-mach dh'ionnsaigh 'n dùin,
'S gabhadh e gu smiùradh fhèin.   96

'S olc a' chuideachd do chàch
Neach nach àbhaist a bhith glan;
Cha chompanach dhaoine as fiach,
Fear le fhiaclan a' spoth chlach   100
Ann an garbhuaic air a ghlùinean,
Le chraos gan sùghadh a-mach;
'S ma leigeas tu 'n deoch ri bheul,
'Na dheaghaidh na fiach a blas.   104

A-mach luchd-cràgairt na h-olainn
Masa h-àill leibh comann ceart!
Druidibh orra suas a' chòmhla,
'S na leigibh an sròn a-steach,   108
Bho nach cluinnear aca stòiridh,
Ach craicinn agus clòimh ga creic,
Cunntas na h-aimsir, 's gach uair
Ceannach uan mun tèid am breith.   112

Suidhidh sinn mu bhòrd gu h-èibhinn,
Gu ceòlach, teudach, gun smalan,
Coibhneil, carthantach ri chèile,
'S na biodh aon den treud 'nar caraibh;   116
Olaibh deoch-slàinte MhicCoinnich,
'S Chòirneil loinneil Ghlinne Garaidh,
Chionn gur beag orra na caoraich
Is luchd-daorachaidh an fhearainn.   120

Dèanaibh gloineachan a lìonadh,
'S gun dìochuimhn air Fear an Earrachd,
Bhon as math leis maireann beò sinn,
'S gun am pòr ud a thighinn tharainn;   124
Nan seasadh uaislean na rìoghachd
Cho dìleas ri càirdeas Ailein,
Cha bhiodh an tuath air a sgaoileadh,
Gan cur gu aoidheachd a dh'aindeoin.   128

NOTES

Source: Dùghalach 1829: 29-33. The song is not in the first edition of MacDougall's work, published in 1798. An important edition of the poem with a Gaelic commentary on the earliest sheep-farmers is found in

D.C.M. [Donald C. MacPherson] 1877: 203-6, which provides some variants and clues to the understanding of the more obscure words. For valuable discussion of MacPherson and the background to the poem, see Cheape 1995.

Tune: No tune is specified in the source, but the song is said to be 'in Gaelic Heroic Measure'. The metre appears to be modelled very loosely on syllabic verse, a metrical form which may have been preserved in use to some extent through the recitation of Gaelic heroic lays. It approximates most closely to double quatrains of *rannaigheacht mhòr* (seven-syllable lines, with monosyllabic end-rhyme between the second and fourth lines) and (towards the end) *rannaigheacht bheag* (seven-syllable lines with disyllabic end-rhyme between the second and fourth lines). The two types of metre are not kept wholly distinct. In the last two verses, eight-syllable lines are evident, reflecting the mixed nature of the metrical pattern.

Date and Context: The reference to the 'splendid Colonel of Glengarry' (line 118) indicates that the song was composed after 1794, when Alexander MacDonell, 15th of Glengarry (who succeeded in 1788), became Colonel of the Glengarry Fencibles. The absence of the poem from the first edition of the poet's work suggests that it may have been composed in or after 1798. D.C.M. affirms 1798 as its date; c. 1800 is reasonable.

The poem was probably composed no later than the early 1800s, as the regiment was disbanded after the Peace of Amiens in 1802, and Alexander MacDonell began to encounter economic problems which did not enhance his image. Faced with growing expenses after the disbanding of the regiment and his marriage in the same year, he began to raise rents, thus becoming more overtly one of *luchd-daorachaidh an fhearainn* ('the raisers of the land-rent'), a course which had already been set by his father. Despite a 10% discount and offers of life tenures, a large number of his tenants surrendered their leases and sought passage to Canada, much to his chagrin (McLean 1991: 128-39).

Ailean Dùghallach (i.e. Allan MacDougall, also known as 'Ailean Dall' ('Blind Allan')) was Glengarry's bard from c. 1798, and his close relationship to the Glengarry family is evidently responsible for his tribute to the chief in lines 117-20. This compliment sits uneasily with the MacDonells' role in the introduction of sheep-farming to their lands; Alexander's father, Duncan, brought sheep-farmers to his estates in 1782 when he leased Glen Quoich to Thomas Gillespie and Henry Gibson, and removals from Glen Quoich began in 1784 (ibid.: 68; for a valuable account of the Gillespies, see Barron n.d.).

The poet's view of Glengarry suggests that he is the victim of external intrusion which he wishes to resist. Of course, the poet must have known that sheep-farmers could not have appeared without the consent of the MacDonell chiefs, and his compliment to Glengarry (if it is more than a rhetorical conceit) must imply that the chief had no liking for the

Lowland flockmasters, despite his family's part in bringing them to their estates. Whether or not Glengarry disliked the Lowland sheep-farmers in general, he certainly had a quarrel with Thomas Gillespie in particular. He and Glengarry fell out over financial matters; Glengarry borrowed money from Gillespie, and mortgaged the estate to him, but a feud developed about repayment. Glengarry even encouraged the stealing of Gillespie's sheep (Barron n.d.: 20).

The poem's aim is not to debate the role of the MacDonell chiefs in fostering new economic practices, but to condemn in the strongest terms the effect that the coming of the shepherds (a term potentially embracing sheep-farmers as well as their servants) is having on traditional Gaelic society. Gaelic society was unaccustomed to the hard-nosed economic determinism which underpinned the shepherds' attitudes, propelled them into an alien culture, and ignored the threat that they posed to distinctively Gaelic cultural values. It is this last point, perceived from the 'receiving end', that fires the poet's indignation. He does not attack the new economic system; he hits out at the symptoms rather than the cause, but he recognises, with an intensity equalled by few Gaelic poets, the power of these economic forces to displace the earlier Gaelic characteristics of Highland society.

11-12 The prophecy (*fàisinneachd*) to which the poet alludes is *Cuiridh peirceall na caora an crann air an fharadh*, 'The jawbone of the sheep will cause the plough to be put on the hen-roost', the hen-roost being the place for storing the plough when it was not in use. This saying, attributed to the Brahan Seer, Coinneach Odhar, is also claimed for Thomas the Rhymer, who lived in the seventeenth century ('The teeth of the sheep shall lay the plough on the shelf') (Nicolson 1882: 159). Allusions to the saying are relatively common in verse of this kind, since it appears to have offered some degree of solace or wider understanding to Highlanders in their predicament: see also Poem 33, line 1.

31 **càirdean:** This form, attested in the source, may be a misprint for *càirdeas* ('friendship'), and is so understood in D.C.M., but it could also be a diminutive form of *caraid* ('friend'), in the sense of 'dear (little) friend'.

39-40 **Frangaich:** Following the French Revolution of 1789, the fear of a similar happening was strong in Britain. The threat of invasion by the French was also prominent in politicians' minds. By the opening years of the nineteenth century, according to Lord Cockburn, 'Invasion became the word', and Volunteers were raised and ships equipped to withstand any such attempt. In Scotland in 1803, the nine Kinghorn Passage Boats were fitted out with carronades, and some herring boats were similarly prepared. See Meikle 1912: 214-5. The poet's desire to see the arrival of the French is fairly radical, given the climate of the time, but probably safely so, since the likelihood of invasion was remote.

44 The saying appears to mean that the poet is reduced to the same low status as cadgers, who travelled on ponies bearing wicker creels; thus

the idiom *air clèibh*, 'mounted on creels'. The creels contained items which they sold at weddings etc. The implied contrast is with the high esteem previously given to poets in traditional Gaelic society; the poet is now *persona non grata*, like the cadgers.

80 **'na dhos:** le moit ('with pride') (D.C.M.).

84 **nam maoidlean:** na maoidlean (Dùghalach); nam maodlaichean (D.C.M.).

96 **smiùradh:** Smearing of sheep was the precursor of modern 'dipping', and involved the application to the fleece of a mixture of butter, Archangel tar and grease, to protect the sheep against ticks and other insects. On large sheep-farms it was a labour-intensive task, performed in autumn; see Hunter 1976: 108-9, and (for a first-hand account of the process) Barron n.d.: 29-30. The implication of the line is that the Lowland shepherds are just like their sheep, especially in having lice and ticks; cf. line 80.

101 **garbhuaic:** garbhuaichd (Dùghalach). D.C.M. understands the word as *gaorr-bhuaic*, which he implicitly derives from *gaorr*, 'entrail juice' and *buaic*, 'dirt, faeces'; thus perhaps 'slimy sheep-dirt'.

117 **MhicCoinnich:** The reference may be to Sir George MacKenzie of Coull, a notable 'improving' landlord: see Cheape 1995: 100. It is much more probable, however, that the poet is referring to MacKenzie of Seaforth, who initially opposed the introduction of sheep-farming to his Kintail estates in the 1780s, and resisted high rentals (Hunter 1995: 23).

122 **Fear an Earrachd:** In 1793 Alan Cameron (1750-1828) of Erracht was given permission to raise the 79th Regiment of Foot, *Rèisimeid an Earrachd*, later known as the Cameron Highlanders (Maclean 1980). This was one of several regiments of Highlanders raised in this period; cf. the Glengarry Fencibles of 1794. The poet obviously approved of the policy of raising such regiments, seeing it as a loyal way of maintaining Highlanders in traditional roles, and contrasting it with the introduction of sheep-farmers to Highland estates. In reality these policies were not mutually exclusive.

2. Aoir air Pàdraig Sellar

Dòmhnall Bàillidh

Sèisd:

Hò 'n ceàrd dubh, hè 'n ceàrd dubh;
Hò 'n ceàrd dubh dhaor am fearann.

Chunnaic mise bruadar,
'S cha b' fhuathach leam fhaicinn fhathast,
'S nam faicinn e 'nam dhùsgadh,
Bu shùgradh dhomh e rim latha.   6

Teine mòr an òrdagh
Is Roy 'na theis-mheadhoin,
Young bhith ann am prìosan,
'S an t-iarann mu chnàmhan Shellair.   10

Tha Sellar an Cùl-Mhàillidh
Air fhàgail mar mhadadh-allaidh,
A' glacadh is a' sàradh
Gach aon nì thig 'na charaibh.   14

Tha shròn mar choltar iarainn
No fiacail na muice bioraich;
Tha ceann liath mar ròn air
Is bòdhan mar asal fhireann.   18

Tha rugaid mar chòrr-riabhaich
Is ìomhaigh air nach eil tairis,
Is casan fada liadhach
Mar shiaman de shlataibh mara.   22

'S truagh nach robh thu 'm prìosan
Rè bhliadhnan air uisg' is aran,
Is cearcall cruaidh de dh' iarann
Mud shliasaid gu làidir daingeann.   26

Nam faighinn-s' air an raon thu
Is daoine bhith gad cheangal,
Bheirinn le mo dhòrnaibh
Trì òirlich a-mach dhed sgamhan.   30

54

Chaidh thu fhèin 's do phàirtidh
An àirde gu bràighe Rosail,
Is chuir thu taigh do bhràthar
'Na smàlaibh a-suas 'na lasair.   34

Nuair a thig am bàs ort,
Cha chàirear thu anns an talamh,
Ach bidh do charcais thodharail
Mar òtrach air aodann achaidh.   38

Bha Sellar agus Roy
Air an treòrachadh leis an Deamhan
Nuair dh'òrdaich iad an compaist
'S an t-slabhraidh chur air an fhearann.   42

Bha 'n Simpsonach 'na chù
Mar bu dùthchasach don mharaich',
Seacaid ghorm à bùth air,
'S triùbhsair de dh' aodach tana.   46

'S i pacaid dhubh an ùillidh
A ghiùlain iad chum an fhearainn-s',
Ach chìthear fhathast bàitht' iad
Air tràilleach an cladach Bhanaibh.   50

NOTES

Source: Sinclair 1890: 200. The present text of the poem was preserved
in Prince Edward Island, and it appears that no version has survived in
Scotland.

Tune: 'Hò 'n clò dubh'.

Date and Context: The poem and its background are discussed in
Grimble 1962: 155-7. The circumstances of the arson described in lines
31-4 of the text are treated ibid.: 5-6. This was the first of the crimes of
which Patrick Sellar, assistant factor to the Countess of Sutherland, was
accused by the prosecution at his trial in Inverness on 23rd April 1816. It
seems likely, as Grimble argues, that the poem was composed soon after
the trial, at which Sellar was acquitted. It is probable that lines 11-14
refer to that acquittal, by which Sellar was left to continue what the poet
regarded as his wolf-like depredations.

The incident involved the home of William Chisholm at Rosal in
Strathnaver, allegedly fired by Sellar, 'with twenty men besides four
sheriff-officers', in June 1814. According to Chisholm, his very elderly
and bed-ridden mother-in-law, Margaret Mackay, was still in the house

when it was set alight, and had to be carried out to a small byre by Chisholm's sister-in-law. She is said to have died five days later.

1-2 Grimble notes (ibid.: 155) that 'the use of the epithet *ceàrd* ['tinker'] clearly refers to Sellar's trial, at which he had discredited Chisholm the chief witness by describing him as a mere tinker.' This further explains the reference, obviously ironic, to Chisholm as Sellar's brother (line 33).

8 **Roy:** According to the poem, he accompanied Sellar to measure parts of the estate (lines 39-42), and this agrees with William Young's description of him as 'the Land Surveyor' (Richards 1982: 311).

9 **Young:** William Young and Patrick Sellar, both from Morayshire, were recruited in 1808 by the Countess of Sutherland, and they 'helped to spawn the massive plans for clearance which were to be executed in the next decade' (ibid.: 202). Grimble notes: 'William Young had already embarked on the scheme of improvement for the south end of the Naver valley before Sellar himself applied for tenancy of the huge sheep farm it was proposed to establish there' (Grimble 1962: 6-7). Young, who was a noted 'improver' before his arrival in Sutherland and had contributed significantly to the development of Burghead and Hopeman, became factor in 1811, and Sellar was appointed his assistant (McKichan 1977: 42-3).

11 **Cùl-Mhàillidh:** Young and Sellar took a lease of a 300-acre farm at Culmailly, near Golspie, and 'improved' it by removing the earlier tenants (ibid.: 43).

43 **'n Simpsonach:** He was evidently a sailor, but I have not identified him. It is possible that he was the master of the packet described in lines 47-8. The reference is indexed (but not explained) as 'A. & D. Simpson' in Grimble 1962: 165.

47-8 This appears to be a reference to the packet service which William Young helped to establish between Burghead and Sutherland in July 1809. The first sailing conveyed both Young and Sellar to Sutherland, apparently for the first time (McKichan 1977: 42).

3. Dìreadh a-mach ri Beinn Shianta

An Lighiche Iain MacLachlainn

Dìreadh a-mach ri Beinn Shianta,
Gur cianail tha mo smuaintean,

A' faicinn na beinne 'na fàsach
'S i gun àiteach air a h-uachdar;   4

Sealltainn a-sìos thar a' bhealaich,
'S ann agamsa tha 'n sealladh fuaraidh.

'S lìonmhor bothan bochd gun àird air
Air gach taobh 'nan làraich uaine,   8

Agus fàrdach tha gun mhullach
Is 'na thulaich aig an fhuaran.

Far an robh 'n teine 's na pàisdean,
'S ann as àirde dh'fhàs an luachair.   12

Far an cruinnicheadh na h-àrmainn,
Feuch a' chaora bhàn le h-uan ann.

Ach, fhir shanntaich rinn an droch-bheairt,
Liuthad teaghlach bochd a ghluais thu;   16

'S iomadh dìlleachdan tha 'n ganntar
Agus bantrach a tha truagh leat;

An dall, an seann duine, 's an òinid
Toirt am mallachd air do bhuaireas.   20

Smuaintich fhèin, nuair thèid thu null bhuainn,
Mar bheir Rìgh nan Dùl do dhuais dhut.

B' fheàrr gun cuimhnicheadh tu tràth air,
Mun tugadh am bàs don uaigh thu.   24

An ceannaich thu le beairteas tròcair?
Cha dèan òr gu bràth a bhuannachd.

Bheil thu 'n dùil gum faigh thu saorsainn
Leis na caoraich 's do chuid bhuailtean?   28

B' fheàrr dhut beannachdan an fheumnaich
Don tugadh tu an dèirc an uaigneas;

B' fheàrr a bheannachdan le dùrachd,
Cridhe bruite gan cur suas dhut.   32

Ge bè àit' am faigh iad fearann,
Mìle beannachd leis na ghluais thu.

Dhùmhlaich an ceò air Beinn Shianta,
Thug a' ghrian a-sìos an cuan oirr';   36

Thàinig duibhre air an iarmailt,
'S cuiridh mise crìoch rim dhuanaig.

NOTES
Source: Gillies 1880: 34-36; Mac-na-Ceàrdadh 1879: 404-5.
   Tune: 'O-hò, na daoine truagha'.
   Date and Context: Alexander MacKenzie (MacKenzie 1966: 232-3)
provides the following description of removals in the vicinity of Beinn
Shiant, Ardnamurchan (1729 feet):
   ·'Down to the second decade of last century it [the land round Beinn
Shiant] supported about twenty-six families, which were distributed over
the component townships of Coire-mhuilinn, Skinid, Buarblaig, and
Tornamona. At one sweep, the whole place was cleared, and the grounds
added to the adjacent sheep farm of Mingary. The evictions were carried
out in 1828, the process being attended with many acts of heartless
cruelty on the part of the laird's representatives. In one case a half-witted
woman who flatly refused to flit was locked up in her cottage, the door
being barricaded on the outside by mason-work. She was visited every
morning to see if she had arrived at a tractable frame of mind, but for
days she held out. It was not until her slender store of food was
exhausted that she ceased to argue with the inevitable and decided to
capitulate...The proprietor at whose instances these "removals" were
carried out was Sir James Milles Riddell, Bart.'
   It is likely that MacLachlan composed this poem shortly after 1828,
perhaps around 1830.
   For further discussion of Sir James Milles Riddell, see Poem 4.
   19 **òinid:** possibly a reference to the 'half-witted woman' in
MacKenzie's account (quoted above).
   25-28 The reference here is to the New Testament story of the rich
man who built his barns, but was unconcerned about his eternal welfare:
see the Gospel of Luke, 12: 13-21.
   29-32 Another New Testament allusion is evident here, namely the
story of the widow's offering: see the Gospel of Mark, 12: 41-44. It is
doubtless used ironically, since it implies that the landlord should give
alms with the self-effacing humility of the widow, rather than the
bombast of the wealthy.

4. Oran Di-molaidh do Riddell Aird-nam-Murchan

Sa mhadainn chiùin Chèitein,
'S mi 'g èirigh gu gnìomh,
Bhiodh smeòrach air gheug
'S i ga bheusadh gu dian;   4
B' e siud an ceòl èibhinn
Ris an èireadh mo mhiann,
Agus greis thoirt ga èisdeachd
Mun èireadh a' ghrian.   8

'S ann a-nis is beag m' fheum
Ged a dh'èireas mi moch,
Lem chaib' as mo lèine,
Dol a reubadh nan cnoc;   12
Cha choisinn mi 'n dèirce
Dhomh fhèin no don bhochd,
'S trì màil rium ag èigheach
Aig an eucoireach olc.   16

Seo a' chomhachag aosmhor
Tha 'n Creag Aodainn seo shìos:
Tha i guidhe 's a' glaodhaich,
'Droch sgaoileadh 'nur gnìomh!'   20
Clann Chamshroin Srath Lòchaidh
Thogadh sròl ris gach crann,
Bheir an Ruidleach an t-òr
As am pòcaibh le cainnt.   24

Ged a dh'fhalbh ar cinn-fheachda,
Gur peacach an tùirn
Ma leigear ar creachadh
Fo mheachainn a' Chrùin,   28
Le maighstirean tuatha
Nach buainticheadh cliù,
'S le balach gun chèireadh
Nach èighear 'na dhiùc.   32

NOTES
Source: MacDonald and MacDonald 1911: 355.

Tune: In the source, the *sèisd* ('refrain') is given as:

Horo ollelo, oll il orro hi, etc.

Cha mhòr nach coma leam cogadh no sìth.

This is the refrain of the song commonly known as 'Cogadh no sìth'.

Date and Context: In the source (p.lxi) the poem is said to have been composed 'about the middle of the 18th century, by an unknown author' and it is stated that this 'proves that the land question is not a new one'. The alleged eighteenth-century dating is accepted in MacLean 1985: 55, but both the style of the poem and its reference to Sir James Milles Riddell show that it belongs to the first half of the nineteenth century.

Sir James Riddell was the proprietor of Ardnamurchan and Sunart, and represented the 'new elite' (Devine 1989) who purchased Highland estates. Although this process dated from the opening years of the nineteenth century in most parts of the Highlands, the Riddells had purchased Ardnamurchan and Sunart as early as 1768 (Macinnes 1994: 14). Lionel Ritchie (Ritchie 1985: 160-1) gives the following assessment of Sir James Riddell's estate policy:

'A social gulf had opened between the Riddells, originally a Linlithgow family and purchasers of land forfeited after the Forty-five, and their Gaelic-speaking tenantry, surviving at the humblest level of existence. The process of social polarisation had doubtless been accelerated by the extensive "improvements" of 1828. The evictions resulting from these changes, together with later removals at Swordles in 1853, have resulted in Riddell's appearance as one of the minor but still reviled actors in the drama of the Highland Clearances. Recent research suggests that earlier views of Riddell have been unduly harsh. Indeed, he appears to have held back from wholesale evictions at a time when mounting rent arrears made them seem a necessary evil. The Riddell estates were seriously affected by the famine which began in 1846 but the proprietor's response was patience in respect of arrears and encouragement of public works. The problems of the estate, after being placed in the care of trustees for a period, were perhaps only solved in 1855 when the Ardnamurchan portion was sold to John James Dalgleish, the Riddells remaining in possession of Sunart. The contemporary estimate of Sir James by his tenants was that, despite his intemperance on the issue of sites, he was an otherwise humane and kindly proprietor.'

The present poem indicates that the sharp rise in rent, apparently three-fold, inflicted by Riddell was deeply resented by at least one of his tenants who would scarcely have described him as a 'humane and kindly proprietor'. Instead, he calls him *eucoireach olc* ('a wicked rogue') (line 16), notwithstanding the sum in excess of £52,000 which the Riddell family had invested in their estates in 'buildings, roads, enclosure, drainage' between 1818 and 1848 (Devine 1989: 117).

25-32 This verse underlines the resentment felt by some Highlanders towards the 'new elite', who lacked the aristocratic blood and trappings of the 'old elite'.

5. Gur Olc an Duine Malcolm

Sèisd:

> Gur olc an duine Malcolm
> 'S gu bràth tha mi ràdh dheth.   2

Nuair a thig na Frangaich
A-nall ga chur ruagadh,
Cò sheasas Malcolm
'S a' ghràisg tha mun cuairt dha?   6

Bidh gach aon dhiubh fiadhaich
Ag iarraidh a bhualadh,
'S bidh mise mi fhèin ann
'S mi sèideadh na tuasaid.   10

Mo chùlaibh, mo chùlaibh,
Mo chùlaibh ris a' bhaile seo,
Mo chùlaibh ris an àite –
'S ann far an d' àraich fada mi.   14

Chan fhaicear sprèidh air buaile,
'S cha chluinnear duan aig banaraich;
Far an robh na daoine,
'S ann tha na caoraich bhuidhe ann.   18

NOTES

Source: The poem is contained in a speech given by the Rev. Donald
MacCallum in London, and reported in the *Oban Times*, 3 January
1885.

Tune: The OT text is preceded by the following vocables which
would identify the tune:

> Hillu hillin o agus o hillin eile,
> Hillu hillin o agus o hillin eile,
> Lailliun o agus o Hugi eile.

Date and Context: The Rev. Donald MacCallum was in London at
a conference of crofter delegates in December 1884, and, in the course of
his speech to the conference, he made reference to the 'gloom and
desolation' which had come upon his native parish of Craignish in

Argyll. According to MacCallum, this change was the result of 'the fierce tyranny of unrestrained landlordism', which was represented at its worst by the actions of the Malcolms of Poltalloch, who held an extensive estate in Argyll, stretching from Mid Argyll to North Knapdale. 'Who,' asked MacCallum, 'has not heard of the heart-rending eviction at Arichonan? Eighteen families were here, on one day, thrown adrift on the cold world. When they resisted the brutality of Martin, the leader of the laird army, who came to turn them out and burn their houses, the fell law of the landlords stepped between. The tyrant and the scourger,' continued MacCallum, 'were let free; the innocent and the down-trodden were locked up for years in the prison of Inveraray.' MacCallum went on to quote 'some verses of a song composed on the evictions'. This suggests that the text, as quoted by MacCallum, was incomplete.

The circumstances leading to the emergence of the Malcolms of Poltalloch as significant landowners in Argyll are examined by Professor Allan Macinnes (Macinnes 1994), who draws attention to their purchases from 'indebted Campbell lairds' and their deep involvement in plantations and slave-trading in the West Indies, whereby they accrued capital for land-purchase and investment.

Emigration from the estates of the Malcolms is on record from at least 1818 (Meek 1988: 22). By the 1840s they were pursuing a vigorous policy of assisted emigration to Upper Canada (Richards 1985: 269). Resistance to their wishes is, however, clearly evidenced by this poem and by the circumstances of the eviction at Arichonan. The township of Kilmory, North Knapdale, was also cleared by force in the summer of 1848, at the same time as Arichonan. The Malcolms requested assistance from the Argyll Constabulary in the clearing of both townships, because 'it was apprehended that the Civil Officers were likely to be deforced as on Similar previous Occasions' (Argyll Constabulary Committee Minutes, 6 July 1848).

Professor Allan Macinnes comments (Macinnes 1994: 28-9): 'It is not altogether surprising that a family such as the Malcolms of Poltalloch who ruthlessly exploited the slave trade in the West Indies, where they regarded the naming of their slaves of a piece with the naming of their livestock, should show limited sympathy in effecting Clearance. Neill Malcolm had to be restrained by his factor, John Campbell, an Inveraray lawyer, from effecting wholesale clearances in his recently acquired estate of Oib in 1801. His grandson Neill, deprived of this restraining influence, instigated the riotous clearing of Arichonan in Knapdale, at the height of the great famine in 1848.'

The song was probably composed soon after the Arichonan eviction in the summer of 1848.

1 **Malcolm:** The 'Malcolm' in question would have been Neil Malcolm of Poltalloch, who succeeded to the estate in 1837 (see Macinnes 1994: 29, quoted above).

3 **Frangaich:** The possibility of an invasion of Britain by the French was anticipated in the opening years of the nineteenth century; see Poem 1, lines 39-40 n. An interest in France appeared in later years, particularly in the period 1848-52, when widespread revolutions were taking place in Europe. Events were set in motion in France in February 1848, when students, workers and national guard forced the abdication of the king and proclaimed the Second Republic. (See Palmer 1986: 141-3, who notes that the revolutions 'sprang from a common background: economic unrest, caused by bad harvests and famine in the countryside and unemployment and recession of trade in the towns.')

The reference to the French in this line is therefore not anachronistic; events in France triggered old hopes and fears more widely in Britain, and stimulated the final phase of Chartist agitation.

18 **bhuidhe:** This breaks the rhyme with *banaraich* (line 16), and Mr Kenneth MacDonald suggests that reading *gheala* for *bhuidhe* would restore the line. Alternatively, we may suppose that some lines of the original text have been lost, and that the present quatrain is made up of couplets from two different quatrains. The adj. *buidhe* is defensible in its application to sheep, since their fleeces were likely to have been stained brown or yellow through smearing (see Poem 1, line 96 n.).

6. [Aoir Choinnich Ghèasto]

Chunnaic mise 's mi 'nam chadal
  Aisling dhen do ghabh mi ioghnadh,
Na *Fenians* a' tighinn a-nall
  A thoirt nan ceann bho na caoraich;   4
Cha bhi claigeann dhiubh ri colainn,
  Thèid an sgaradh bho gach aon dhiubh,
Thèid an sgrios bho thràigh gu monadh;
  An sin thig sonas air an t-saoghal.   8

Chunnaic mise Coinneach Ghèasto,
  'S mòr an treud a bha ga ruagadh,
E a-mach am Bràighe Buidhe,
  Lasraichean teine mun cuairt dha;   12
E ri èigheach is ri rànaich,
  'Gheibh sibh na tha 'n dàn 's mun cuairt dhomh,
'S ma leigeas sibh dhomh mo bheatha,
  Gheibh sibh mo thaighean is mo chruachan.'   16

NOTES

Source: These verses, which probably formed part of a longer poem, were collected by Miss Jo MacDonald in 1972-73 from the recitation of Mr John Budge, Lochalsh, who was a native of Borve, Skye (d. 1981). (I am grateful to Mr Budge's daughter, Mrs A. MacVicar, Inverness, for details.)

Tune: No tune is specified in the source.

Date and Context: Kenneth MacLeod, who owned the estate of Greshornish and Orbost, was an indigo planter in India, where he acquired a considerable fortune (Nicolson 1994: 241). He used his wealth to acquire the estate after he returned to Skye. He donated £30,000 to the Gesto Memorial Hospital, Edinbane. He died, unmarried, in 1869. The poem was probably composed in the 1860s (see line 3 n.).

3 **Fenians:** The Irish Republican Brotherhood, otherwise known as the Fenian organisation, was founded simultaneously in Dublin and New York in 1858. The Fenians 'believed that Britain would never concede independence [to Ireland] except to physical force, and they therefore prepared by secret military organisation for an armed uprising when Britain should be at a disadvantage.' A rising was attempted in 1867, but it was 'no more than a gesture', although the Fenian movement alerted Gladstone to the seriousness of affairs in Ireland (Moody and Martin 1984: 278-9).

In this poem, the Fenians are given the role of 'liberating invaders' usually assigned to the French (see Poems 1, lines 39-40 n., and 5, line 3 n.).

This is one of the very few surviving references to Irish nationalistic politics and political groupings in this entire corpus of Gaelic verse.

7. 'Venus' nan Gàidheal

Tha mi 'n seo air an tulaich
  Aig bun a' bhruthaich leam fhèin,
'S mi ri smaointinn mum chàirdean,
  'S mar a tha mi 'nan dèidh;   4
Dh'fhalbh m' athair 's mo mhàthair,
  'S mo bhràithrean gu lèir,
'S ged a chluinnear mo ghàire,
  'S ann troimh àilgheas nan deur.   8

Nuair dh'fhalbh 'Venus' nan Gàidheal,
  Siud an àireamh bha mòr,
Bha ceithir cheud 's a dhà dhiubh
  Air an càradh 'na com;   12
Nan robh soirbheas 'nam fàbhar
  Gan toirt sàbhailt' a-nunn,
Rìgh nan Dùl bhith gan teàrnadh
  Thar sàile nan tonn.   16

Ach bha a' ghaoth 'nan aghaidh,
  'S dh'èirich boil air a' chuan;
'S nuair dhùmhlaich na frasan,
  Mar an fheannag ghlas bha an tuar;   20
Na siùil-chinn 's iad gan sracadh,
  Lùb na cruinn àrda a-nuas;
A h-uile aon 's iad ri acain –
  Bha sgeul aca bha cruaidh.   24

Thàinig sgeula don dùthaich
  Nach robh an cunntas dhiubh beò;
Dh'fhàg sin mi fo thùrsa,
  Mo chridhe brùite le bròn;   28
Gun do chaill iad an cùrsa
  'S gun do dhùmhlaich orra an ceò,
Na cruinn chaola gan rùsgadh,
  'S fear an stiùiridh fo leòn.   32

Tìr mòr fo mo chasan,
  Dh'fhalbh an t-airtneal 's an sgìos;
H-uile aon aig an robh stòras
  Chuir e mòrchuis an gnìomh;   36

Dh'fhàg iad mis' ann am ònar
  Air tulach bhòidheach san fhraoch;
'S ann am bruadar a thòisich mi,
  'S dh'fhalbh mo chòmhradh sa ghaoith.   40

Am bruadar chunnaic mi am chadal,
  Thu bhith agam, a ghaoil;
Nuair a dhùisg mi sa mhadainn,
  Sin a' bharail bha faoin;   44
Ged tha mi car tamaill
  'Nam laighe san fhraoch,
'S mòr mo dhùil ri dhol thairis
  Do dh'fhearann nan craobh.   48

NOTES

Source: This poem was collected by Donald M. MacCuaig, Bowmore, Islay, from the late Duncan MacCalman 'during one of the many nights we spent together singing and reciting songs and melodies', and a copy was published in the *Ileach*, 7 February 1987. It was subsequently printed in Newton 1988: 189-90. The text was also known to the late Gilbert Clark, Port Charlotte, who recited part of it to me in Tiree in the early 1980s. I am very grateful to Mr MacCuaig for supplying a copy of the text as published in the *Ileach*, together with a manuscript draft and a recording of the tune. The present text follows the order of that in the *Ileach*, but obvious misreadings are corrected from the manuscript version.

Tune: The tune used by Mr MacCuaig appears to be a variant of that of 'The Braes of Strathblane' (known in Gaelic as 'Aodann Srath Bàin'). I am grateful to my colleague, Dr James Grant, for identifying the melody.

Date and Context: The identity of the composer is unknown, but he or she was evidently a member of one of the families who emigrated on the ship 'Venus'. Norman Newton (Newton 1988: 189), following Mr MacCuaig's introductory note in the *Ileach*, states that the ship sailed from Port Ellen, Islay, to Canada in 1862, but I have found no independent corroboration of this.

If the dating is correct, the emigrants are to be identified with the 400 or so who left Islay, and chiefly the district of the Oa, in 1862-63; the close correspondence between this number and the 402 who were in the 'Venus's' hold (line 11) is noteworthy. Emigration from the Oa was encouraged by John Ramsay of Kildalton who cleared tenants from Killeyan in 1862, and provided assisted passages; see Ramsay 1969: 36-41 and Storrie 1981: 145-7. See further Poem 8.

33-6 The difficulty of understanding these lines as they stand suggests that part of the song may have been lost in transmission or that individual words may have been altered. If we make a minor emendation to line 33, and read it as

Tìr mòr fo *an* casan ('With the mainland under *their* feet')

the lines make much better sense, and would apply to the emigrants rather than the poet. The point would be that, having got dry land under their feet, those who had the means were able to overcome their weariness, and to use their resources in the New World. By contrast, the composer of the song was left at home with no comparable prospects. This, together with the loss of kin and sweetheart, induced him or her to contemplate emigration.

In Mr MacCuaig's manuscript draft, lines 33-40 form the last verse of the song, but this does not remove the difficulty with line 33.

8. Fios chun a' Bhàird

Uilleam MacDhunlèibhe

Tha a' mhadainn soilleir grianach,
'S a' ghaoth 'n iar a' ruith gu rèidh;
Tha an linne sleamhainn sìochail
On a chiùinich strì nan speur;   4
Tha an long 'na h-èideadh sgiamhach,
'S cha chuir sgìos i dh'iarraidh tàmh;
Mar a fhuair 's a chunnaic mise,
A' toirt an fhios seo chun a' Bhàird.   8

Seo crùnadh mais' a' mhìos
San tèid don dìthreabh treudan bhò,
Do ghlinn nan lagan uaigneach
Anns nach cuir 's nach buainear pòr,   12
Leab-innse buar nan geum –
Cha robh mo roinn diubh 'n-dè le càch;
Mar a fhuair 's a chunnaic mise,
Thoir am fios seo chun a' Bhàird.   16

Tha mìltean sprèidh air faichean,
'S caoraich gheal' air creachain fhraoich,
'S na fèidh air stùcan fàsail,
Far nach truaillear làr na gaoith;   20
An sìolach fiadhaich neartmhor
Fliuch le dealt na h-oiteig thlàith;
Mar a fhuair 's a chunnaic mise,
Thoir am fios seo chun a' Bhàird.   24

Tha an còmhnard 's coirean garbhlaich,
Còrs na fairg' 's gach gràinseach rèidh,
Le buaidhean blàths na h-iarmailt
Mar a dh'iarramaid gu lèir;   28
Tha 'n t-seamair fhiadhain 's neòinean
Air na lòintean feòir fo bhlàth;
Mar a fhuair 's a chunnaic mise,
Thoir am fios seo chun a' Bhàird.   32

69

Na caochain fhìor-uisg' luath
A' tighinn a-nuas o chùl nam màm
Bho lochain ghlan' gun ruadhan
Air na cruachan fad' on tràigh;　　　　　36
Far an òl am fiadh a phailteas,
'S bòidheach ealtan lach gan snàmh;
Mar a fhuair 's a chunnaic mise,
Thoir am fios seo chun a' Bhàird.　　　　40

Tha bogha mòr an t-sàile
Mar a bha le reachd bithbhuan,
Am mòrachd maise nàdair
'S a cheann-àrd ri tuinn a' chuain –　　　44
A rìomball geal seachd mìle,
Gainmhean sìobt' o bheul an làin;
Mar a fhuair 's a chunnaic mise,
Thoir am fios seo chun a' Bhàird.　　　　48

Na dùilean, stèidh na cruitheachd,
Blàths is sruthan 's anail neul,
Ag altram lusan ùrail
Air an laigh an driùchd gu sèimh,　　　52
Nuair a thuiteas sgàil na h-oidhche
Mar gum b' ann a' caoidh na bha;
Mar a fhuair 's a chunnaic mise,
Thoir am fios seo chun a' Bhàird.　　　　56

Ged a roinneas gathan grèine
Tlus nan speur ri blàth nan lòn,
'S ged a chìthear sprèidh air àirigh,
Is buailtean làn de dh'àlach bhò,　　　60
Tha Ile 'n-diugh gun daoine,
Chuir a' chaor' a bailtean fàs;
Mar a fhuair 's a chunnaic mise,
Thoir am fios seo chun a' Bhàird.　　　　64

Ged thig ànrach aineoil
Gus a' chaladh 's e sa cheò,
Chan fhaic e soills' on chagailt
Air a' chladach seo nas mò;　　　　68

Chuir gamhlas Ghall air fuadach
Na tha bhuainn 's nach till gu bràth;
Mar a fhuair 's a chunnaic mise,
Thoir am fios seo chun a' Bhàird.   72

Ged a thogar feachd na h-Alb',
As cliùiteach ainm air faich' an àir,
Bithidh bratach fhraoich nan Ileach
Gun dol sìos ga dìon le càch;   76
Sgap mìorun iad thar fairge,
'S gun ach ainmhidhean balbh 'nan àit';
Mar a fhuair 's a chunnaic mise,
Thoir am fios seo chun a' Bhàird.   80

Tha taighean seilbh na dh'fhàg sinn
Feadh an fhuinn 'nan càrnan fuar;
Dh'fhalbh 's cha till na Gàidheil;
Stad an t-àiteach, cur is buain;   84
Tha stèidh nan làrach tiamhaidh
A' toirt fianais air 's ag ràdh,
'Mar a fhuair 's a chunnaic mise,
Leig am fios seo chun a' Bhàird.'   88

Cha chluinnear luinneag òighean,
Sèisd nan òran air a' chlèith,
'S chan fhaicear seòid mar b' àbhaist
A' cur bàir air faiche rèidh;   92
Thug ainneart fògraidh uainn iad;
'S leis na coimhich buaidh mar 's àill;
Leis na fhuair 's a chunnaic mise,
Biodh am fios seo aig a' Bhàrd.   96

Chan fhaigh an dèirceach fasgadh
No 'm fear-astair fois o sgìos,
No soisgeulach luchd-èisdeachd;
Bhuadhaich eucoir, Goill is cìs;   100
Tha an nathair bhreac 'na lùban
Air na h-ùrlair far an d'fhàs
Na fir mhòr' a chunnaic mise;
Thoir am fios seo chun a' Bhàird.   104

Lomadh ceàrn na h-Oa,
An Lanndaidh bhòidheach 's Roinn MhicAoidh;
Tha 'n Learga ghlacach ghrianach
'S fuidheall cianail air a taobh;   108
Tha an Gleann 'na fhiadhair uaine
Aig luchd-fuath gun tuath, gun bhàrr;
Mar a fhuair 's a chunnaic mise,
Thoir am fios seo chun a' Bhàird.   112

NOTES
Source: Livingston 1882: 151-5.
   Tune: 'When the kye comes hame'.
   Date and Context: The poem was first published in 1863 as a
broadsheet 'printed in double columns by Wm. Gilchrist, Printer,
Howard Street, Glasgow' (MacLean 1915: 166). It was probably
composed shortly after the estate policy of John Ramsay of Kildalton set
in train the departure of a number of Islay folk from the Oa (line 105), on
board emigrant ships bound for Canada, in 1862-63 (Storrie 1981:
145-7). It is highly likely that Livingston was among those who, in 1862-
63, contributed 'a spate of angry or sarcastic letters to the press, written
over nom de plumes. They were thought to come largely from Islaymen
long settled comfortably in Glasgow, who accused John Ramsay of
"enforced removals"' (Ramsay 1969: 40-1). See also Poem 7.

   14 The reference in this line is to Mrs Blair, mother of the Rev. Robert
Blair, editor of Livingston 1882. The poem is composed as if she were
sending 'a message to the poet' from Islay. Mr Blair senior had resigned
his farm of Lòn Bàn, near Bowmore, at Martinmas 1863 (Livingston
1882: 152). The alternative title given to the poem by the poet is 'Oran
Bean Dhonnachaidh' ('The Song of Duncan's Wife').

   41 The line evidently contains an oblique reference to Bowmore,
known in Gaelic as Am Bogha Mòr.

   43 **Am mòrachd:** The source reads a' mòrachd, but it makes better
sense (as Mr Kenneth MacDonald suggests) to emend as shown in the
edition; thus 'in the majestic greatness of nature's beauty' – surely one of
the most concise and evocative lines in nineteenth-century Gaelic verse.

   81-8 Margaret Storrie comments (Storrie 1981: 178): 'The ruins that
one sees today are often all that is left of "swollen clusters deserted
almost immediately after a period of vigorous but unhealthy growth". In
Islay today these groups of ruins are to be seen in many places, the
highest degree of concentration being the Rinns, around the Oa and in
the upper parts of the Glen.' See the notes on lines 105, 106, 107, 109.

   99 **soisgeulach:** Itinerant preachers of various evangelical per-
suasions, but chiefly Baptist and Independent, were active in Islay in
the first half of the nineteenth century. They attracted strong followings

in the Rinns and the Oa, areas which were later significantly depopulated; see Meek 1991: 76.

105 **ceàrn na h-Oa:** the promontory of the Oa, in the south-west of Islay, immediately west of Port Ellen.

106 **An Lanndaidh:** This is generally used nowadays as a kenning or poetic name for the island if Islay. Here, however, it appears to denote a particular district of the island. Mr Donald MacCuaig kindly informs me that the name was used of the Rinns; but it seems likely that it once referred to a specific district beyond *Roinn MhicAoidh* ('Mackay's Division'), which has now become the standard Gaelic name for the Rinns. The poet's use of *An Lanndaidh* alongside *Roinn MhicAoidh* seems to confirm the connection, but it also demonstrates that the names once denoted two different districts.

107 **an Learga:** probably Largie. In the Middle Ages, Islay was divided into three parts, one of which was Largie and Oa in the south. Lands in 'Oa and Largie of Islay' were granted to John MacIan of Ardnamurchan in 1499; see Munro and Munro 1986: 230-1. Largie probably lay centrally, between the Oa and the Glen; see next note.

109 **an Gleann:** the Glen, extending eastwards from Bridgend, and upwards to Ballygrant.

The most noticeable reductions in rural population, through clearance and removal, assisted emigration and the creation of planned villages, took place in the Rinns, the Glen (including what was probably part of Largie) and the Oa; in the Rinns, population displacement occurred mainly in the period 1824-35 (when Walter Campbell of Shawfield still owned Islay); in the Glen and the Oa, the decline of holdings with more than two tenants occurred after the Potato Famine of 1846. Clearing in the Glen was taking place by 1848, when James Brown, an Edinburgh accountant, administered the estate after the bankruptcy of the Campbells, and removals continued thereafter when the Campbells' estate was broken up and sold in portions to new landlords, including John Ramsay who purchased Kildalton and Oa (1855-61). Population decline in the Glen and the Oa was most marked between 1848 and 1863. See the maps in Storrie 1981: 128-9, 136-7.

9. Oran air Fear
a bha a' Fuadachadh nan Gàidheal

An uair a thig an t-eug ort,
Leam fèin gur math, O raithill ò.

Cuiridh sinn air dèilidh thu
Led lèine bhric, O raithill ò.   4

Togaidh sinn gu h-uallach thu
Air guaillibh fhear, O raithill ò.

Cha tèid nì air d' uachdar
Ach buachar mairt, O raithill ò.   8

'S a-chaoidh cha chinn an t-eòinean ort
No am feòirlinn glan, O raithill ò.

Ach cinnidh foghanain is feanntag
Aig ceann do chas, O raithill ò.   12

Nuair thèid spaid den ùir ort,
Bidh an dùthaich ceart, O raithill ò.

Bidh gach bochd is truaghan
A' bualadh bhas, O raithill ò.   16

Nam faighte air an tràigh thu
An àite stamh, O raithill ò;

Gum biodh fear no dhà ann
A ghàireadh mach, O raithill ò.   20

Cha chuirte cist' no anart ort
Ach lèine bhreac, O raithill ò.

Gu bheil cridhe spìocach
Ad chliabh a-steach, O raithill ò.   24

Tha d' aodann mar am miaran,
A bhlianaich bhric, O raithill ò.

'S e an t-òr a bha san laoighcionn
Chuir daoine as, O raithill ò;   28

74

Or na seiche ruaidhe,
'S cha bhuaidh cho math, O raithill ò.

Nan cailleadh tu chlach bhuadhach,
Bhiodh d' uain glè thearc, O raithill ò.   32

Mo mhallachd fhèin thar chàcha
Gu bràtha leat, O raithill ò.

NOTES

Source: The *Oban Times*, 3 February 1883. The song is known in other sources, including MacDonald and MacDonald 1911: 289, where it is entitled 'Oran do Dhroch Bhàillidh' ('Song to a Bad Factor'). The MacDonald (MacD) text, which is shorter than that in OT, includes lines 1-16 of the above edition, with some variant readings, and with the couplets in a different order. According to the editors of MacD (p.xlvi), the text was probably 'added to in different localities'.

The OT text is the oldest and longest of the extant texts. MacD has 11 couplets, with three couplets which are not wholly attested in OT, although they echo the sentiments and sometimes the phrasing of the earlier version. These are:

> Togaidh sinn air còmhlaidh thu,
> Is còmhlan leat, ho raill ò.

('We will lift you on to a board / and a group of people along with you.')

> Cuiridh sinn san uaigh thu,
> 'S a' chlach bhuadhach leat, ho raill ò.

('We will put you in the grave / and the efficacious stone with you.')

> Cha bhi gal nam pàisdean ann,
> No gàirich bhan, ho raill ò.

('There will be no crying of children, or wailing of women.')

Tune: OT gives the *fonn* as:

> A chòtain duibh, o hùillein,
> 'S a thriùbhsair ghlais, O raithill ò.

Date and Context: The editors of MacD note that 'the original factor is believed to have been on the Ardnamurchan estate'. An Ardnamurchan origin is not inconceivable: there is a tradition that ascribes the song to Dr John MacLachlan of Rahoy (MacLean 1985: 56).

However, if the couplets about the deer (lines 27-30) were part of the original text, it is unlikely that the song could have been composed before 1867, when a deer-forest of 22,000 acres was formed in Ardnamurchan (Orr 1982: 172). Given the distribution of deer forests (ibid.: 168-80), Ardnamurchan would not have been the only possible district of origin. Nevertheless, an earlier core of couplets, originating in Ardnamurchan, may have existed, to which those on the deer might have been added later, there or in another district.

Although MacD claims that a 'bad factor' is the subject, the OT title is less specific, referring only to one who was 'evicting Highlanders'. Such a person could just as easily have been a landlord. We should probably not seek a specific identification; the song probably operated on the principle that, if the circumstances coincided, it could be applied to the 'bad landlord' or 'bad factor' in any district.

3 Cuiridh iad air còmhlaidh thu ('They will put you on a board') (MacD).

7 d' uachdar-sa (MacD).

10 feòirnein (MacD).

12 air do chramhlaich ghlais ('on your grey skeleton') (MacD).

15-16   Cha bhi bantrach 's truaghain ann.
A bhualadh bhas, ho raill ò.
('There will be no widow or poor souls / to strike (i.e. wring) their hands.') (MacD).

The form of the couplet in MacD has a superficial ring of authenticity when ,compared with OT, but it may represent a late attempt to bring the sense of the lines into keeping with customs of keening and lamenting. The reading in OT is consistent with the theme of rejoicing as portrayed in satirical elegies on the deaths (or alleged deaths) of undesirable individuals. See Poem 10.

25-6 Perhaps translate as: 'Your face resembles a thimble, made of pock-marked lean meat'.

31-2 The implication is that the landlord or factor is using supernatural power to increase the size of his flock. I know of no other reference to the use of a *clach bhuadhach* in this context.

10. [Cumha a' Bhàillidh Mhòir]

Uisdean Ròs

Tha sgeul anns an dùthaich, 's tha sinn sunndach ga
h-èisdeachd,
Gu bheil am Bàillidh 'na shìneadh, 's gun trìd air ach lèine,
'S e gun chomas na bruidhneadh, gun sgrìobhadh, gun
leughadh;
'S gu bheil cùl-taice nan Ileach 'na shìneadh 's
chan èirich.   4

'S nuair thèid iad don bhàta nì sinn gàir' a bhios èibhinn;
'S nuair chruinnicheas sinn còmhla bidh sinn ag òl air a
chèile
Uisge-beatha math Gàidhealach, fìon làidir is seudar;
'S cha bhi sinn tuilleadh fo chùram on a sgiùrsadh a'
bhèist ud.   8

Gum bi a' Factor air thoiseach san t-sloc sa bheil Sàtan,
'S Aonghas Mòr as a dheaghaidh, 's lasair theine ri
mhàsan,
Leis na rinn thu de ainneart air mnathan 's air pàisdean,
'S an sluagh bha san dùthaich rinn thu sgiùrsadh
far sàile.   12

'S nuair a chualaig iad an Canada gun do chaidil a'
bhèist ud,
Chaidh an tein'-èibhinn fhadadh is chaidh bratach
ri geugan;
'S ann an sin a bha làn aighear, 's iad a' tachairt ri chèile,
'S chaidh iad uil' air an glùinean 's thug iad cliù gun
do dh'eug thu.   16

NOTES

Source: The poem and the introduction were recorded in 1976 by the
late Eric Cregeen from Donald Morrison, Ardtun, Isle of Mull. The
recording is in the School of Scottish Studies, SA 1976/54A. The text was
published in *Tocher*, 24: 310-11. The introduction is as follows:

'Donald Morrison: "There was this old man, according to traditional
story, he was evicted from his croft, and then he got a small 'rookery'

beside a burn or small river. And he was there all his days but he always regretted that he was evicted from his croft. And the Factor died. Uisdean Ròs they called him and he said, when the Factor died: Tha sgeul anns an dùthaich..." '

Tune: The source does not specify a tune.

Date and Context: John Campbell of Ardmore (Islay), who farmed at Ardfeenaig in the Ross of Mull, was the Chamberlain of the Duke of Argyll's lands in Mull and Iona from 1845 until his death in 1872. He was also factor of Tiree from c. 1846 to 1864. In these islands he gained a very unsavoury reputation as a merciless and oppressive agent of estate policy, especially at the time of the Potato Famine. His notoriety as an evictor was compounded by his alleged partiality towards the people of his native island of Islay.

It is more than evident that Campbell had the capacity to arouse strong, unfavourable feelings among tenants who were exposed to his power. His allegedly overbearing manner is reflected in the two names by which he was known in Tiree and Mull – *Am Bàillidh / Factor Mòr* ('The Great Factor') and *Iain Dubh Caimbeul* ('Black John Campbell'). Within his own class and family circle, however, he was naturally highly regarded; a song in his praise, composed by his wife, is found in Mac-na-Ceàrdadh 1879: 9-11. Another complimentary poem, composed by 'Fear-siubhail' ('Traveller'), was published in Glasgow in 1868, as a pamphlet entitled *Moladh do Mhaighsteir Iain Caimbeul Bailidh ann an Airdfineig 'am Muile*. It refers to Campbell's kindness at the time of the Famine, when he is said to have brought meal across from Ireland in his own boat. (I owe this reference to Mr Robin Campbell, Surrey.)

The present poem is far from complimentary. It is evidently not a mock elegy, but a blistering satire, intended as a fitting 'send off' for Campbell, when, allegedly to the great relief of many, he died in the late summer of 1872. The composer, Uisdean Ròs, is apparently to be identified with a certain Eugene Rose (or Ross) who held part of a croft at Ardtun in the 1840s. The poem stands in contrast to the sentiments expressed by Campbell's family at the time of his death: see further MacArthur 1990: 138-9.

5 Campbell's body was taken by boat from Mull to Islay for burial.

10 **Aonghas Mòr:** Angus MacNiven was Campbell's ground officer and right-hand man. He was one of several Islaymen whom Campbell introduced to Mull, and his strict adherence to his master's policies was deeply resented. So too was the preferential treatment that he received from the Factor Mòr. He was given the crofting land at Tiraghoill as a farm, and the crofters were displaced to poor land on Ben Lee, a mile or so to the east of Bunessan. He too was lampooned in Gaelic verse. One verse and the refrain of a song attacking him have survived in oral transmission in the Ross of Mull to the present day. I recorded these fragments from John Campbell, *Teonaidh Chailein*, in Bunessan in July 1991:

Sèisd:
Cùm bhuam an seicealair
'S gun dannsainn 'Beic a' churraic odhair'.   2

Aonghas Mòr MacCrìthein,
Seicealair na tìre;
Gur h-e a thogadh m' inntinn
  E bhith sìnt' an Cille Chomain.   6

Refrain:
Keep the trouble-maker away from me
so that I can dance 'The obsequious slant of the dun cap'.   2

Big Angus MacNiven
is the trouble-maker of the land;
how it would elate my mind
  if he was stretched out in Cille Chomain.   6

Cille Chomain (line 6) is a well-known graveyard in Islay. The verse and refrain were transmitted to John Campbell by the Morrisons of Ardtun, who had connections with Islay through Mrs Donald Morrison. It is thought that the song was composed in Islay, where MacNiven's reputation was equally unflattering.

11. Manitoba

Iain MacIlleathain, Bàrd Bhaile Mhàrtainn

Sèisd:

Gur muladach mise 's mi an seo gun duin' idir
A thogas, no thuigeas, no sheinneas leam dàn;
Le dùrachd mo chridhe, soraidh slàn leis na gillean
A sheòl thar na linne gu Manitobà.   4

Bu ghrianach ar madainn nuair bha sinn 'nar balaich,
Gun chùram, gun ghearan, gun teannachadh màil;
Le ceòl is làn aighear, cha laigheadh an smalan
Air a' chomann a bh' againn am Baile nam Bàrd.   8

Mi 'm shuidhe gu h-uaigneach air tulaichean uaine,
Tha nithean gam bhuaireadh nach cualas le càch;
Mi caoidh nam fear sunndach bha ceanalta, cliùiteach,
Dh'fhàg eilean an dùthchais 's an cùl ris gu bràth.   12

'S nuair ràinig a' mhadainn gu dol air an aineol,
'S a thionail gach caraid a bh' aca san àit',
Chan urra mi aithris am bròn a bh' air m' aire
'S an cùl ris a' bhaile sa mhadainn Di-màirt.   16

'S e faileas na daoine: 's nach sgarach an saoghal –
'S e 's fasan dha daonnan bhith caochladh gach là.
'Nar coigrich air uachdar, cha mhaireann 's cha bhuan
 sinn,
Is mìltean de thruaghain gam fuadach thar sàil.   20

Tha luchd fearainn shaoir anns an àm seo ro-ghaolach
Air stòras an t-saoghail a shlaodadh bho chàch;
'S bidh innealan baoghalt' sa Ghàidhealtachd daonnan
Gu fògradh nan daoine, 's cur chaorach 'nan àit'.   24

Chan fhaic mi san àm seo ach caoraich air bheanntan;
Chan eil anns gach gleann ach fear Gallda no dhà;
'S am beagan a dh'fhan dhiubh air rudhachan mara
Gan iomain gu cladach 's gam feannadh le màl.   28

Tha 'n òigridh ghrinn uallach an-diugh air am fuadach;
Tha deas agus tuath taighean fuar agus fàs;
Chan fhaic mi a' ghruagach dol feasgar don bhuaile,
'S cha chluinn mi a duanag 's i cuallach an àil.   32

Luchd fhèileadh is osan is bhonaidean cocte
Bha riamh air am moladh air thoiseach sna blàir,
Tha iad gan cur thairis gu dùthaich mhì-fhallain,
'S gun nì air an air' ach am fearann chur fàs.   36

Cha labhair mi tuilleadh mu euchd nam fear curant'
Do Bhreatainn fhuair urram 's gach cumasg is spàirn;
'S e daoradh an fhearainn a dh'fhàg sinn cho tana,
'S gun chuimhn' air Sebastopol 's Balaclabhà.   40

NOTES

Source: Cameron 1932: 164-5. This version differs in a number of ways
from the more recent text of Hector Kennedy, reproduced with valuable
notes in Mackay 1979: 78-81. The most significant difference is the
preservation of two quatrains in Kennedy's version (henceforward
referred to as K). These are included as lines 13-20 of the present edition.
They add significantly to the body and elegiac tone of the poem,
providing more detail and placing it firmly within the conventions of
verse concerned with *caochladh* ('adverse change'). These quatrains
are also attested in the version preserved in Sinclair 1900: 111-3, but with
less convincing readings for some lines.

K, however, does not attest the second and fifth quatrains of the
present text. K also offers variant readings in several lines, and the most
significant are noted below.

Tune: The tune is given in Mackay 1979: 78.

Date and Context: The poem was composed when a group of
MacLeans emigrated from Balephuil, Tiree, to Manitoba in 1878.

4 **thar na linne:** air an t-slighe ('on the way, voyage') (K). K's
reading seems less ornate, and may represent the original phrase.

7 **Le ceòl is làn aighear:** Ach sunndach, làn aigheir ('But in good
spirits and full of mirth') (K).

8 **Baile nam Bàrd:** a poetic kenning for the township of Balephuil,
which was noted for its unusually high number of active poets; see
Cregeen and MacKenzie 1978: 13.

12 Sinclair 1900 reads: 'S mi smaointinn air an-iochd luchd-fearainn le
'm màil ('and I reflecting on the cruelty of the landowners with their
rents'). This is a less specific and less satisfactory form of the line.

16 **cùl ri:** The phrase '(cuir) cùl ri' ('turn one's back on') carries none

of the pejorative connotations associated with the English 'equivalent'. It occurs in other Gaelic poems describing a separation from one's native place, sometimes under pressing circumstances.

37-40 In K this quatrain takes the following form:

> Cha labhair mi tuilleadh ma euchd nam fear duineil
> Ach ruigidh mi Ruisia 's mullach Alma;
> 'S e daoiread an fhearainn chuir na Gàidheil an tainead:
> 'S gun chuimhn' air Sebastopol 's Balaclava.

('I shall say nothing more about the deeds of the brave men, but I will go so far as to mention Russia and the Heights of Alma: it is the weight of the rent that has left the Gaels few in numbers: forgotten are Sebastopol and Balaclava.')

The main allusions in both versions of the quatrain are to the principal battles and sieges of the Crimean War (1853-56), in which Highland regiments participated. K gives more detail, referring to Russia and Alma in line 38. Hostility between the Turks and the Russians sparked off the conflict, which drew in the British and French after the destruction of the Turkish fleet. The siege of Sebastopol by a British and French force of some 50,000 men lasted for a year from September 1854. The battle for the strategic Heights of Alma took place on 20th September 1854. The battle of Balaclava was fought on 25th October 1854, and was noteworthy for the brave role of the 93rd Highlanders under the command of Sir Colin Campbell. The regiment repulsed a Russian attempt to seize the British base (Woodward 1939 edn: 267-92; Palmer 1986: 39, 88-9, 258). MacLean believed that the Highlanders had been ill rewarded for their bravery.

40 Sinclair 1900 reads: "S a dh'fhàg iad cho tana an gleannaibh nan sàr' ('and made them so scarce in the glens of the fine men'). It is highly probable that this is the result of 'improvement' by the editor.

12. Bochdan na Rìoghachd

Calum Caimbeul MacPhàil

Tha bochdan na rìoghachd
  Fo bhinn a tha cruaidh,
Aig uachdarain fearainn
  'S fo chìs aig an tuath: 4
An dèirc chan fhaod iad iarraidh,
  'S an obair tha i gann,
'S gun nì ach taigh nam bochd,
  'S b' fheàrr bhith crocht' na ann.   8

Tha Gàidhealtachd na h-Alba
  Gu dearbh 'na h-adhbhar bròin,
Far an robh na mìltean
  De ghrinn ghillean òg',   12
Seann daoine fiachail
  Is fial mhnathan còir',
Is caileagan bu chùbhraidh
  Na 'n driùchd air an lòn.   16

Càit a bheil na daoine
  Bha taobh nam beann àrd',
Le beagan cruidh is chaorach
  Air raon mar a b' àbhaist,   20
Nach diùltadh an dèirce
  Don fheumnach 'na chàs,
'S a bheireadh cuid na h-oidhche
  Le coibhneas is blàths?   24

Tha riaghladairean na dùthcha
  Mar stiùir aig an nàmh,
A' fògradh nan laoch,
  'S a' toirt chaorach 'nan àit';   28
Gheibh Sasannaich na Beurla
  Gach nì mar as àill,
'S thèid na Gàidheil a sgiùrsadh
  Gu dùthchannan fàs'.   32

Nuair thòisicheas an streupaid
   Thig feum air a' bhochd;
Bidh daoin' uaisle gan glaodhaich
   Bhàrr aodann nan cnoc;   36
Freagraidh Mac Talla iad,
   'Chan eagal duibh sa chàs,
Is pailteas chaoraich-mhaola
   Ri aodann a' bhlàir.'   40

Comanndairean gan stiùireadh
   A dhùthaich nan Gall,
Le casan fada, caola,
   Is cuirp ghoirid fhann;   44
Sùil nach seasadh cruadal
   Is gàirdean gun fheum,
'S ma chuir sibh cùl ri Gàidheil,
   Fhuair sibh gàrlaich 'nan dèidh.   48

Bidh taighean-mòr' 'nan luaithre
   Is uaibhrich gun cheann,
'S an teaghlaichean gan ruagadh
   Bhàrr guaillean nam beann;   52
Oladh iad an leòr
   As gach tobar a tha geur
A dh'fhosgail iad don bhochd –
   Gheibh deoch as dhaibh fhèin.   56

Bha gàrradh an Eden
   'S bu rìgh e thar chàich,
Gus an tàin' an nathair lùbach
   Le cùmhnantan bàis;   60
Thuit an sin a challaidean,
   'S bha mhillsearachd dhaibh geur,
'S tha an nathair sin an tràth-s'
   Cur nan Gàidheal as a chèil'.   64

Ma their thu gu bheil mi cruaidh
   Air daoin'-uaisle an tràth-s',
Tilg sa mheidh-thomhais iad,
   Is mothaich mar a tha;   68

Mur eil eucoir a' snàmh
  Thar cheartas is ga bhàthadh,
Fuilingidh mi mo sgiùrsadh
  A dùthaich nan Gàidheal.   72

NOTES

Source: The *Oban Times*, 16 November 1872; later reprinted in MacPhàil 1947: 5-7.

Tune: This is not specified in the source.

Date and Context: The poet's main concern is the effect of the Scottish Poor Law as formulated in 1845. The law recognised two categories: the able-bodied poor, ineligible for relief, and the deserving poor. Maintaining the poor in the Highlands required a substantial contribution from landlords. The poet implies that the landlords' failure to meet the real extent of their obligation led to the emigration of the poor. In lines 5-6, he alludes to the exclusion of the able-bodied poor from any relief, a circumstance which led to further poverty, especially if work was scarce. In line 4, he draws attention to the exploitation that followed from the restrictions on poor relief, and implies that the able-bodied poor would have been given hard labour and low wages by farmers who were aware of their need for work. The poet argues that the real value of poverty-stricken Highlanders was as defenders of Scotland.

13. Oran Muinntir Bheàrnaraidh

Murchadh MacLeòid, Glaschu

Ceud fàilt' gu muinntir Bheàrnaraidh
    O bhàrd a mhuinntir Leòdhais;
Bu sibh fhèin na h-àrmainn
    A bhiodh tàbhachdail sa chòmhraig;   4
B' e adhbhar bròin is cràidh
    Gum faiceadh Pàrlamaid ur seòrsa
Gar sgiùrsadh as ur fàrdaichean,
    'S ur n-àite bhith aig òisgean.   8

A shluagh mo chridhe, 's truagh nach mise
    Bha nur measg nuair thòisich
Na coin gur ruagadh, an dùil ur fuadach
    Null thar chuan bho ur n-eòlas;   12
Am fear a thàinig leis na bàirnigidh
    Air àilgheas Dhòmhnaill,
A ghortachadh cha b'fhiach leibh e,
    Ach riab sibh dheth a chòta.   16

'S mi bha èibhneach nuair a leugh mi
    Mu ur n-èirigh còmhla,
Ri guaillibh chèile, 's rinn sin feum dhuibh –
    Ghlèidh sibh 'n grèim bu chòir dhuibh –   20
Bhon thug Sir Seumas dhuibh am feur
    Bha aig ur sprèidh air mòintich;
Chan fhuadaichear neach tuilleadh dhibh
    Gun fuil an cuim a dhòrtadh.   24

Is glan a chaidh sibh an òrdagh
    Air a' mhòintich moch Di-haoine;
A-steach gu bràighe Steòrnabhaigh,
    Bu bhòidheach luchd mo ghaoil-sa;   28
Pìob nan dos ri ceòl dhuibh,
    Is gille còir cur gaoth innt',
'S Mac Talla bh' anns na creagan
    Ri toirt freagairt air gach taobh dhi.   32

Bha gach maor is siorram
   'S an luchd-lagha bh' anns an àite
Air chrith le geilt nuair chunnaic iad
   Na curaidhean ri meàrsadh;   36
Gu coibhneil thug sibh cuireadh dhaibh,
   'S gun cluinneadh iad mar bha sibh
Gur sàrachadh le ainneart
   Aoin de ainglibh dubha Shàtain.   40

Nuair dh'innis sibh don t-siorram
   Mu na dh'fhuiling sibh de dh'fhòirneart,
'S a cheasnaich e gach fear agaibh
   Mun earraid 's mun a' chòta,   44
Ràinig sibh am Matsonach,
   Sa chaisteal san robh chòmhnaidh,
Is chuir sibh iolach suas an sin
   A chual' e staigh 'na sheòmar.   48

Nuair a chunnaic e tre uinneig
   Na bha muigh ga iarraidh
De threun-fhir throma dhèanadh pronnadh,
   Nam bu chron bu mhiann leibh,   52
Thàinig agus dh'èisd e ribh,
   'S am Beurla rinn sibh sgial dha,
Mar bha sibh air ur sàrachadh
   Fo làimh a dhroch fhear-riaghlaidh.   56

Isean salach nead na h-iolair'
   Le ghob guineach millteach,
'S iomadh uan a rinn e tholladh –
   'S tric am fuil air ingean;   60
Ach innsidh mise dha a chunnart,
   Mura sguir e bhìdeadh –
Thèid a thilgeil leis a' ghunna
   Shloc nach urr' e dhìreadh.   64

Dòmhnall dona, bronnach, brùideil,
   Dòmhnall gnùgach, ciarghlas,
De Rothaich ghortach Bhaile Dhubhaich –
   B' olc an cliù 's an gnìomh iad;   68

Gus an tàinig thu do Leòdhas,
  Cha robh bròg a riamh ort –
Sgiathan fad' air ablach còta
  Còmhdachadh gach sliasaid.   72

Sguiridh mise bhith ga leantainn;
  An còrr cha chan mi 'n tràth seo;
'S e guth na tha Leòdhasaich an Glaschu,
  'S tha sinn pailt an àireamh –   76
Mura leig e dheth a chleachdadh,
  A' creachadh sluagh ar n-àite,
Thèid trì-fichead againn dhachaigh,
  'S clachaidh sinn gu bàs e.   80

NOTES

Source: MacLeod 1962: 28-30.
  Tune: 'Moladh Chabar Fèidh'.
  Date and Context: The song was inspired by the sequence of events
which concerned the crofters of the island of Bernera, Loch Roag, Lewis,
in the spring of 1874, and resulted in the so-called 'Bernera Riot' in
Stornoway in April of that year. Three Bernera crofters were tried at
Stornoway Sheriff Court in July 1874, and were acquitted. At another
trial the sheriff officer involved in the dispute was fined for assault. The
fine of the officer, the acquittal of the men, and the subsequent dismissal
of Donald Munro, Chamberlain of Lewis, made this a particularly
significant happening.
  The dispute centred on the summer grazings normally used by the
islanders of Bernera. These were originally on Beann a' Chualain, in
Uig, on the Lewis mainland. The crofters lost their first lot of grazings in
1872. These became part of the sporting estates of Morsgail and
Scaliscro, and they were given moorland which once belonged to the
farm of Earshader. They were then instructed to build a dyke, seven
miles long, to demarcate their grazings from the Scaliscro estate. Having
done so, they were then informed that they were to lose the grazings, and
were to receive the grazings of the farm of Hacleit in Bernera. The
Bernera crofters were unwilling to move, since they were not happy with
the Hacleit grazings, and they were visited by Donald Munro,
Chamberlain of Lewis, in an attempt to persuade them to accept the new
offer. It is alleged that Munro threatened to evict them if they did not
agree. Subsequently, on 24th March 1874, a sheriff officer from
Stornoway, Colin MacLennan, arrived in Bernera to serve 58
summonses of removal. In the evening he was attacked by a crowd of
youngsters, and allegedly threatened to shoot them. The following
morning he was involved in a scuffle with a group of men, and the

officer's coat was torn (as mentioned in lines 13-16 of the poem).

When the matter was reported in Stornoway, it was decided to arrest those who were alleged to have assaulted the sheriff officer. Remarkably, one of the men, Angus MacDonald, was in Stornoway with a companion when the Police Superintendent was on his way to make the arrests in Bernera. He was recognised, and a major incident – the Bernera Riot – occurred, in which the police were obstructed in their attempt to take him to the Police Office. Later a task-force of 130 Bernera men set out for Stornoway in order to free MacDonald, but they met him on his way home. They then went to Stornoway, where they sought a meeting with the proprietor of Lewis, Sir James Matheson. Their request was granted, and, through an interpreter, they told him of the threats of eviction made by Donald Munro. The march to Stornoway and the conversation with Sir James Matheson form the core of the poem (lines 25-56).

After the trials in Stornoway, the Bernera men were reinstated in their grazings in Earshader. For detailed accounts of the Bernera affair, see *Trial* 1874; MacAmhlaigh 1980; and MacPhail 1989: 12-17.

The poem was probably composed between April and July 1874. It may have been composed before the trial, since it does not refer to it directly, nor does it mention the downfall of Donald Munro. The poet was resident in Glasgow when he heard of the march of the Bernera men to Lews Castle, a point which suggests a date of composition not much later than April 1874.

14 **àilgheas Dhòmhnaill:** See lines 57-72 n.

21 **Sir Seumas:** Sir James Matheson, proprietor of Lewis. Matheson purchased Lewis from Lady Stewart MacKenzie of Seaforth in 1844.

57-72 The subject of the invective is Donald Munro, Chamberlain of Lewis until he was formally discharged from office on 8th July 1875, a year after the Bernera trials. A native of Tain, Munro came as a solicitor to Stornoway in 1842, and was appointed Chamberlain in 1853. He held numerous other offices, but he was particularly notorious for his role as Chamberlain. His high-handed actions were sometimes executed without the knowledge of Sir James Matheson, as was the case with the serving of the Bernera eviction notices. For a brief summary of his career, see MacPhail 1989: 13; for a fuller account, see Grant 1992.

67 **Rothaich:** the family of Munros to whom Donald Munro belonged: see previous note.

14. Spiorad a' Charthannais

Iain Mac a' Ghobhainn

O Spioraid shoilleir shàr-mhaisich,
A Spioraid ghràsmhoir chaoin,
Tha riaghladh anns an àros sin
Tha uile làn de ghaol,   4
Nan gabhamaid gu càirdeil riut
Gad fhàilteachadh gu caomh,
'S e siud a bheireadh àrdachadh
Do nàdar clann nan daoin'.   8

Nam b' eòl dhuinn thu 'nad mhaisealachd,
'S nam b'aithne dhuinn do luach,
'S e siud a bheireadh inntinn dhuinn
Os cionn an t-saoghail thruaigh;   12
Gur sona iad fhuair eòlas ort,
'S len còmhnaich thu gu buan;
'S ann tromhad tha na sòlasan
Tha 'n Tìr na Glòire shuas.   16

'S tu phàirticheadh gu h-èifeachdach
Rinn gnè nam flaitheas àrd;
An àite greann na h-eucorach
Bhiodh maise 's sgèimh nan gràs;   20
'S tu sheargadh gnè na truaillidheachd
'S a nuadhaicheadh ar càil;
'S tu thogadh chum nan nèamhan sinn
Le tarraing threun do ghràidh.   24

O Spioraid chaoimh nan gràsalachd,
Nam biodh tu tàmh 'nar còir,
'S tu dh'fhuasgladh oirnn 's a shlànaicheadh
An dream tha cnàmh fo leòn;   28
'S tu thogadh cridh' nam bantraichean
Gu seinn le aiteas mòr,
'S nach fàgadh gu neo-choibhneil iad
An gainntir dorch a' bhròin.   32

'S tu mhùchadh teine 'n naimhdeis
San t-sùil as gràinde colg;
'S tu rèiticheadh 's a chiùinicheadh
A' mhala bhrùideil dhorch;   36
'S tu thogadh neul na h-aingidheachd
Bharr gnùis nan aintighearn' borb,
'S a bheireadh gionaich saoibhreis uap'
'S gach aimhleas tha 'na lorg.   40

'S tu bheireadh beachdan fìrinneach
Don t-sluagh mu rìoghachd nèimh;
'S tu bheireadh soisgeul fìorghlan dhuinn,
Mar dh'innseadh e bho chèin,   44
'S nach fàgadh tu air luasgadh sinn
Le foirmean truagh nam breug,
A dhealbhadh gu h-eas-innleachdach
Tre mhìorun luchd nan creud.   48

Nan tigeadh saoghal dòibheairteach
Gu eòlas glan ort fhèin,
'S e siud a dhèanadh sòlasach
Na slòigh tha ann gu lèir;   52
An sin sguireadh foill is fòirneart ann,
Is sguireadh còmhstri gheur;
Bhiodh mealltaireachd air fògradh as,
Is theicheadh neòil nam breug.   56

Ach 's eagal leam gu d' thrèig thu sinn,
'S do nèamh gun d' theich thu suas;
Tha daoin' air fàs cho eucoireach,
'S do ghnè-sa fada uap';   60
Tha seiche ghreannach fèinealachd
Gan eudachadh mun cuairt;
Chan eòl dhomh aon nì reubas e
Ach saighead Dhè nan sluagh.   64

Ah! Shaoghail 's fada tuathail thu
On uair sin anns na thrèig
Do charthannas is d' uaisleachd thu,
'S a ghabh thu Fuath is Breug;   68

Mar inneal-ciùil neo-cheòlmhor dhut
Gun teud an òrdagh rèidh,
Cha seinn thu pong le òrdalachd,
'S cha deòin leat dol air ghleus.   72

Gun claoidhear am fear suairce leat
Tràth bhuadhaicheas fear olc;
Gun slìobar am fear suaimhneach leat,
'S gum buailear am fear gort';   76
Gur fial ri fear an stòrais thu,
'S gur dòit' thu ris a' bhochd;
Gur blàth ri fear a' chòmhdaich thu,
'S gur reòt' thu ris an nochdt'.   80

Chan eil aon nì dhut nàdarrach
Rin canar àgh air nèamh.
Chan fhaighear gnìomh gu bràth agad
Rin can an t-Ard Rìgh feum;   84
Ach 's leat na h-uile dìomhanas,
'S a' phian tha teachd 'nan dèidh;
Do dhòrainnean 's do ghàbhaidhean
Cha tàrr mi chur an cèill.   88

Gur leatsa neart nan aintighearnan
Is gèimhlichean nan tràill;
Gur leat guth treun nan ainneartach,
'S guth fann an fhir tha 'n sàs;   92
Gur leatsa spìd is uamharrachd
An t-sluaigh tha 'n ionad àrd,
'S a mheasas cho mì-fhiùghail sinn
Ri sgùilleach air an tràigh.   96

Gur leat am batal dèistinneach
Le toirm a reubas cluas;
Tha glaodh a' bhàis 's na pèine ann
Gu nèamh ag èirigh suas;   100
Nuair thèid na prionnsan fòirneartach
Dhan spòrs an cogadh cruaidh
A chosnadh saoibhreis eucoirich
An èirig fuil an t-sluaigh.   104

Gur leat an togradh aimhleasach
'S na miannan teinteach caothaich
A bheir bhàrr slighe na còrach sinn,
Air seachran gòrach claon;   108
A dhùisgeas gaol na truaillidheachd
Is fuath do nithean naomh';
A neartaicheas 's a luathaicheas
An truaighean air clann daoin'.   112

Gur leat an creideamh buaireasach
A dhùisgeas gruaim is greann;
An creideamh nach dèan suairce sinn,
'S nach dèan ar n-uabhair fann;   116
An creideamh th'aig na diadhairean,
Lem miann a' chòmhstri theann:
'Nan làimh-san dh'fhàs a' Chrìosdalachd
Mar bhiasd nan iomadh ceann.   120

An searmonaiche prèisgeil ud,
'S ann dh'èigheas e le sgairt
Gur mallaicht' sinn mur èisdear leinn
Ra chreud-san, an tè cheart;   124
An àite bhith sìor èigheach rinn
Mur dleasdanas 's gach beart,
A dhèanamh daoine cèillidh dhinn
An làthair Dhè nam feart.   128

An Crìosdaidh dubhach, gruamach ud
A chnuasaicheas gu dian,
A chuireas aghaidh chràbhach air
Mar fhàidh ann an nial,   132
'S e dèanamh casgairt uamhasaich
Air uamharrachd 'na chliabh,
Chan aithnichear air 'na dhèiliginn
Gun do ghèill Apolleon riamh.   136

An duine caomh a dh'èireas suas
Gu nèamh air sgiath a' ghràidh,
Cha deasbair dian mu chreudan e,
'S cha bhi e beumadh chàich;   140

Chan Easbaigeach 's cha Chlèireach e,
Cha Ghreugach e 's cha Phàp,
Ach fear a' chridhe dhaondachail
Sam faighear gaol a' tàmh.   144

O Charthannais, gur h-àlainn thu,
A ghràis as àirde luach!
Ach 's lìonmhor nach toir àite dhut
Gu bràth 'nan cridhe cruaidh.   148
Nan deònaicheadh a' cheòlraidh dhomh
Mo chomas beòil car uair,
Gun innsinn pàirt de ghnìomharan
Nam biasd thug dhutsa fuath.   152

Cha robh do ghnè-sa 'n Dòmhnall bochd,
Am fear bu rògaich goill,
Bha 'n dùil gum biodh gach Lèodhasach
Air fhògaradh don choill.   156
Ach phàigh e pàirt de dhòibheairtean,
Is gheibh e 'n còrr a thoill;
Gun aithnich e gu dòrainneach
Gur feàrr a' chòir na 'n fhoill.   160

Cha robh do ghnè-sa riaghladh
Ann am broilleach iarainn cruaidh
Nam bàillidhean 's nan tighearnan
Chuir sìos an tìr mu thuath.   164
Bu charthannach na fàrdaichean
Bha seasgair, blàth innt' uair;
'S tha tìr nan daoine còire 'n-diugh
'Na fàsach dòbhaidh, truagh.   168

Gun chuir iad fo na naosgaichean
An tìr a b' aoidheil sluagh;
Gun bhuin iad cho neo-dhaondachail
Ri daoine bha cho suairc.   172
A chionn nach faodte 'm bàthadh,
Chaidh an sgànradh thar a' chuain;
Bu mhiosa na bruid Bhàbiloin
An càradh sin a fhuair.   176

Gun mheas iad mar gum b' shnàthainn iad
Na còrdan gràidh bha teann
A' ceangal cridh' nan àrmann ud
Ri dùthaich àrd nam beann.   180
Gun tug am bròn am bàs orra
'N dèidh cràbhaidh nach bu ghann,
'S an saoghal fuar gan sàrachadh,
Gun ionad blàth dhaibh ann.   184

A bheil neach beò san linn seo
Leis an cuimhn' an latha garbh
'S na chuireadh an cath uamhann –
Waterloo nan cluaintean dearg?   188
Bu tapaidh buaidh nan Gàidheal ann,
Nuair dh'èirich iad fon airm;
Ri aghaidh colg nan treun-fheara,
Gun ghèill ar naimhdean garg.   192

Dè 'n sòlas a fhuair athraichean
Nan gaisgeach thug a' bhuaidh?
Chaidh taighean blàth a' charthannais
'Nam baidealaich mun cluais;   196
Bha 'm macaibh anns an àraich
'S iad a' teàrnadh tìr gun truas;
Bu chianail staid am màthraichean,
'S am fàrdaichean 'nan gual.   200

Bha Breatann dèanamh gàirdeachais,
Bha iadsan dèanamh caoidh.
Cha robh an tìr an àraich ac'
Na dhèanadh sgàth bhon ghaoith;   204
Gach fuiltean liath is luaisgean air
Le osag fhuar a' ghlinn,
Na deuraibh air an gruaidhean,
'S an fhuar-dhealt air an cinn.   208

A Bhreatainn, tha e nàireach dhut,
Ma dh'àirmhear ann do sgeul
Gun bhuin thu cho mì-nàdarrach
Rid fhìor-shliochd àlainn fhèin;   212

An tìr bha aig na gaisgich ud
A theasairg thu 'nad fheum,
A thionndadh gu blàr-spòrsa
Do na stròdhailich gun bheus.   216

Nach dìblidh cliù ar mòr-uaislean,
Na fir as neònaich mèinn?
Carson a tha iad mòrchuiseach,
'S iad beò air spòrs gun chèill?   220
Nan còmhdaicheadh na ruadh-chearcan
Lem buachar uachdar slèibh,
'S e siud a b'fheàrr a chòrdadh riu
Na sràidean òir air nèamh.   224

O criothnaich measg do shòlasan,
Fhir-fhòirneirt làidir chruaidh!
Dè 'm bàs no 'm pian a dhòirtear ort
Airson do leòn air sluagh?   228
'S e osnaich bhròin nam bantraichean
Tha sèid do shaoibhreis suas;
Gach cupan fìon a dh'òlas tu,
'S e deòir nan ainnis thruagh.   232

Ged thachradh oighreachd mhòr agad,
'S ged ghèill na slòigh fod smachd,
Tha 'm bàs is laghan geur aige,
'S gum feum thu gèill da reachd.   236
Siud uachdaran a dh'òrdaicheas
Co-ionnan còir gach neach,
'S mar oighreachd bheir e lèine dhut,
'S dà cheum de thalamh glas.   240

'S e siud as deireadh suarach dhut,
Thus', fhir an uabhair mhòir,
Led shumanan 's led bhàirlinnean,
A' cumail chàich fo bhròn;   244
Nuair gheibh thu 'n oighreachd shàmhach ud,
Bidh d' àrdan beag gu leòr;
Cha chluinnear trod a' bhàillidh ann,
'S cha chuir maor grànd' air ròig.   248

'N sin molaidh a' chnuimh shnàigeach thu,
Cho tàirceach 's a bhios d'fheòil,
Nuair gheibh i air do chàradh thu
Gu sàmhach air a bòrd.   252
Their i, ''S e fear miath tha 'n seo,
Tha math do bhiasd nan còs,
Bhon rinn e caol na ceudan
Gus e fhèin a bhiathadh dhòmhs'.'   256

NOTES

Source: MacLeòid 1916: 76-84.

Tune: The metre is that of Dugald Buchanan's hymn, 'Fulangas Chrìosd' (MacLean 1913: 5-13). The tune is given in MacLeòid 1916: 76.

Date and Context: This song was composed soon after the events in Bernera in the spring of 1874 (see Poem 13). The extent of the poet's reflections on the principal defect which, in his view, underlies landlords' and factors' policies sets this poem apart from all others in the nineteenth century; its significance is discussed in the Introduction. The poem is noticeably lacking in specific detail, but it develops a powerful argument based on a specifically Christian perspective; the Spirit of Kindliness can be none other than the Holy Spirit whose absence, even within the hearts of practitioners of outward̶   ̶ion, leads to conflict. When the Spirit of Kindliness disappear̶   ̶ is taken by the spirit of self-interest, which generates ̶   ̶resentation has a wide, and even timeless, applicat̶

136 **Apolleon**̶   ̶velation 9: 11. Apollyon is best know̶   ̶ Bunyan's *Pilgrim's Progress*, ̶   ̶miliation. Christian eventua̶   ̶unter.

153 **D**̶   ̶Aunro: see Poem 13, lines 25-56.

188 **Water**̶   ̶8th June 1815, and marked the final defeat̶   ̶apoleon. The British army was led by the Duke̶   ̶er 1986: 302). Highlanders had a distinguished part̶   ̶nd it is commemorated in the name of at least one Highland̶   ̶Waterloo in Skye) where veterans settled.

193-200 The referen̶   ̶o evictions taking place while Highland men were in action in the British imperial army may allude to the notorious clearance at Greenyards, Easter Ross, in 1854. It was alleged that, as the clearance proceeded, 'some of the men of Greenyards were currently serving in the 93rd Regiment at Sebastopol' (Richards 1982: 462). The execution of clearances at the time of the Crimean War was deeply resented throughout the Highlands: see also Poem 11.

15. Oran Luchd an Spòrs

Iain Mac a' Ghobhainn

Is muladach mise 's nach faod mi,
Alba, cliù ceutach a luaidh ort;
'S grànda ri innse do bheusan,
Bhuin thu cho neo-ghnèitheil is suarach.   4
Ged a bha an sliochd agad sàr-ghrinn,
Ochan! bu mhàthair gun truas thu;
Thilg thu do chlann bhàrr do bhroillich,
Gu rùm do na bodaich a thruaill thu.   8

Bodaich a thruaill thu gu mòr,
Bhon a bha 'm pòca làn òir;
Roghnaich thu bodaich an airgid,
'S chuir thu air falbh na fir chòir.   12

Chuir thu air falbh na fir chòir,
Rìgh! cha b' e chòir ach an eucoir;
Eadar iad 's dùthaich an eòlais,
Tha fairgeachan mòra a' beucadh.   16
Muinntir gud shaoradh bhon fhòirneart,
Rachadh gu deònach san t-sreupa;
Muinntir dol eadar thu 's toisgean
Chuireadh 's a chosnadh an treun-chath.   20

Muinntir gu tric anns na blàir
Dhòirt am fuil chraobhach gu làr;
'S leibideach phàigh thu an duais dhaibh,
Dh'fhògair thu uat iad gu bràth.   24

Cò nise thèid dàna 'nad adhbhar?
Tha Gàidheil nan euchd air an ruagadh;
Nam biodh iad an guaillibh a chèile,
Cò tha fon ghrèin chuireadh ruaig orr'?   28
Nise bhon chuir thu air chèin iad,
Cha 'dùthaich nan treun' à seo suas thu;
Dùthaich nan ruinnsearan Sasannach,
Dùthaich nam madraidh 's nan ruadh-chearc.   32

Nuair dh'èireas an cogadh 's an t-àr,
'S a thèid luchd nan gadhar gu blàr,
'S mòr m' eagal gun gèill iad sa chùis sin,
Ged 's sgiobalt' a chiùrras iad geàrr.　　　　　　　36

Tha Gàidheil a-nis air an sgiùrsadh
Gun adhbhar à dùthaich an àraich,
Peanas luchd-uilc ac' ga ghiùlan,
Ged is ann cliùiteach a bha iad;　　　　　　　40
Air seachran sna fàsaichean dorcha,
Measg allmharach borba na fàs-choill,
A' tilgeil an saighdean gu millteach
Gud chridhe le cinnt tha ro-bhàsmhor....　　　　　　　44

Bha uair gum b' e aiteas cheann-feadhna,
Còmhnaidh nan daoine bhith teann orr';
B' ait leò bhith faicinn gach taobh dhiubh
Fàrdaichean faoilte nan gleanntan;　　　　　　　48
Thionndaidh na h-uile car claon oirnn,
Thàinig oirnn caochladh bhon àm sin;
Rinneadh ar gleannan fuar fàsail,
Dh'fhairich sinn làmhan nan aintighearn'.　　　　　　　52

Làmhan nan aintighearnan truagha
A chuir as am fearann an sluagh,
Daormainn an ionad nan àrmann,
A chinnich le fàrdaichean fuara.　　　　　　　56

Dh'fhalbh uainne na ceannardan uasal
Anns an robh suairc agus fìrinn;
Thàinig 'nan àite luchd fuadain;
Chuir iad don-bhuaidh air an tìr seo.　　　　　　　60
Thàinig luchd-brachaidh an eòrna,
Staillearan dòite nam pìoban,
Rinn beairteas air creachadh luchd-pòite,
A' cur an dubh-dhòlais air mìltean.　　　　　　　64

Siud na gàrraich a tha
An àite na muinntir a bha
A' riaghladh air Gàidhealtachd Alba;
Chan urrainn g' eil sealbh dhuinn an dàn.　　　　　　　68

Bha cuid aca malairt an òpium;
Thionail iad mòran de ionntas;
Dh'fhairich na Sìnich an dòibheairt;
Sgrios iad na slòigh leis a' phuinnsean;　　　　　72
Muinntir gun choibhneas, gun tròcair,
Duilich an leòn anns a' chuinnseas –
An èirig na rinn iad de robaireachd,
Thoill iad an stobadh le cuinnsear.　　　　　76

'S cianail fear saoibhir 's e baoth,
Gun fhios de chàradh chloinn daoin',
Ged chuireadh e mìltean gu truaighe
Gu mealtainn aon uair de spòrs chaoich.　　　　　80

An tì sin a dh'atas mar uamh-bhiasd,
A' fàs suas an uamharrachd stòrais,
'S fìor chulaidh eagail measg sluaigh e,
Mur bi a ghluasadan stòlda.　　　　　84
Mar gharbh-lebhiàtan nan cuantan,
'S fìor chulaidh uamhais ri spòrs e;
Faodaidh aon bhuille de eàrra
Dochann is bàs thoirt air mòran....　　　　　88

'N Tì shocraich bun-daingeann na talmhainn,
'S a thug am muir gailbheach gu òrdagh,
'N Tì shuidhich bun-daingeann nan àrd-bheann,
'S a dh'àrdaich am bàrr gu na neòil orr':　　　　　92
'N Tì chuir ùir air an aigeal,
'S a sgaoil brat maiseach an fheòir air,
Nuair chunnaic e 'n domhain seo crìochnaicht',
Dh'iarr gun lìonte le slòigh e.　　　　　96

Eiridh fear-riaghlaidh nan dùl,
'S tagraidh e fhathast a' chùis;
'S thèid uamhar luchd nan cairt odhar
Le bruaich an t-sluic dhomhain 'nam brùchd.　　　　　100

NOTES
Source: MacLeòid 1916: 123-6.
　Tune: This is not specified in the source.
　Date and Context: The poem is a general indictment of Scotland as
a nation which has, in the poet's view, rejected its own people in favour

of strangers, especially those with financial resources. The latter have purchased Highland estates, and displaced the older patriarchal chieftains. The poem tends to romanticise the 'old elite' (cf. Poem 16), and to condemn by contrast the 'new elite' (as in lines 57-64). The poet does not consider why the 'old elite' left the Highlands, or why they should have sold out to the 'oppressors' whom he despises. The paradox that the new elite made money, while the old elite lost it, is not explored in the poem. For a discussion of the changing ownership of Highland estates, see Devine 1989 and 1994: 63-83.

There is no indication of the date of the poem, but it may have been composed around the same time as Poem 14. However, it has to be said that Smith's critique in this poem seems much more conservative and much less analytical than that presented in Poem 14.

26 **Gàidheil nan euchd:** The source reads *Gaidheil nan eug*, but this does not make good sense. In lines 25-36, the poet shows that he regards the Highlands chiefly as a reservoir of fighting men. He makes it clear that the maintenance of this fighting force is, in his view, vital to the interests of Scotland. It is ironic that Smith and other Gaelic poets were happy to accept that Highlanders should be heroically killed in imperial conflicts but not evicted (with minimal bloodshed) from their homes.

42 **allmharach borba:** It is striking that Smith, who was so keenly aware of exploitation in Poem 14, should himself fall victim to a prejudiced perception of the 'natives' in other lands, and should apply to them one of the epithets used of the Scottish Gaels by their external oppressors.

61 **luchd-brachaidh an eòrna:** It is not clear whom the poet had in mind, but the description would fit, among others, John Ramsay of Kildalton, who purchased the Port Ellen distillery in Islay, and became a distiller of note. He made his first purchase of land in Islay in 1855, and by 1862 owned the lands of Kildalton and Oa. See Ramsay 1969.

69 **malairt an òpium:** The reference is to James Matheson, whose business enterprises were said to include opium-trading in the East.

16. Na Croitearan Sgiathanach

Niall MacLeòid

Gur bochd leam an cunntas
Tha nochd as mo dhùthaich,
Mo dhaoine gan sgiùrsadh
   Aig ùmaidhean Ghall;   4
Le bataichean rùisgte
Gan slacadh mar bhrùidean,
Mar thràillean gun diù dhiubh
   Gan dùnadh am fang.   8.

An sluagh bha cho càirdeil,
Cho suairce 's cho bàidheil,
Rinn uachdarain stràiceil
   Am fàsgadh cho teann;   12
Tha saors' air am fàgail,
Tha an raointean 'nam fàsaich,
'S na caoraich an àite
   Nan àrmann sa ghleann.   16

Gun chuimhn' air na fiùrain
A dhìon dhuinn ar dùthaich,
Le an airm-chogaidh rùisgte
   Thug cùis dhe gach nàmh;   20
Fo dhaorsa nach lùbadh,
Ach ceartas nach diùltadh,
Is dh'fhàg iad an cliù sin
   Gun smùr aig an àl.   24

Na suinn a bha calma,
Bu shunndach a dh'fhalbh iad
Fo bhrataich na h-Alba,
   'S a dhearbh iad an làmh;   28
Chan ioghnadh ge searbh leinn
'S ged dhùisgeadh e fearg dhuinn,
An sliochd bhith gan dearmad,
   'S gan tearbadh bhon àit.   32

Bha 'n uair-sin ar sinnsir
Fo uachdarain rìoghail;
Bha uaisle 'nan inntinn
   Le fìrinn is gràdh;   36
Bha 'n cànain cho binn dhaibh
'S an càirdeas gun dìth dhaibh;
An cogadh no 'n sìth dhaibh
   Bha dìlseachd 'nan gnàths.   40

Bha 'n dachaigh 's an còmhnaidh
Le an sluagh mar bu chòir dhaibh,
'S iad fiosrach is eòlach
   Mun dòigh anns gach càs;   44
Nuair thachradh iad còmhla
Sa chlachan Di-dòmhnaich,
Cho coibhneil gam feòraich,
   Gu còmhraiteach blàth.   48

Iad fhèin 's an cuid dhaoine
Cho seasmhach 's cho aontach,
Mar theaghlach cho gaolach,
   Nach sgaoileadh ach bàs;   52
Chan airgead no caoraich
Bha dhìth air na laoich sin,
Ach gaisgich gun chlaonadh
   Nach aomadh sa bhlàr.   56

Cha robh uisge no mòinteach
Fo dhìon no fo chòmhdach,
'S bha saors' agus sòlas
   Aig òigridh na tìr;   60
Cha robh bàillidhean spòrsail
Gam feannadh le fòirneart,
'S a' gearradh an lòin diubh
   Gun tròcair, gun suim.   64

Ach, dùisgibh, mo chàirdean,
'S bhur dùthaich na fàgaibh,
Ach seasaibh gu làidir
   Ga teàrnadh le buaidh;   68

Bhur sinnsirean dh'fhàg i
Mar dhìleab gu bràth dhuibh,
Is dìonaibh-s' an tràth-s' i
    Don àl a thig uaibh.   72

Chan ann le mì-riaghailt,
Ach tuigseach is ciallach,
Gun lùbadh, gun fhiaradh
    Am briathran no 'n gnàths;   76
Tha mìltean is ceudan
A sheasas mar dhìon dhuibh,
Gu 'm faigh sibh nas miann leibh
    De shliabh nam beann àrd'.   80

Thèid crìoch air gach fòirneart,
'S bidh biadh agus stòras,
Bidh sìth agus sòlas
    A' còmhdach na tìr;   84
Bidh fuinn agus òrain
Gu binn aig an òigridh,
'S na rìbhinnean bòidheach
    Mun chrò len crodh-laoigh.   88

Gach oighr' agus bàillidh
Gun fhoill no gun àrdan,
Rin daoine cho càirdeil
    Mar bha iad bho thùs;   92
'S bidh Gàidheil gun àireamh
An dùthaich nan àrd-bheann,
Cur mais' air an àite,
    'S a' fàs ann an cliù.   96

NOTES

Source: MacLeòid 1975: 131-4.
    Tune: This is not specified in the source.
    Date and Context: Because of its general vagueness, it is difficult to date this poem precisely. It was published in the first edition of the poet's work in 1883, and it could have been inspired by events either at Braes or in the poet's native district of Glendale (see Poems 20, 21 and 22).
    The circumstances alluded to in the first verse, together with the reference to high ground in lines 79-80, could suggest that it was more

probably a response to the fracas at Braes in Skye on 19th April 1882, the so-called 'Battle of the Braes'. The 'battle' involved a detachment of Lowland policemen under the overall command of Sheriff William Ivory, who formed a task-force to remove 'agitators' from Peighinn a' Chorrain. They were attacked by local people as they took their captives through the defile leading out of Braes, and the police baton-charged the local defenders, including women, on the upper slope. The agitation at Braes was caused by the loss of the crofters' common grazing on Ben Lee (see MacPhail 1989: 38-52). See further Poem 17.

MacLeod's poem is noteworthy for its romantic portrayal of an earlier Golden Age, in which such violence and its causes were unknown. MacLeod attributes the difference to the arrival of a new class of landlords, whom he describes as *uachdarain stràiceil* ('pompous landlords', line 11), and whose actions contrast with those of their predecessors, *uachdarain rìoghail* ('regal landlords', line 34), who mixed happily with the local population at church, and loved to hear the Gaelic language. The new landlords are non-Gaels who are not sympathetic to the *mores* of earlier days; they are the initiators of clearance; they are heedless of, and ungrateful for, the loyalty of Highlanders in battles on behalf of the Empire, and they restrict access on their estates. The poem does not explain why matters changed, but suffuses cause and effect in a warmly romantic glow, in which the darker shades of modern landlord oppression are painted against the softer colours of Highland virtues.

While sympathetic to the crofters' cause and anxious to restore the lost harmony, MacLeod disapproves of the actions of his own fellow-islanders, whose 'disorder' affronts him (and one senses that the poem may be a kind of 'shock response' to the first major confrontations in Skye). He advocates (lines 73-80) a well-mannered, civil campaign. His final prophecy of an imminent return to the earlier Golden Age, if such advice is followed, suggests that he has yielded too far to his innate romanticism, but, in fairness, it must be noted that apocalyptic visions of the Highland 'end-times' were by no means unique to MacLeod.

17. [Dùbhlan Fir a' Bhràighe]

Niall Ceannaiche

Ma thig maor oirnn à Port Rìgh
    'S gun Achd an Rìgh 'na làimh aige,
Seallaidh sinne nach e 'n t-sìth
    A nì sinn ribh sna h-amannan;   4
Ach am batal thoirt da-rìribh,
    Dìleas bidh 'n t-àrd-cheannard oirnn;
'S a' chlach as àirde tha sa phrìosan,
    Islichear an ceann aice.   8

Bidh tuilleadh againn Dòmhnall Bàn,
    Bidh Teàrlach, bidh Dòmhnall Ruadh againn;
Gum bi Coinneach air an sàil,
    Iain Dubh – tha a nàdar buaireasach;   12
Fios a dh'ionnsaigh Dhòmhnaill Ràghnaill
    Air an t-sràid 's e sguairigeadh,
A bheir an t-saighdearachd bharra chàich,
    'S air an ceann bidh Ruairidh ann.   16

Bidh 'n fhuil rìoghail ['n] seann Iain Stiùbhard,
    'S iomadh tùirn san d'fhuaireadh e;
Ged tha 'n aois a' toirt a lùths as,
    Dùrachdail sa chruadal e,   20
Dìon an fhir a th' air a chùlaibh,
    Sùil aig far a ghualainn orr';
O, gheibh e urram 'na mo dhùthaich,
    'S fuil a' Phrionnsa gluasad ann.   24

NOTES

Source: These verses were composed, as part of a longer poem, by Neil MacPherson, known locally as Niall Ceannaiche ('Neil the Merchant'), from Braes in Skye. They were transmitted by the Skye bard, Calum Nicolson, Braes, and recorded from him by the Danish ethnomusicologist, Thorkild Knudsen, at a seminar in the School of Scottish Studies, Edinburgh, on 13th June 1968. They were subsequently published in Knudsen 1969. (I am very grateful to Professor Bill

106

Nicolaisen, University of Aberdeen, for putting me in touch with Mr
Michael Chesnutt, Head of the Department of Folklore, University of
Copenhagen, who kindly identified the source and supplied a copy of the
text.)

Miss Jo MacDonald obtained fragments of a further verse from Mr
William MacDonald, Braes, in 1972-73:

Thèid fios a chur dh'ionnsaigh MhicAidh
Nuair ....
....
....   28
Gach smear is crodhan tha gu h-àrd
A' teàrnadh nuas mu Bhealltainn;
Thèid coin is gillean chur ['n]an sàil;
Thèid taigh Iain Bhàin a shealltainn dhaibh.   32

(Notice will be sent to MacKay
when   28
every bit of marrow and hoof on the hill
will be coming down around May Day;
lads and dogs will be set to their heels;
Fair-haired John's house will be shown to them.)   32

Tune: This is given in Knudsen 1969.

Date and Context: The most likely time for the composition of the
poem was the period between the 'Battle of the Braes' on 19th April 1882
and May Day of that year. After the six Braes men had been taken to
Portree and put in prison, the possibility of going to Portree and
storming the jail was considered by their fellow crofters in Braes, and this
seems to be the context of the allusion in lines 7-8. This intention was
later abandoned on the advice of the local schoolmaster. The frag-
mentary verse is of great value in setting the context and suggesting the
date for the poem. MacAidh (line 25) was John MacKay, farmer of
Home Farm, Portree, who had a lease of Ben Lee, the area of outrun
which was at the centre of the Braes dispute. His lease was due to expire
at Whitsun 1882, and agitation, including a rent-strike, was initiated by
the Braes crofters within the preceding year. There was talk of bringing
his cattle down from the hill by force, as is reflected in lines 30-31. Iain
Bàn (line 32) was a shepherd whose house on Ben Lee, while being built,
was apparently knocked down by the crofters of Olach and Achadh na h-
Anaid. This dispute was, however, resolved, and the house was
completed prior to 1882. Here it is a symbol of the power of the people
(MacDhòmhnaill 1980: MacPhail 1989: 38-30).

The verses shed interesting light on the local perception of the so-
called Battle of the Braes. Niall Ceannaiche threatens a 'real battle' (line
5) if an official comes from Portree, and this suggests that the Braes
people viewed the celebrated 'battle' as a relatively small affair. In
contemplating a further attack, Niall Ceannaiche points to the heroic

qualities of the potential soldiers, and his style is close to that of formal Gaelic panegyric.

Mr William MacDonald was able to identify for Miss MacDonald some of the individuals named in these verses. They are as follows:

9 **Dòmhnall Bàn:** Donald MacLeod was grandfather of Alexander Nicolson, formerly lecturer in Gaelic at Jordanhill College of Education.

10 **Teàrlach:** Teàrlach Mòr, otherwise Charles Matheson, brother of Dòmhnall Ruadh.

11 **Coinneach:** grandfather of Willie MacDonald.

13 **Dòmhnall Raghnaill:** Donald Matheson, grandfather of the Braes postman in the 1970s.

16 **Ruairidh:** Roderick Matheson, said to have been a 'peaceful man'.

17 **Iain Stiùbhard:** a great-grandfather of Calum Nicolson.

18. Aoir na Bàirlinn

Calum Caimbeul MacPhàil

Seinneam aoir don Bhàirlinn ghionaich,
'S tric chuir bior an cridh' a' Ghàidheil;
Dh'fhàg i tìr nan Gàidheal gun sonas,
Riaghailt an Donais is a chàirdean;   4
Thàin' i 'm bliadhna 'n Eilean Sgiathach
Dh'iarraidh pàirt den t-sluagh ga fhàgail,
Toirt àithne neo-sheirceil chruaidh
Bhith deas gu gluasad Là Fhèill Bhrèanainn.   8

Cha d'fheòraich i an robh neach eile
Bheireadh fasgadh dhaibh 'nam fàrdaich;
Nan robh iad uile mar bha ise,
Cha robh nithean ach am bàs ann;   12
Cha d'èisd i ri gearan na h-Aoise
No idir ri caoineadh nam pàisdean;
Thilg i 'n acair as a grèim,
Is dh'fhàg i iad air tuinn an àrdain.   16

Thilg i mar bhàta gun stiùir iad,
Gun chairt-iùil, gun siùil, gun ràmhan,
Gan tulgadh air cuan a' mhì-cheartais,
Is iomaghaoth nam beartach gan sàrach;   20
Sibhs' tha sàbhailt' anns a' chaladh,
Nach dèan sibh tarraing ri ur càirdean;
Seasaibh gramail, fearail, dìleas –
Cuim a strìochdamaid mar thràillean?   24

Seasaibh calma, mar aon Chomann,
Cumaibh coinneamhan 's gach àite;
Bithibh gleusda, gach curaidh
Sa bheil srad de fhuil a' Ghàidheil;   28
'S mura dèan iad reachd gar còmhnadh,
Cha mhiosa do Dhòmhnall na Pàraig;
Feumaidh ceartas leud is astar,
'S lann nach smachdaich ceilg gu bràth e.   32

109

NOTES

Source: MacPhail 1947: 9-10. I have not been able to find an earlier version of the text.

Tune: This is not specified in the source.

Date and Context: The poem was evidently composed in response to events in Skye in the early 1880s, perhaps in 1881. In March 1881 Fraser of Kilmuir made threats of eviction against tenants in Valtos who refused to pay their rents. The serving of summonses and notices, carrying the threat of eviction, was also evidenced at Braes and Glendale in 1881-82. See, in general, MacPhail 1989: 31-60.

8 **Là Fhèill Bhrèanainn:** Saint Brendan's festival day is 16th May.

25 **aon Chomann:** The reference is probably to the Federation of Celtic Societies, founded in 1878. It met in Glasgow on 6th May 1881, and a motion expressing sympathy with the Valtos tenants was passed (ibid.: 33).

29 **reachd:** This is early recognition of the need for a law or statute to protect Highland crofters.

30 The reference is to the plight of Highland crofters, represented by *Dòmhnall* (Donald), and their Irish counterparts, represented by *Pàraig* (Patrick). Transl. 'Donald will share the same fate as Patrick' (lit. 'Donald will be no worse off than Patrick').

31-2 Transl. 'Justice needs to be executed widely and speedily, and requires a blade to prevent treachery from ever overcoming it.'

19. Oran eadar Tuathanach agus Uachdaran

Calum Caimbeul MacPhàil

Tuathanach

Cha mhòr nach b' fheàrr bhith marbh fon fhòid
  Na 'm fògradh th' aig na h-uachdarain oirnn;
Maoir is bàirlinn air ar tòir
  A-nis 's gach dòigh nach dualach dhuinn;   4
Cas-chrom an lagh a' toirt dhaibh còmhnaidh,
  'S chan eil dòigh nach buail iad sinn,
'S mur seas ar càirdean sinn sa chàs,
  Gun toir an nàmhaid buaidh oirnn.   8

Uachdaran

Nam biodh sibh umhalta dom reachd,
  Gun smachdaichinn gu h-uasal sibh,
Ach bhon a rinn sibh aramach,
  Gum faigh sibh gleac nach buadhaich leibh;   12
Gheibh sinn saighdearan on Chrùn
  A smùideas thar nan cuantan sibh,
Is thèid ur fearann a chur fàs –
  Bidh caoraich bhàn' is tuath mhòr ann.   16

Tuathanach

Cuin nach tug sinn riamh a chòir
  Anns gach dòigh don uachdaran?
Nach do phàigh sinn riamh am màl
  'S a' chàin ged bha e cruaidh oirnn?   20
O nach mùthadh tu do dhòigh,
  'S tu feuchainn dòighean tuathail oirnn,
Cha ghèill a h-aon againn sa chàs,
  Cho fad 's bhios làmh an gualainn dhuinn.   24

Uachdaran

An uair bheir mise sibh gu cùirt
  Bidh ùin' agaibh air smuaineachadh;
Thèid ur càradh anns a' phrìosan
  Gu cinnteach, 's cha bhi fuasgladh ann;   28
Chì sibh an sin nach fealla-dhà
  Bhith dèanamh tàir air m' uaisle-sa;
Nuair a thèid ur sròn fo ghlais,
  Gun tuig sibh smachd nan uachdaran.   32

NOTES

Source: The *Oban Times*, 28 April 1883. The full *OT* text contains seven verses, of which the first four are presented in the present edition. The remaining three verses cover the following themes: *Tuathanach* points to the upper hand of landlords in the law courts; *Uachdaran* puts forward the landlords' demand for the crofters' immediate submission and underlines their folly in holding out against landlords' resources; and *Tuathanach*, in conclusion, describes the supportive role of *'Fionn'* (Henry Whyte) as Secretary of the Federation of Celtic Societies and of *an t-Ollamh Mac Gill' Ios'* (probably Dr H. Cameron Gillies) in assessing the landlords' real strength.

Tune: This is not specified in the source. This poem is more likely to have been recited than sung.

Date and Context: The poem reflects the increasing use of police, soldiers and the courts in the landlords' attempts to vindicate the law and resolve agitation on their estates. It was probably composed after the 'Battle of the Braes' in April 1882.

20. Thàinig Sgeula gu ar Baile

Alasdair MacIlleathain

Thàinig sgeula gu ar baile
Gu robh am poilios tighinn gar glacadh,
Tighinn a-staigh 'n a' Ghleann le astar,
   'S chuir siud gaiseadh 'na ar crìdh.   4

Chaidh an Dùdach Mhòr a shèideadh,
Chaidh na pìobairean ri gleusadh,
Dh'fhairich mi cailleach ag èigheach,
   'Clann nan Gàidheal, O cha till!'   8

Ged a b' eagal b'fheudar gluasad
'S ar làrach a sheasamh le cruadal,
Fear le bata 's fear le buailtean,
   'S fear le cuaille cabar-saoidh.   12

Siud far an robh sealladh àlainn,
Dìreadh ri bruthach an Fhàsaich,
Brataichean ri crannaibh àrda
   'S iad a' snàmh gu sèimh sa ghaoith.   16

Thàinig oirnne curaidh chalma,
'S iad cho aontaichte gu falbh linn,
Muinntir Sgianaidin is Chaileaboist,
   'S iad cho armaichte rinn fhìn.   20

Dh'fhalbh sinn leotha mar a thoill iad,
Gan cur a-nall far crìoch na h-oighreachd;
Nuair a ràinig sinn an taigh-seinnse,
   Gu robh 'n oidhch' againn 's sinn sgìth.   24

NOTES

Source: This song was recorded by Allan Campbell (then a producer at BBC Radio Highland) from the singing of John MacLeod, Glendale, in 1982. The song was presented as part of a very informative Gaelic radio programme on the Glendale Land League which was produced by Allan Campbell, and subsequently broadcast.

    Tune: The BBC recording preserves the tune of the song. The metre is that of 'Olaidh sinn deoch-slàint' an oighre'.

Date and Context: The song gives a very vivid picture of a 'crofters' army' on the march, and preparing to give battle to a detachment of police. Circumstances very similar to those of the song were described thus by Neil MacLean, *Niall Alasdair Dhòmhnaill*, the son of the composer, from Milovaig, Glendale, in an interview with Allan Campbell in 1982:

'Fhuair iad fios, co-dhiù, gu robh leth-cheud poiliosman a' tighinn à Glaschu, agus thuirt iad riutha fhèin, "Coinnichidh sinn iad aig Cnoc an t-Sìthein!"

"S tha àit' uamhasach freagarrach ann a shin aig Cnoc an t-Sìthein; tha *bottleneck* ann far a faigheadh tu cothrom air daoine: tha rathad mòr sìos fon a' chnoc, sìos pìos. Bha làn-chothrom ac' air am bataradh ann a shin.

'Chruinnich iad uamhas – a chuile duine bha *able-bodied* ann an Gleann Dail: 's cha bu bheag na bh' ann an uair ud agus...

'Aig Cnoc an t-Sìthein: agus chruinnich iad clachan, dùn chlach, a chlachan a bhiodh freagarrach airson an tilgeadh air na...Thug iad fad feasgair a' cruinneachadh chlach. Bidh e colach gur h-e na clachan a th' ann chon a' latha 'n-diugh, nan sealladh tu gu math. Cha deachaidh na cùirn sin...cha deachaidh cach a thoirt asda riamh. 'S dòch' gu bheil iad a' feitheamh ris an ath *Land League*!'

('They got word, anyway, that there were fifty Glasgow policemen coming from Glasgow, and they said to themselves, "We'll confront them at *Cnoc an t-Sìthein!*"

'And there's a very suitable place there at *Cnoc an t-Sìthein*; there's a bottleneck there where you could get a good chance at them; the main road passes below the hill, a bit down. They had full scope for battering them there.

'They gathered a great crowd – everyone who was able-bodied in Glendale; that was no small number in those days and...

'At *Cnoc an t-Sìthein*: and they gathered stones, mounds of stones – the kind of stones that would be suitable to throw at...They spent a whole evening gathering stones. It's likely that these stones are there to this day, if you looked carefully...These cairns...not a single stone was ever taken off them. Perhaps they're waiting for the next Land League!')

Neil MacLean goes on to relate how the police were informed on board the steamer at Carbost that the Glendale men were waiting for them at *Cnoc an t-Sìthein*. They then decided to continue to Dunvegan, and make a flanking movement against the crofters. It is not clear from the recording how the incident ended, but it seems that the police did not advance, and that the Glendale men were prepared to go only as far as the estate boundary to meet them.

It is difficult to find a perfect match in the written and oral accounts of police interventions in Glendale. It is not clear which intervention is described in extant Gaelic sources, as there was more than one skirmish of this kind in the district. John MacLeod, after singing the song, relates how a crowd of Glendale men met a sixty-strong contingent of police, and began to attack them with bags of mud from the ditches (cf. Poem 21). The police, some of whom were bleeding, were forced to retreat to Dunvegan.

MacLeod's account bears a striking similarity to an event recorded elsewhere as having occurred on 20th January 1883. On that occasion, a crowd from Glendale, armed with sticks, gathered to meet a contingent of (allegedly) 50 policemen who were rumoured to be coming to the district. The police disembarked from the steamer 'Dunara Castle' at Dunvegan. According to MacPhail 1989: 59, 'discretion proved the better part of valour, and the officers of the law retreated, the Glendale and Dunvegan police constables taking refuge in Dunvegan Castle.'

The song describes this incident or one very similar to it, seen from the crofters' perspective. In the light of oral tradition still known to his father, Mr Archie Campbell, Allan Campbell warns against the possibility of exaggeration in the numbers of police (the song itself being silent on this point), and urges caution in accepting the term 'police' at face value. Events at Braes tended to colour the interpretation of happenings at Glendale.

For the background to events in Glendale, see Poem 22.

5 A large horn which was used to warn the communities of the approach of police or soldiers is still preserved in Glendale.

11-12 For verification of the type of 'army' and weapons described in the song, it is worth comparing the description given by Alexander MacVicar, police constable at Glendale, of the crowd which went to meet Sheriff Officer MacTavish on 16th January 1883 (see Poem 21 for full reference):

'I was at Station the time the Milivaig and Glendale tenants got the warning that they were coming. The horn was blowing in all directions and the people running towards the road throughout the glen. I saw the Milivaig tenants running past, each of them armed with new sticks made for the purpose.'

21. MacThàbhais an t-Sumanaidh

'A' Chreag Mhòr'

MacThàbhais an t-sumanaidh,
Cha bhàirlig e tuilleadh sinn;
Cha mhòr nach d'fhuair e bàs
    Nuair dh'fhàg sinn e 'm Brunigil.   4

'S i bean taigh-seinns' an Dùine
Thug dhuibh an uidheam ghiùlain;
A Rìgh, b' e 'n t-ioghnadh liomsa
    'Na smùr nach do chuireadh e.   8

Gum faca mis' thu 's drèin ort
A' dol a-mach am bràighe,
'S na gillean ['s iad] ag èigheach,
    'Tha Seumas is curag air!'   12

An curag nach robh àlainn
'Na shìneadh bho Fhèill Màrtainn
An atharnaich bhuntàta,
    'S b' e 'n tràill air na chuireadh e.   16

Gu robh do phàigheadh daor dhut
Ged ghabh thu leis an daoraich;
Gum b' fheàrr dhut buain a' mhaoraich
    Na maoirneachd cho cunnartach.   20

Nuair ghabh iad an ratreuta,
'S a thòisich iad air Seumas,
Bha h-uile fear ag èigheach,
    'B' e 'm beud thu bhith fulang uainn.'   24

Nuair thàinig iad 'na chòmhdhail
'S a nochd iad ris a' chòmhlan,
Thubhairt cuid dhiubh, 'Glacadh beò e,
    Am poll-mòna gun cuir sinn e.'   28

Ach ghabh iad dòigh a b' fheàrr:
Cha mhòr nach deach a bhàthadh;
Bha 'm poca dubh 'na phlàsda
    Gu chàradh ma mhuineal-san.   32

116

Bha Aonghas Dubh à Ròag
Air Tormod 'g iarraidh tròcair,
'S nuair thàinig an luchd-tòrachd,
    Gun d'fhòsaigeadh uile iad.   36

Thubhairt Tormod is e rànaich,
'Nach muladach a tha mi;
'S e gillean Mòr Ni Phàraig
    A thàmailtich buileach mi.   40

'Bha fear an dèidh a chèile
Air fastadh agam fhèin dhiubh,
'S nuair thionndaidh iad 'nan reubail,
    Chan èisdeadh iad tuilleadh rium.'   44

NOTES

Source: The *Oban Times*, 20 June 1885. Close variants of three verses, lines 1-4, 13-16 and 37-40, were collected by Miss Jo MacDonald in Glendale, Skye, in 1972-73.

Tune: No tune is specified in the source, but the metre is that of 'An Dòmhnallach Urramach': see Mac-na-Ceàrdadh 1879: 467-9.

Date and Context: The poem refers to events on and around 16-19th January 1883, when Sheriff Officer James MacTavish from Glasgow, accompanied by two concurrents and 14 policemen under the charge of Sergeant MacKenzie from Kingussie, was sent to Glendale to serve notices of interdict on the crofters who had put their cattle on the farm of Waterstein (MacPhail 1989: 59). MacTavish and his companions were met by a crowd of Milovaig and Glendale tenants, as the Glendale police constable, Alexander MacVicar, described in a letter (17 January 1883) to the Chief Constable of Inverness-shire:

'The crowd met them at the Glendale Bridge and immediately turned them. I saw them pushing and shoving Mactavish and throwing pail fulls of water and gutters [i.e. mud, probably taken from ditches] about his head. They had also an old bag full of gutters and they were striking them with this. I could not recognise them at the distance. They drove them in this manner until they put them off the Estate. They then turned to the Ground Officer's house and took Angus MacLeod the Sheriff Officer at Roag out of the house and put him on the Road. This MacLeod came with Mactavish as a witness, but being informed he was threatened by the tenants he remained there until Mactavish would return' (Highland Regional Archive, Ref. HRA/R13/J4). (I am grateful to Mr Robert Steward, Highland Regional Archivist, for providing a copy of the letter.)

See also Poems 20 and 22.

4 **Brunigil:** This was on the boundary of the MacLeod estate, near Skinidin.

12 **curag:** This was probably the sheriff officer's cape. It may have been his official garb, but it is known that, on other occasions, officers did employ cloaks or capes to disguise themselves.

33 **Aonghas Dubh à Ròag:** This may be a reference to Angus MacLeod, the sheriff officer who accompanied MacTavish; see the letter quoted above.

37-44: These lines may reflect the tensions created locally by the Glendale troubles, especially between the agitating crofters and others who were less inclined to agitate. So far I have been unable to identify the individuals who are mentioned.

22. Duanag don Triùir Ghàidheal a th' ann am Prìosan Dhun Eideann

Alasdair MacIlleathain

Feuch nach bi sibh an gruaim rium
  Ged nì mi 'n duan seo fo bhròn
Mun sgeul ùr a fhuair sinn
  A chuir oirnn smuairean is leòn;   4
Ar càirdean caomh agus suairce
  Am prìosan duaichnidh gun dòigh –
Cliù nam fiùran sin seinneam
  Dh'fhalbh à Eilean a' Cheò.   8

Ged a thèid mi ga luaidh dhuibh,
  Chan eil mo bhuadhan air dòigh;
Tha iomadh nì ga mo bhuaireadh –
  Tha m' aigne buairte gu leòr;   12
Ach sheasainn leibh ri uchd cruadail
  'S ri bàs nam buadhaicht' e oirnn –
Cliù nam fiùran sin seinneam
  Dh'fhalbh à Eilean a' Cheò.   16

Bu sibh na gaisgich nach lùbadh,
  'S tha an cliù sin 'nur còir;
Daoine aigeannach, sunndach,
  Gu dìreadh stùc is bheann mòr;   20
Daoine fòghlamaicht' bhuail,
  Ged fhuair sibh dùbhlan sa mhòd –
Cliù nam fiùran sin seinneam
  Dh'fhalbh à Eilean a' Cheò.   24

Is iomadh latha 'nur dùthaich
  A chaith sibh ùine gu leòr
Air bhur lìonadh le cùram
  Mu staid na dùthcha 's an t-slòigh;   28
'S fearann àitich ur sinnsir
  An-diugh 'na fhrìthean 's 'na lòin
Air feadh dhùthchannan eile
  'S air feadh Eilean a' Cheò.   32

119

O, gur sinn tha fo chùram,
 Tha ar n-ionndrainn cho mòr,
Pàirt de mhuinntir ar dùthcha
 Fo ghlasan dùint' an taigh-mhòid,   36
Ann am prìosan a' Chalton
 Le breith bhacach nan Lords,
'S na daoine ghabhadh an leisgeul
 Nochd an Eilean a' Cheò.   40

Ach 's fàth misneach faraon dhuinn
 Uaislean 's laoich feadh gach slòigh,
'S luchd-lagh àrd bhith rim faotainn
 An comann caomh ar luchd-fòir;   44
Dhearbh iad sin a bhith dìleas
 Anns gach nì mar bu chòir;
Tha iad eudmhor gun leth-bhreith
 Do mhuinntir Eilean a' Cheò.   48

Tha am bàillidh le dìcheall
 A' cleachdadh innleachdan seòlt';
Thig e uairibh gu dìblidh
 Gu bannan sìth a chur oirnn,   52
An dùil gum pàigh sinn am màl dha
 'S gum bi sinn càirdeil gu leòr,
'S nach bi cuimhn' air nì eile
 A bh' ann an Eilean a' Cheò.   56

Ach, a bhàillidh, a dhuine,
 Cha do thuig thu air chòir
Nàdar muinntir na dùthcha
 Ged tha thu 'n dùil a bhith seòlt';   60
Oir nuair thàrlas dhaibh aomadh
 Tha iad mar aon anns gach dòigh,
'S cha chuir gealtair gu breislich
 Muinntir Eilean a' Cheò.   64

Fhuair sibh reachd air a sgrìobhadh –
 Tha siud cinnteach gu leòr –
Nach faodadh duine no feudail
 A dhol thoirt ceum feadh ur feòir;   68

Bhac sibh dhinn na cos-cheuman
   A bh' aig na treubhan on tòs,
Aig gach àl, ged a theirinn,
   A bh' ann an Eilean a' Cheò.   72

An reachd a bh' againn cha trèig sinn,
   'S cha leig sinn eug i dhar deòin,
Dh'aindeoin bagradh a shèidear
   No thig 'nar dèidh air ar tòir;   76
Siùbhlaidh sinn na cos-cheuman
   Mar bhios ar feum a' toirt oirnn,
Gus an duine mu dheireadh
   A bhios an Eilean a' Cheò.   80

Bha na h-uachdarain fearainn
   Ann an aighear 's an ceòl,
Iad gach latha gu suaimhneach
   'S am mnathan guanach le sròl;   84
Càrnadh beairteis is saoibhreis
   Do an cloinn a bhiodh beò –
Toradh saothair dhaoin' eile
   Bh' ann an Eilean a' Cheò.   88

Nuair a thàinig na h-uaislean
   'S an t-uachdaran òg,
Cha d'fhàg iad taigh gun a chnuasach –
   O, bu shuarach an dòigh;   92
Thuirt iad rinne le beag-chuis –
   Mar gun creideamaid sgleò! –
''S gasda 'n cothrom sa bheil sibh
   Ann an Eilean a' Cheò.'   96

Cuiream crìoch air an duan seo,
   Ged tha e luath leam air dòigh;
Tha iomadh nì ga mo bhuaireadh
   De na truaighean tha oirnn;   100
Ach ma bhios mi san àite,
   'S gun tig càch thugainn beò,
Nì mi duanag bheag eile
   Do mhuinntir Eilean a' Cheò.   104

NOTES

Source: The *Northern Chronicle*, 18 April 1883. It was published in the *Northern Chronicle*, which was not a pro-crofter paper, 'because it has literary merit and represents the feelings of Skye crofters only too truly. They shut out the landlords' side of the question, and think they can be a law unto themselves. The poet, A. MacLean, praises the men in jail, and tells of their supposed wrongs.'

Tune: The source does not provide a tune.

Date and Context: The three Glendale men, whose imprisonment inspired this poem, were John MacPherson (later known as the 'Glendale Martyr'), John Morrison and Donald MacLeod. They were later joined by a fourth crofter, Malcolm Matheson, who happened to be in Stornoway, training with the Royal Naval Reserve. Their trial was held in Edinburgh on 15th March 1883, and they were sentenced to two months' imprisonment. The poem appears to have been composed soon after the verdict became known in Glendale.

The troubles in Glendale affected primarily the townships of Upper and Lower Milovaig and Borodale, which were situated on the estate owned by the Rev. Hugh MacPherson, the nephew of the previous owner, Sir John MacPherson MacLeod, who had died in 1881. The new owner was an absentee, and the administration of the estate was in the hands of trustees. Until October 1882 the factor for the estate was Donald MacDonald of Tormore, whose actions were the main cause of discontent among the crofters. From October 1882 the factor was John Robertson, proprietor of the estate of Greshornish in Skye.

The troubles centred on (1) the severe restrictions imposed by Tormore on the tenants of the Glendale townships, preventing them from 'trespassing' on his farms on the Glendale estate, when gathering driftwood, and restricting their ability to find suitable harbourage for their boats, etc.; and (2) the lease of the farm of Waterstein, which had been held by Dr Nicol Martin of Boreraig and Husabost until it expired at Whitsun 1882. Martin did not renew the lease, and it was given to MacDonald of Tormore. Despite the crofters' efforts to secure the farm for themselves, the trustees confirmed Tormore in the lease, but, as relations worsened, he abandoned his contract when he demitted the factorship. Frustration among crofters impelled them to put their cattle to graze on the Waterstein farm. They refused to accept notices of interdict in June 1882, and their ongoing defiance of the law resulted in the dispatch of police and sheriff officers to the estate early the following year. This led to sporadic confrontations (see Poems 20 and 21). Matters did not improve when Robertson became factor, since he intensified efforts to remove the Milovaig cattle and sheep from Waterstein. Eventually the gunboat *Jackal* was dispatched in February 1883, and the leaders of the crofters' resistance were persuaded to surrender by a civil servant, Malcolm MacNeill, who was on the gunboat.

The men who were thus arrested and imprisoned in Edinburgh were from Lower Milovaig. The poet, Alexander MacLean, was closely associated with the crofters' actions. For a full account, see MacPhail 1989: 52-61.

It is interesting that the poet has refrained from providing specific detail, such as the names of the prisoners, as if he were trying to keep a step back from the proceedings.

57 **a bhàillidh:** The factor who is addressed is probably MacDonald of Tormore, though by this stage the factor was John Robertson. Tormore was most obviously involved in the posting of notices of trespass and in the actions leading to the issuing of interdicts.

89-92 The *uachdaran òg* is likely to be Hugh MacPherson. The condition of their houses was a cause of considerable distress to the crofters, partly because the restrictions on the estate made it difficult for them to obtain suitable thatching material.

23. [Fàilte a' Choimisein]

Teàrlach MacFhionghain

Ho-rò, cha bhi mulad oirnn,
  Tuilleadh cha bhi èis oirnn,
Coimisean tighinn dhan dùthaich,
  An dùil gun dèan e feum dhuinn.   4

Nuair thèid gach nì an òrdagh dhuinn,
  'S thèid còraichean a leughadh,
G' eil mapaichean am pasgadh ac',
  Dealbh nan croit gu lèir ac'.   8

Gheibh sinn Heall is Greallainn,
  Feall is Druim Shlèite,
Oismaigearaidh is Sgòr,
  Is thig sinn beò gun èis ann.   12

Seall sibh fhèin Cnoc Oth thall,
  'S gach tobhta bhòidheach rèidh ann;
Chì sinn fhathast ceann orra,
  'S b' e m' annsa bhith an tè dhiubh.   16

Sguiridh sinn den ghiomaireachd,
  Oir 's tric ro-fhliuch ar lèintean;
'S fheàrr gu mòr bhith tuathanachas,
  'S a' ruamhar pàirce rèisgnich.   20

NOTES

Source: The song was recorded by Miss Jo MacDonald in Kilmuir, Skye, in 1973.

Tune: This is not specified, but the metre of the song is close to that of 'Ho-rò, chan eil cadal orm'; see Mac-na-Ceàrdadh 1879: 334-6.

Date and Context: As it stands, the text of the song does not identify the commission to which it refers, but it seems likely that it is the Royal Commission, established in March 1883 'to inquire into the conditions of crofters and cottars in the Highlands and Islands of Scotland', and now best known as the 'Napier Commission', from the name of its chairman, Lord Napier and Ettrick. Its other members were: Charles Fraser-Mackintosh, MP for Inverness Burghs; Donald Cameron of Lochiel, Conservative MP for Inverness-shire; Sir Kenneth MacKenzie of

Gairloch; Alexander Nicolson, a Skyeman who was Sheriff of Kirk-cudbright; and Donald MacKinnon, Professor of Celtic at the University of Edinburgh. The Commission was active in Skye in May 1883, and heard evidence at several locations in the island.

Despite initial misgivings about the composition of the Commission, which was perceived by the pro-crofter lobby as being too obviously representative of the landlord interest through the presence of two major landowners, Cameron of Lochiel and MacKenzie of Gairloch, it was welcomed by Highland crofters generally, as this song and Poem 24 indicate. On the whole, crofters were inclined to expect too much from it; it did not restore lost holdings, as Charles MacKinnon hoped, and as many were encouraged to believe; nor did it condemn landlordism, as John MacLean of Tiree desired. Its recommendations for the development of crofting townships, with some degree of protection, fell short of providing the essential security which crofters requested, and three members recorded dissent on several key points. Nevertheless, the gathering of evidence and its expeditious publication in April 1884 in a massive Report constituted a major presentation, testified eloquently to the crofters' plight, and helped to set the scene for the introduction of the Crofters' Holdings (Scotland) Act of 1886. See Cameron 1986 for an excellent summary of the Commission's work and its monumental Report.

9-16 The place-names are those of vacant crofts in the Kilmuir area. Some witnesses to the Commission were asked to 'specify in public the areas of land near their township which their people would like' (Cameron 1986: 123).

24. Teachdairean na Bànrighinn

Iain MacIlleathain, Bàrd Bhaile Mhàrtainn

O, seinnibh cliù nan Teachdairean
On t-seachdamh là den mhìos sin;
Ceud soraidh slàn thar chuantan leis
A' Chomann uasal rìoghail.   4

Ach saoghal buan don Bhànrighinn
Thug don Chomann àithne rìoghail
Gu teachd don eilean uaigneach seo
Air uchd a' chuain gu h-ìosal.   8

Tìr Bhàrr-fo-Thuinn nan garbh-thonnan,
An t-eilean ainmeil, fiachail;
Gu buan tha fuaim na fairge ris;
'S e nis as ainm Tir-ìdh dha.   12

Thug sinne sgeul na còrach dhaibh;
Bha chuid bu mhò dheth sgrìobhte,
Le gearan seasmhach, sònraichte,
Den chuid bu bhòidhche 'n fhìrinn.   16

Tha dòchas math is dùil agam
Gun dèan an Diùca sìth rinn,
'S gun èirich grian na h-ùr-mhadainn
A nì gach stùc a dhìreadh.   20

Ged tha an t-eilean cliùiteach seo
Don Diùc an-diugh toirt chìsean,
Cha b' ann le ceart no cruaidh lannan
A fhuaireadh e le shinnsre;   24

'S e cuilbheartan is lùbaireachd,
Is sodal-cùirt' is slìobadh,
Is rìoghalachd ar triathan-ne
Chuir e fo riaghladh millteach.   28

Mar luing bha sinn gar cuan-luasgadh,
'S gach fadadh-cruaidh a' strì rith';
Ach gheibh i caladh sàbhailte,
Ma bhios na Gàidheil dìleas.   32

Nuair bheir iad suas an teachdaireachd,
Bidh luchd an fhearainn dìte,
'S thig meas air *Tìm an Obain*
Anns gach baile mòr san rìoghachd.   36

NOTES

Source: The *Oban Times*, 22 November 1884. The present version is derived from three sources: lines 1-20 and lines 29-36 from *OT* and Cameron 1932: 162-4 (which is broadly consistent with *OT*), and lines 21-28 from Sinclair 1900: 118-20. The lines taken from Sinclair 1900 are consistent with the poet's views in other songs (see Poem 35), and were probably omitted from Cameron and *OT* because of their attack on the Duke of Argyll. For further evidence of verses of MacLean's songs surviving beyond the standard printed texts, see Poems 11 and 30.

The present edition omits the four quatrains preceding the last verse in the source texts. These verses are a generalised excursus on the plight of the Highlands.

Tune: This is specified in *OT* as 'Clachan Ghlinn-da-ruail'. For a modern setting of the tune, see *A' Chòisir Chiùil*, Part II: 27.

Date and Context: The song was composed shortly after the Napier Commission visited Tiree on 7th August 1883. The Commission met in Kirkapol Parish Church. See also Poem 23.

2 Bidh reachdan math ri 'n linn ann (Sinclair 1900). This reading looks like an editorial 'poeticising' of the specific detail in the line as represented in Cameron's version.

12 'S e Tiriodh ainm r'a innse (Sinclair 1900).

25. [Moladh Henry Seòras]

Molaidh sinn Henry Seòras,
    Canaidh sinn òran 's urram dha;
Canaidh, 's ann dhuinn bu chòir siud,
    Molaidh gu deònach, duineil e.   4

Sgrìobh e leabhar mu chòirean,
    'Soirbheachadh Mòr is Uireasbhaidh';
Chuir e crith air na fir mhòra
    Feadh na Roinn Eòrpa 's Ameirioga.   8

Obair is fearann 's iùl-riaghlaidh
    An làmhan dhaoin' iargalt' fuileachdach,
Tàir air a' bhochd 's air a' Chrìosdaidh
    Sìor dhol am meud sa h-uile àit'.   12

Chuir e fios-fithich an cèill dhaibh,
    Dh'innis e 'n call 's an cunnart dhaibh;
Cunntas le gille 'na dheann-ruith –
    'Am pailteas a th' ann cha bhuin e dhuibh.'   16

Theagaisg e reachd do gach reubal –
    'Dèan mar dhut fhèin dod choimhearsnach';
Gràdh an co-dhàimh ri gach creutair –
    Siud mar lagh Dhè is dhuine dhuinn.   20

Fhuair iad cho fad' an toil fhèin dhinn,
    Is duilich dhaibh gèilleadh buileach dhuinn;
Cluinnidh iad tuilleadh o Henry
    Is cuideachd nan teang' mun sguir sinn dhiubh.   24

Mòr-shluagh na cruinne air èirigh,
    Dh'ionnsaich an èiginn tuigse dhaibh;
Crìoch air gach cogadh is eucoir,
    Is bràithrean gu lèir mar rugadh sinn.   28

Cuideachdan Ghlaschu 's Dhun Eideann,
    Cuideachdan Eirinn 's Lunnainn leinn;
Dùthaich is baile le chèile,
    Muinntir tìr chèin – 's bidh a' bhuil orra.   32

NOTES

Source: The *Oban Times*, 13 December 1884. The composer, given as 'MacL.', has not been identified.

Tune: This is not specified in the source.

Date and Context: Henry George (see Index 2) was interested in the Irish and Highland land questions, and visited Scotland in February 1884. He went to Braes, Skye, but did not make much of an impact. At a meeting in the City Hall, Glasgow, on 18th February he advocated the proclamation of 'the grand truth that every human being born in Scotland has an inalienable and equal right to the soil of Scotland – a right that no law can do away with, a right that comes from the Creator who made earth for man and placed him upon the earth'. This resulted in the formation of the Scottish Land Restoration League, based on George's tenets, and supported by John Murdoch (MacPhail 1989: 95-6).

The song was probably composed soon after the meeting in Glasgow.

26. Oran mu Chor nan Croitearan

Dòmhnall MacFhionghain, Glaschu

Sinn tha neo-shunndach an dùthaich nan Gall,
  Le snigh air mo shùil, 's beag an t-ioghnadh tha ann,
'S gach pàipear san dùthaich toirt cunntais san àm
  Mu chor ar luchd-dùthcha an dùthaich nam beann.   4

On Bhut ann an Leòdhas gu Maola Chinntìr,
  Na h-eileanan mara, na srathan 's na glinn,
Le màil iad gam feannadh 's am fearann nach fhiach,
  Na sgreabagan tana, ged 's reamhar am prìs.   8

'S mòr anns bheil brìogh dheth aig sìolaibh nan Gall,
  'S clanna nan Gàidheal gun àite dhaibh ann,
'S ma dh' iarras iad fearann, 's e gheibh iad san àm
  Coin-lomhainn 'Fir Shasainn' a sparradh a-nall.   12

Gam feannadh 's gan ruagadh gun truaighe tha chlann,
  Bidh bàillidh cur cruaidh riu gach uair le choin sheang,
A chumail nan uachdaran shuas anns an Fhraing,
  Na baigearan uasal, 's an uaisle air chall.   16

'S tha damh a' chinn chabraich ann fhathast gu leòr,
  Tha am bradan san abhainn gu bras-charach beò,
Gu spuirt do 'Fhir Shasainn' thig pailt air an tòir,
  'S ma bheanas sinn fhèin dhaibh, tha am prìosan
      mar sròin.   20

'S mas lagh e, cha cheartas, an reachd rinn iad fhèin;
  An Tì sin a chruthaich na h-uile fon ghrèin,
Cha d'òrdaich e riamh dhaibh gach sian dhiubh dhaibh
      fhèin,
  Gach bradan is fiadh agus eunlaith nan speur.   24

'S i mo shoraidh le dùrachd a dhùthaich nam beann
  Gun soirbhich gach cùis leo bhon dhùisgeadh a clann;
Tha eachdraidh toirt cunntais, cha mhùchar a cainnt,
  Gur gaisgeil gu 'n cùl iad an àm rùsgadh nan lann.   28

Ged 's tearc a tha càirdean nan Gàidheal san streup,
  Tha gràinnean nach tàir dhiubh sa Phàrlamaid fhèin,
'S ged 's dorcha an iarmailt, 's na siantan tha breun,
  Na neòil thèid an riasladh, 's thig grian air an speur.   32

NOTES

Source: The *Oban Times*, 31 January 1885.

  Tune: 'Cogadh no sìth'.

  Date and Context: The generalised nature of the poem makes it difficult to determine precisely when it was composed. It may reflect the overall mood of disappointment following the publication of the Napier Commission Report in April 1884. The 'Highland question' was prominent in the newspapers following the troubles on the Kilmuir estate and the arrival of a military expedition in Skye on 16th November 1884 (MacPhail 1989: 115-6).

  Nevertheless, the poem is significant because, in lines 29-32, it anticipates the first sparks of political optimism, created by the extension of the franchise in 1884 and the stronger efforts of existing pro-crofter Members of Parliament. These developments were to pave the way for the return of the crofters' candidates at the General Election of November-December 1885 (see Poem 29).

27. Bratach nan Croitearan

Dòmhnall MacDhòmhnaill, Grianaig

Bratach nan croitearan tapaidh,
  Nach robh gealtach ga cur suas,
Slàn don làimh a dheilbh sa bheairt i –
  'S gur tiugh, gasda chaidh a luadh.   4

'S e suaicheantas 'Ceist an Fhearainn' –
  Thigibh 's leanaibh i gu cruaidh;
Eiribh o gach gleann is caladh,
  'S cha dèan carachd a toirt uaibh.   8

Fàilte air MacCaluim, an diùlnach,
  Tha ga giùlan thar nan stuagh;
Chìthear e an camp 's an cùbaid
  Mar reul-iùil air ceann an t-sluaigh.   12

Ghoid na h-uachdarain mhì-dhìleas
  Còraichean ar sinnsir uainn,
'S dh'fhàg iad lom gun fhonn gun nì sinn –
  Cha robh dìreadh againn suas.   16

Ach gheibh sinne ceannard làidir
  Thèid don Phàrlamaid gu luath;
Bithidh ar sròl aig deagh MhacPhàrlain,
  'S cha toir nàmhaid oirre buaidh.   20

'S cha bhi e a-nis 'na ònar
  A' tagairt còraichean an t-sluaigh;
Bithidh ri ghualainn Mac-an-Tòisich,
  'S thèid e còmhla ris 'nan gruaig.   24

NOTES
Source: The *Oban Times*, 10 October 1885.
  Tune: This is not specified in the source.
  Date and Context: The song is an indicator of the optimism which preceded the General Election of November-December 1885, as crofters' candidates and their supporters canvassed in the Highland constituencies. As the location of the poet indicates, Highlanders resident in the Lowlands took a keen interest in events.

The poem is one of several from this period which use the banner as a rallying-symbol for pro-crofter voters: see Meek 1995 for further examples of 'banner poems' associated with the campaign of Donald Horne MacFarlane (line 19). Banners were used extensively by crofters in their campaign for land-rights, especially at times of public demonstration or protest, notably in Glendale in Skye. Banners carried emblems and slogans such as 'Liberty', 'Down with the Landlords' etc.

The crofters' leaders who are mentioned in the poem are listed in Index 2.

28. Croitearan Leòdhais

Murchadh MacLeòid, Brù, Barbhas

'S e 'n t-iongantas as mìorbhailich
Bha riamh an Eilean Leòdhais,
Na daoine bochda riaghladh ann,
'S na tighearnan gan cur fodhp';   4
Tha iad an-diugh le fialachd
A' tighinn a dh'iarraidh bhòts,
'S chan fhaigh iad uainn am bliadhna iad
Ge brèagha an cuid sgeòil.   8

A Chlann nan Gàidheal, còmhnaibh mi,
'S gun tòisich sinn ri roinn,
'S gun can sinn ris na h-uachdarain
Iad a dh'fhuireach uainn a-chaoidh;   12
'S gun seas sinn mar bu dual dhuinn
Le ar guaillean dlùth ri chèil',
'S gun toir sinn uile buaidh orr'
Le fear na gruaige rèidh.   16

Nach b' e 'n Dotair Dòmhnallach
An t-òlach air an ceann;
'S ann dha as aithn' na dòighean
San toir e chòir gu ceann;   20
'S tha mise nise dòchasach
A slòigh an eilein duinn,
Gun toir iad dha na bhòtaichean
'S gun seas e chòir don cloinn.   24

Ach fhuair e nis na bhòtaichean
'S tha dòchas agaibh fhèin
Gun seas e nis ar còraichean
An aghaidh luchd an fhòirneirt ghèir;   28
'S tha mise guidhe tròcair dhut
Ma dheònaiches tu fhèin
Nach till thu ris an t-seòrsa
Tha an còmhnaidh ris a' bhreug.   32

134

Is aithne dhuibh Nobhàr sin,
'S tha ghnùis ro-àlainn òg,
'S chan fhaicear e sa Phàrlamaid
Airson an àit'-s' ri bheò;   36
Chan eil sinn airson uachdarain
Bhith riaghladh anns a' chùirt,
'S cha chreid sinn an cuid bhriathran
Gus am faic sinn gnìomh air tùs.   40

Tha oighreachd aig Nobhàr sin,
'S chan fheàirrd' e i san àm,
Na daoine bochd' gan sàrachadh,
Gun àrach ac' don cloinn;   44
'S cha toir e sreath bhuntàta dhaibh
A bheir an tràth gu ceann –
'S e 'g iarraidh staigh don Phàrlamaid
Gu ar n-àite sheasamh ann!   48

Tha feadhainn de mo chàirdean
Le Nobhàr anns a' chùis,
Is bha siud 'na shaothair fhàs dhaibh,
'S cha b' fheàirrd' iad e 'nan cliù;   52
Cha d' fhuair iad air na nàbaidhean
A thàladh air an taobh,
'S tha iad an-diugh cho tàmailteach
Gan càineadh feadh na dùthch'.   56

An-diugh gur mis' tha uasal
As an t-sluagh dom buin mi fhèin,
Gach fine 's treubh 's na bhuaineadh iad –
Cha d'fhuaireadh iad fo ghèill;   60
Is ged tha daoine suarach
A' cosnadh duais dhaibh fhèin,
Tha Siorrachd Rois a' buadhach,
'S na h-uachdarain fo ghèill.   64

Bu tàmailteach le uaislean
Nuair chualas leo an sgeul,
Na daoine bochd' a' buadhach
Bha suarach aca fhèin;   68

'S gun choisinn siud do uachdarain
Bha uasal asda fhèin
Bhith gealltainn dhuinne duaise,
Nan cuirte suas iad fhèin.　　　　72

Ach ma tha sinn bochd, gun d'fhuaireas
Sinn na b'uaisle na iad fhèin,
Is thugadh iad an duaisean
Don t-sluagh a tha leo fhèin;　　　　76
Cha chog sinn airson tuarasdail,
Ach bheir sinn buaidh gu treun,
Is bidh ceartas dhuinn 'na shuaicheantas,
'S cha ghabh sinn duais na brèig'.　　　　80

Tha breitheanas ro-uamhasach
'Na thuarasdal don bhrèig;
Thug Iùdas fhèin a mhallachd oirr'
Ge b' eagalach a ghnè;　　　　84
'S an duine reic am fearann,
Dh'fhuiling peanas mar an ceudn';
Thuit e marbh mar shamhladh,
'S a leannan as a dhèidh.　　　　88

ᐟNach duilich cor ar naomhairean
Ma dh'fhaodar sin a ràdh,
Mar chaidh iad leis na h-uachdarain
Bha cur an t-sluaigh gu bàs?　　　　92
Na prìosanaich cha d'fhuasgail iad
Mar fhuair iad anns an àithn',
Ach chaidh iad leis na cìobairean
Bha cur na tìre fàs.　　　　96

Nach innis sibh dhomh, a naomhairean,
Na smaointean bh' agaibh fhèin
Nuair bha sibh tràth an ionracas
Toirt aonta don a' bhrèig?　　　　100
Na dh'fheòraich sibh da-rìribh dhith
Gach nì chuir sibh an cèill?
Mur d' fheòraich cuim a dhìtear e,
'S an fhìrinn air a thaobh?　　　　104

Ach 's ann bha 'n duin'-uasal ann,
A lean an sluagh 's gach ceum,
Greenfield an duin'-uasal –
Cha mhealladh duaisean e;   108
Bha fìrinn air mar shuaicheantas,
'S do uaislean cha do ghèill,
'S cha ghabhadh e le tuarasdal,
'S e 'g amharc suas gu nèamh.   112

Ach ciod chuir don àite thu,
A Nobhàr tha gun suim,
Nuair dh'fhuadaich thu do luchd-àiteachaidh,
'S a dh'fhàg thu iad ro-ghann?   116
Tha fèidh is caoraich bhàn' agad,
Is cuir do làmh 'nam làimh,
'S mur cuir iad thu don Phàrlamaid,
Chan àrdaich mis' thu chaoidh.   120

NOTES

Source: This poem was published in two sections in the *Oban Times*, the first on 17 April 1886, and the second on 24 April 1886. The composer is given as the 'Lews Bard', identified in the second published section of the poem as Murdo MacLeod, Bru, Barvas.

There is a version of the poem in MacLeòid 1916: 210-2, but it does not give the name of the poet, nor does it include the verses condemning the clergy in the *OT* text (lines 89-104 in the present edition).

The present edition follows the first section of the *OT* text, but omits two of the more rhetorical anti-clerical verses following line 104. In five further verses (also omitted from this edition), the poet puts the Highlanders' plight before the Queen, refers to emigration to Quebec, exhorts the landlords to restore the land to the people as a way of ensuring their election to Parliament, warns that there will be real confrontation if they do not, and comments on the present antipathy to sheep. The *OT* version concludes with lines 113-20 of this edition. Line variants from MacLeòid 1916: 210-2 are given below (MacL).

Tune: The tune is not specified in either source, but the metre is very close to that of Dugald Buchanan's hymn, 'Fulangas Chrìosd', and the first line is identical with the fifth line of Buchanan's hymn (MacLean 1913: 5). It is possible that the hymn and the song share the same tune.

Date and Context: The poem was obviously composed at the time of the General Election of November-December 1885, with specific reference to the candidates for Ross and Cromarty. However, the existing text seems to consist of verses composed both before and after the result of the election was known. The first three verses (lines 1-24) are a form of *brosnachadh*, urging Lewis voters to support Dr Roderick MacDonald, while two verses condemn Munro-Ferguson of Novar who had previously held the constituency. Part of the poem (lines 25-32, 65-72) appears to have been composed after MacDonald's victory was known, since it refers to his success and to the landlords' discomfiture. The poet alleges that bribery played a significant part in Munro-Ferguson's campaign. The poet's perspectives are more significant than his versecraft, which is banal in parts.

8 'tha 'n cuid sgeòil (MacL).
10 a' roinn (MacL).
16 léith (MacL).
21 cur dòchais (MacL).
22 an slògh (MacL).
23 gach voté (MacL).
25 gach voté (MacL).
26 agam féin (MacL).
27 a' chòir dhuinn (MacL).
28 an aghaidh fòirneirt ghéir (MacL).
29 dhuit tròcair (MacL).

41 **Nobhàr:** Ronald Crauford Munro-Ferguson of Raith and Novar came of a landed family, and, although he was a Liberal, he was unacceptable to the crofters because of his landed interests (MacPhail 1989: 149).

59 iad *omitted* (MacL).
60 toirt géill (MacL).
64 cha ghéill (MacL).
73 Ged 'tha sinn bochd (MacL).
74 uasal seach (MacL).
77 airson duaise (MacL).
79 'Us ceartas 's e ar suaicheantas (MacL).

83 **Iùdas:** Judas Iscariot bought a field with the reward received for betraying Christ, but 'there he fell headlong, his body burst open, and all his intestines spilled out'; see the Book of Acts 1: 18.

85-8: The reference is to the New Testament characters, Ananias and Sapphira, who were both implicated in deception over a land transaction, and paid for it with their lives; see the Book of Acts 5: 1-11.

86 Bha peanas ás a dhéidh (MacL).

89-104 The identity of the *naomhairean* is not immediately evident, nor are the specific grounds of the attack. However, it is probably relevant that, in the 1884 by-election in Ross and Cromarty, Munro-Ferguson was supported by two distinguished Free Church ministers, Dr Gustavus Aird of Creich and the Rev. Murdo MacAskill, who succeeded the Rev. Dr John Kennedy as minister of Dingwall Free Church. Dr

MacDonald contested the by-election, but came third, the winner being Munro-Ferguson (MacPhail 1989: 153-4). The poet implies that ministers were supporting Munro-Ferguson again in the 1885 election. In Sutherland, Free Church ministers were supporting the Marquis of Stafford in that election; see further Poem 29.

105 Nach b' e sud an t-uasal (MacL).

107 **Greenfield:** The Rev. James Greenfield (1831-99) was inducted as minister of Stornoway Free Church of Scotland in 1872. He became Senior Minister in 1894 (Ewing, I: 177).

109 'S e fìrean 'tha ro-shuairc' e (MacL).

111 aon duais uath' (MacL).

29. Co-dhiù Thogainn Fonn nan Gaisgeach

Iain MacIlleathain, Maol Buidhe

Sèisd:
Co-dhiù thogainn fonn nan gaisgeach
Anns gach àit' an òlainn drama;
Co-dhiù thogainn fonn nan gaisgeach.　　　3

'S e Dotair Dòmhnallach tha mi 'g ràidhtinn –
Is mac croiteir e gun àicheadh;
Thug e buaidh air Fear Nobhàr,
　　A Taigh na Pàrlamaid chùm e mach e.　　　7

Ach gur e mo cheist an t-uasal
Sheas gu dìleas anns a' chruadal;
Thug e nise uile buaidh orr',
　　'S tha e shuas a dheòin no dh'aindeoin.　　　11

Bha na ragaichean an còmhnaidh
A' sìor ruith le an cuid bòilich,
Ag innse air a h-uile dòigh
　　Gun tugadh Nòbhar òg dhuinn ceartas.　　　15

Ach gur e mo cheist an t-àrmann
A fhuair urram mòr nan Gàidheal;
Thug e buaidh air a nàmhaid,
　　'S bheir e bhàn dhuinn màl an fhearainn.　　　19

Tha Dotair Dòmhnallach làn cruadail;
Dh'èirich Leòdhas bhon taobh tuath leis,
Siorramachd Rois nam fearaibh cruaidh –
　　'S e 'n t-Eilean Dubh chùm suas a' bhratach.　　　23

'S ann a tha mo cheist air Ruairidh
A fhuair urram bhon taobh tuath seo,
'S tha e nis am measg nan uaislean
　　Chum bhith cumail suas a' cheartais.　　　27

Bha 'n Dòmhnallach Camashron air thùs ann –
'S mòr tha bhailtean air a chùram;
Ma gheobh esan uile dhùrachd,
　　Cha bhi cùram oirnn à ceartas.　　　31

Dotair Clarc an sàr dhuin'-uasal,
'S mòr bu mhisde sinne uainn e;
Air Mac-na-Ceàrda thug e buaidh,
   'S bheir e bhuainn am fuachd 's an t-acras.   35

Tha Jesse Collings air ar cùlaibh
Gu ar seasamh aig na cùirtean,
'S chan eil bàillidh fon a' Chrùn
   Bheir màl dùbailt' bhuainn an ath-bhliadhn'.   39

Na Cataich nach do sheas cho cruaidh
'S bu chòir dhaibh aig àm a' chruadail,
Bhiodh aca Sutharlanach suairce
   Chuireadh gruaim air Diùc 's air Marcuis.   43

Ach gur sinne tha gu stàideil
Le Dotair Dòmhnallach 's MacPhàrlain,
Friseal Mac-an-Tòis', an t-àrmann;
   'S ann tha tàir aig muinntir Chataibh.   47

NOTES

Source: The text of the poem, which was reproduced in Barron 1976: 346-7, is derived from the *Scottish Highlander* newspaper. A cutting of the newspaper text can be found in the Mulbuie Land League Minute Book, which records the appointment of the poet, John MacLean, Drynie Park, Mulbuie (by Muir of Ord), in the Black Isle, as poet to his local branch of the Highland Land Law Reform Association.

   Tune: 'Co-dhiù thogainn fonn mo leannain'.

   Date and Context: The poem was composed primarily to celebrate the victory of Dr Roderick MacDonald (see Index 2) in the General Election of November-December 1885, and is thus to be dated to December 1885. For an account of the land agitation in Easter Ross, see Gibson 1986. For the elections in the Highlands generally, see MacPhail 1989: 147-68.

   6 **Fear Nobhàr:** MacDonald defeated the sitting Liberal candidate, Munro-Ferguson of Novar, by 4,942 votes to 2,925. The victory was received with particular enthusiasm because MacDonald had contested the seat in 1884, and had been defeated by Novar. Although Novar posed as a radical, he did not win support generally, and the poet's sentiments in lines 12-15 reflect the prevailing view that he and his supporters were not to be trusted (MacPhail 1979: 390-1; Meek 1977c: 349-50).

   12-15 The allusion is to the newspapers (*ragaichean*, line 12) which supported Novar's candidature.

   23 The extant Minute Book of the Mulbuie Branch of the Highland

Land Law Reform Association demonstrates that the Black Isle had a very vigorous body of supporting crofters.

29 The Northern Burghs was the larger of the two burgh constituencies in the crofting counties. It consisted of Wick, Cromarty, Tain, Dingwall, Dornoch and Kirkwall. Hence the poet's reference to Cameron's extensive responsibility. The other burgh constituency, Inverness Burghs, comprised Inverness, Forres, Fortrose and Nairn (MacPhail 1979: 368). For Cameron, see Index 2.

30 This line reflects the fact that Cameron gained his seat by a very narrow majority of 923 votes to 868 over the official Liberal candidate, John Pender of Minard Castle, who had held it since 1872 (ibid., 392).

33 The poet alludes to the accusation that Clark was a 'carpet-bagger' (MacPhail 1979: 391). For Clark, see Index 2.

34 **Mac na Ceàrda:** Clark defeated the Liberal candidate, Major Sinclair, younger of Ulbster, by 2,110 votes to 1,218 (ibid.).

36 **Jesse Collings:** See Index 2.

40-3 The people of Sutherland (*Na Cataich*, line 40) failed to return Angus Sutherland (referred to as *Sutharlanach*, line 42) as their M.P. For Sutherland, see Index 2.

43 **Diùc is Marcuis:** The reference is to the Duke of Sutherland and his eldest son and heir, the Marquis of Stafford, the so-called 'Radical Marquis'. The Marquis, after some ten years of silence during his representation of the constituency, was suddenly converted to radical land reform in the autumn of 1884. The publication of his proposals to ameliorate crofters' conditions was sanctioned by his father (MacPhail 1979: 386-9). See further the note on Angus Sutherland in Index 2.

30. Do Dhòmhnall MacPhàrlain

Iain MacIlleathain, Bàrd Bhaile Mhàrtainn

Sèisd:

Tìr nam beann, nan gleann, 's nam breacan,
Tìr nam beann, nan gleann, 's nan gaisgeach;
Fàilt' is furan Dhòmhnaill MhicPhàrlain,
An dùthaich nam beann àrd 's nam breacan.　　　　4

Saoghal buan le buaidh is rian dhut,
Gu bhith dol gun dàil a riaghladh
Dùthaich mhaiseach nam fear fialaidh,
　　Nan earb, nam fiadh is nam bradan.　　　　8

Thug an sluagh le urram spèis dhut,
A dh'aindeoin luchd-tuaileis brèige,
Is rinn iad àite-suidhe rèidh dhut
　　An St Stèphen's ann an Sasainn.　　　　12

Moch Di-ciadain bha sinn deònach
Gu bhith dìleas dhut sa chòmhstri;
Bàta b' fheàrr chaidh riamh a sheòladh,
　　Cha tigeadh i a chòir a' chaladh.　　　　16

Thug sinn bàt' air uallach guaille
Cheann Loch Ghot, 's b' e port a' chruadail,
Dhol gu Muile nam beann fuara
　　Dh'aindeoin doineann cuain is gaillinn.　　　　20

Ghabh an t-*Eileanach* a cùrsa,
Gearradh geal nan tonnan dùbh-ghlas;
Shaoil mi gum b' e Ceap an Dùidsich
　　Fearann Mhuile dlùth air Stafa.　　　　24

Gàidheil an Rois Mhuilich fhuair sinn
Cridheil, coibhneil, aoibheil, uasal;
Sìol nam fear as fhad on chualas,
　　Chuireadh ruaig, 's as dian a leanadh.　　　　28

143

Siud da-rìribh là a' chruadail,
Earraghàidheal uil' aig tuasaid;
Anns an fhicheadamh blàr bha buaidh leat,
    'S lean thu 'n ruaig le luchd nam breacan.   32

An ath Dhi-luain bha sgeula gàirdeachais
Air feadh uile chloinn nan Gàidheal;
Is bha a beanntan agus àrdain
    'S iad le barrachd gràidh a' lasadh.   36

Teintean mòr' air beanntan uaine;
Pìobairean a' cluich gu h-uallach;
Is guth-gàirdeachais an t-sluaigh ann
    Togail fuinn a ghluais Mac Talla.   40

Bidh na bàird a' dèanamh òran;
Anns gach coill' gun seinn na smeòraich;
Chan eil fear dom buin an ceòl sin
    Ach luchd-tagair còir an fhearainn.   44

Tha do chàirdean leat gud chòmhnadh
Gu bhith seasamh taobh na còrach –
Teàrlach Friseal Mac-an-Tòisich,
    'S an t-Urramach òg MacCaluim.   48

Tha iomadh Ahab foilleil, dalma
An-diugh an Gàidhealtachd na h-Alba;
Is b' fheàrr gum faicinn fuil gach cealgair,
    Is a charbad fo na madaibh.   52

Thigeadh *Tìm an Obain* sàbhailt'
Mar chalaman Nòah don àiric,
Le fios gu bheil an tuil air tràghadh
    Ged a chuir i fàs an talamh.   56

Seo a' bhliadhna ùr don Bhànrighinn,
Do Ghladstone is do Dhòmhnall MacPhàrlain,
Dhol gu toirt do na Gàidheil
    Dàimheachd làidir 'nan cuid fearainn.   60

'S guidheam buaidh le Dòmhnall MacPhàrlain,
Fear deagh iùil air cheann nan Gàidheal,
Mar bha Maois o shean san fhàsach
    A' toirt chàich gu Tìr a' Gheallaidh.   64

NOTES

Source: The primary source of the present edition is Cameron 1932: 173-5. Variant readings are provided by a text of ten quatrains (omitting lines 33-40 and 49-64 of the present edition) in MacCallum 1912: 148. MacCallum's version (the earliest known to date) probably derives from a text published in a contemporary newspaper, but I have been unable to locate the source. Another valuable text has been provided by Hector Kennedy, and is printed in Mackay 1979: 92-3 (K). Although significantly shorter than the text in Cameron, containing only the refrain and four of Cameron's thirteen verses, K preserves two very important quatrains which are not attested in Cameron. They occur as the first two quatrains of K. They are included in the present text as the last two quatrains (lines 57-64). Lines 57-60 are also attested, although in a variant form, in Sinclair 1900: 115-17.

Tune: The tune is given in Mackay 1979: 92.

Date and Context: The song commemorates the achievement of Donald H. MacFarlane in winning the constituency of Argyll at the General Election of 1885. The voting extended from Monday 24th November to Friday 4th December. The voting-station for the Tiree crofters was at Bunessan, and this called for the sea journey which the poet describes. It is a striking measure of the crofters' determination to use their newly-acquired franchise that they were prepared to travel to Mull on a stormy winter's day to cast their votes in favour of MacFarlane. See Meek 1995.

The reference to Gladstone and MacFarlane in lines 57-64 raises an interesting question about the period of composition of the poem. After the General Election of November-December 1885, the Conservative government of Lord Salisbury remained in office, and was not defeated until 21st January 1886, when it fell as a result of a resolution put forward by Jesse Collings (see Index 2). The poet may have composed these verses in December 1885, and hazarded a guess that Gladstone and MacFarlane would continue the campaign for crofters' rights; but it is more likely that he added the quatrains when it became known that Gladstone was setting up his third Ministry. The poem as a whole may thus have been composed over a period from early December 1885 to late January 1886. It is perhaps significant that MacCallum's text does not include those verses which describe the reaction to MacFarlane's victory; these may have been a slightly later addition (by the poet) to his first version, and we may thus need to envisage three stages in the creation of the poem as we now have it.

7 **Dùthaich mhaiseach:** Cameron reads 'Dùthcha mhaisich', which looks like an editorial emendation. This is confirmed by MacC.

10 Dh'aindeoin olc luchd-tuaileas bréige (MacC).

12 **St Stèphen's:** a reference to St Stephen's Chapel in the Palace of Westminster. The Commons met there from 1547 to 1843.

15 Ach am bàt' a b'fheàrr a sheòladh (MacC).

18 **Loch Ghot:** Gott Bay, where the present Tiree pier is located. It seems that the stormy weather prevented the steamship concerned (see line 21 n.) from using the small harbour at Scarinish, where ships usually anchored, and that she came into Gott Bay. The voters were ferried out to her in small boats.

21 **an t-*Eileanach*:** The MacCallum steamer, *Hebridean*, was chartered by MacFarlane to take voters from Coll and Tiree to the polling stations.

23-4 These lines may be translated, 'I thought that the Dutchman's Cap was the land of Mull close to Staffa' or 'I thought that the land of Mull close to Staffa was the Dutchman's Cap'.

25 There were close links between Tiree and the Ross of Mull in this period. The Tiree men were evidently given hospitality by the people of the Ross, and this verse acknowledges their kindness.

26 **uasal:** suairce (MacC).

28 A chuireadh an ruaig 's a leanadh (MacC).

29 B' e Diciadain lath' a chruadail (MacC).

30 'S Earraghàidheal riut aig tuasaid (MacC). This is probably a superior reading to that in Cameron, since the subtle use of *riut* ('Argyll was contending against you') implies (quite correctly) that strong forces were ranged against MacFarlane.

31 Anns an fhichead blàr (MacC).

42 **na smeòraich:** an smeòrach (MacC).

47 The line follows MacC. Cameron reads: *Am Frisealach is Mac-an-Toisich*, which suggests that the editor may have misconstrued the line as containing the names of two individuals.

47-8 For Fraser-Mackintosh and MacCallum, see Index 2. The Rev. Donald MacCallum did not stand as a candidate in the 1885 General Election, but it is likely that he was canvassing for the Land League in Tiree. He was well known in the islands for his support of the crofters; see Meek 1977a; 1987.

49 **Ahab:** a reference to King Ahab in 1 Kings 21: 1-16. When depicting social and political conditions in the Highlands, crofters' leaders frequently referred to Biblical stories and characters. 'Ahab' represented the avaricious landlord. For Ahab's death and the reference to his blood which flowed from his chariot, see 1 Kings 22: 35-8. Note the Biblical allusion to the Flood in line 54, and also the comparison between Donald MacFarlane and Moses in lines 63-4. For further discussion of the use and influence of the Bible in the Land Agitation, see Meek 1987.

31. Slàinte Dhòmhnaill 'IcPhàrlain

Iain MacIlleathain, Bàrd Bhaile Mhàrtainn

Deoch-slàinte Dhòmhnaill 'IcPhàrlain;
Is uasal, suairce, bàidheil thu;
Tha dùrachd Chloinn nan Gàidheal leat
    A h-uile là, ged dhealaich sinn.   4

'S ro-lìonmhor àit' san òlar
Ann an tìr nan gleann 's nam mòr-bheann i,
Deoch-slàint' an uasail mhòralaich,
    'S a chuirear òr ga ceannach dha.   8

Is òlaidh sinn le dùrachd i
An tìr an fhraoich gu dùthchasach;
On as urram mòr dar dùthaich e
    Thu dhol do chùirt nan Sasannach.   12

Duin'-uasal measail, iomraiteach,
Mar thobar glan nach tiormaicheadh,
Ged bha na h-uiread ioraghaill
    Aig MacFhionghain 's aig Poltalloch riut.   16

Rinn Earraghàidheal dearmad ort
Le mheud 's a bh' ann de chealgairean;
'S e sin an-diugh rinn Sgairinis
    Bhith cho ainmeil ri Sebastopol.   20

Ri gailleann 's doineann geamhraidh,
Ged rinn Earraghàidheal ceannard dheth,
'S e rinn an t-olc na mealltairean
    'S na thàinig ann de shliomairean.   24

Na laoich as fhad' on chualas iad
Air muir 's air tìr bhith cruadalach,
San eilean ìosal, uaine seo,
    An t-àit' bu dual dan seanairean.   28

'S an caraid riamh bha dìleas dhuinn
'S a leig mu sgaoil na prìosanaich,
Bidh urram fad gach linn aige;
    Tha beannachd tìr na gainneimh leis.   32

NOTES

Source: Cameron 1932: 169-70.

Tune: The tune is not specified in the source.

Date and Context: The poem was evidently composed soon after Donald MacFarlane had failed to gain re-election as M.P. for Argyll in the General Election of 15th July 1886. The reference in line 28 to MacFarlane's obtaining the release of the prisoners could suggest that a verse was added, or that a couplet was refashioned, after the Tiree prisoners (see Poem 35) had been liberated in January 1887. If so, this would indicate that MacFarlane remained active on the crofters' behalf even after his defeat.

13-24 MacLean thought that a 'dirty tricks' campaign had been orchestrated against MacFarlane by MacKinnon of Balinakill and Malcolm of Poltalloch (see Index 2). The allusion to his integrity (line 14) rebuts allegations of the kind made in Poem 32, to the effect that MacFarlane was an unprincipled opportunist, disingenuous and even dishonest in his dealings with his constituents. MacLean prefers to believe that the other two contenders packed the county with lackeys who spread smears about MacFarlane. It is, however, noticeable that MacLean makes no mention of MacFarlane's adherence to Roman Catholicism or to the critical issue of his commitment to Irish Home Rule.

19-20 The sending of police to Tiree (to servce notices of interdict on the crofters who had put their cattle on Greenhill farm in May) had been delayed, partly through the tactics of the Duke of Argyll, so that Malcolm of Poltalloch would have every opportunity to win the seat. With MacFarlane's departure and the return of a Conservative government, the way was clear for the initial dispatch of police in July 1886 and subsequent military intervention (MacPhail 1989: 189). The police were quartered in Scarinish, the main village and harbour in Tiree.

32. Oran na h-Election

'An Tàillear Crùbach'

Buaidh is piseach gu bràth do
Earraghàidheal nan gaisgeach;
Chuir iad cùl ri MacPhàrlain,
Ris a' Phàpa 's ri Gladstone;   4
Chuir iad cùl ris na gàrlaich –
Gillean Phàrnell – 's rin cleachdadh;
Tha i nis mar bu dual dhi
A' togail suas na gorm-bhrataich –   8
　　　An *Union Jack*.

Guma buan an duin'-uasal
A fhuair a' bhuaidh anns a' chaonnaig;
Guma buan mar an ceudna   12
Na sheas gu treun air a thaobh ann;
Cluinntear cliù Earraghàidheal
An-diugh 's gach àite san t-saoghal;
Sheas i dlùth agus dìleas   16
Air taobh na fìrinn 's an Aonaidh;
　　　'S nach eil sin math?

Nall am botall, a Mhàiri,
'S cuir a làn anns gach glaine,   20
Chum gun òl sinn air slàinte
Fir mo ghràidh, Fear Pholltalaich;
B' e fhèin smior an duin'-uasail;
Chan eil truailleachd fa-near dha;   24
'S beag air aimhreit is tuasaid;
'S e sìth is suairceas bu mhath leis
　　　An duine mhath.

Tha meas mòr agus cliù air   28
Anns an dùthaich mar dhuine;
Tha e iochdmhor is truasail
Ris an tuath th' ann an gainne;

149

Tha e iriosal, bàidheil,   32
Coibhneil, càirdeil, ro-gheanail
Ris gach ìosal is uasal;
'S e fhèin mo luaidh de na fearaibh –
    Mo ghille glan.   36

Dòmhnall Adhairc MacPhàrlain,
Siud an t-àrmann tha spòrsail;
Fhuair e bean ann an Eirinn
'S thug e spèis airson òir dhi;   40
Chuir e buileach a chùl ri
Dòigh a dhùthcha o phòs e;
B' fheàrr leis tionndadh 'na Phadaidh
Gu bhith tabaid 's a' dòrnadh   44
    Aig Donnybrook.

Nuair bha Dòmhnall 'na òigfhear,
Siud an t-òlach bha cràbhach;
Bhiodh e an cuideachd nan 'daoine',   48
'S b' i an Eaglais Shaor bu lag-tàimh dha;
Ach b' fheàrr le Dòmhnallan diadhaidh
A bhith fo sgiathan a' Phàpa;
Dh'fhàg e uaidhe na 'daoine'   52
'S an Eaglais Shaor, 's lean e Pàrnell
    'S chan ann gu rath.

Ann an Aird nam Murchan a' chnòdain,
An Liosmòr le chuid meanbh-sprèidh,   56
Ann am Muile nam mòr-bheann,
'S an Tiriodh còmhnard na gainmhich,
Ann an Colla 's an Còmhal,
An Ile bhòidheach 's a' Mhorairne,   60
Ann an Lathurn' 's san Oban,
Bha meas air Dòmhnall gus na dhearbh e
    Nach robh e math.

Ged a dh'iarradh na daoine   64
Na tha de mhaoin air an domhain,
Theireadh Dòmhnall gum faodadh
Iad siud fhaotainn gan roghainn;

Gheall e fearann gu leòr dhaibh,   68
Sprèidh is stòras as t-fhoghar;
Ach 's e 'Geallam 's cha toiream'
A bh' aig mo Dhòmhnallan laghach –
        Mo ghille math.   72

Ged tha Dòmhnall cho bialach,
Milis, briathrach ri daoine,
Leigeil air a bhith fialaidh,
Cha tug e riamh dad de mhaoin dhaibh;   76
Ged tha mìltean bonn òir
A' dol 'na phòcaid gach bliadhna
Chan fhaigh bochdan na dùthcha
Na cheannaicheas fiù a' phuinnd shiabainn   80
        On duine mhath.

Is iomadh fear a bheir stiallan
Agus iallan ro fhada
As an leathair aig càch   84
A-chum a chàirdean a thatadh;
Seo an dòigh a th' aig Dòmhnall –
Tha e còir mar tha Gladstone;
Tha e chearta cho fialaidh ri   88
Coileach liath Iain 'ic Eachainn
        Mu bhiadh an eich.

NOTES
Source: The *Northern Chronicle*, 16 November 1887. The poem was
published under the pen-name of 'An Tàillear Crùbach' ('The Lame
Tailor').
    The identification of 'An Tàillear Crùbach' remains unclear, but it
may be worth noting that MacFarlane was strongly attacked in the run-
up to the 1885 election by the Rev. Neil Taylor, Free Church minister in
Dornoch, who, in a letter to the Argyll electorate, regarded him as 'a
Papist and a pervert from Presbyterianism' (MacPhail 1989: 157).
Taylor (1830-89) was a native of Kilmun, Argyll. Ordained in Dundee in
1860, he was translated to Dornoch in 1882 (Ewing 1914: I, 337).
    Tune: 'Oran na Feannaig'.
    Date and Context: In the source the poem is prefaced by a letter to
'muinntir mo dhùthcha' ('the people of my region'), which claims that
'This is a song made last year to MacFarlane when the people of the
county turned their backs on him. More or less all were singing it this
time last year.'

The letter sets out the poet's objections to MacFarlane. These objections are as stated in the poem, but the religious dimension is even more heavily stressed, especially MacFarlane's conversion to Catholicism, for which his wife is said to be responsible. The writer goes on: 'It is a bad business when people noted for their devotion to the church go along with the like of [Charles] Bradlaugh and Stuart Glennie, who publicly raise their voices against Jesus Christ.' The writer, who is a devoted Unionist, castigates the Gaels for becoming *dearg Eireannaich* ('dyed-in-the-wool Irishmen'). It is their identification with Ireland that makes them want MacFarlane as an M.P., and the poet claims that if all sensible men who respect themselves and their country stand against Ireland, everything will be all right.

It is highly likely that the points mentioned in the letter and in the song were significant factors in MacFarlane's defeat in July 1886. Contrast this with Poem 31. 'An Tàillear Crùbach' seems to have been afraid that MacFarlane would make a political 'come-back' (as, indeed, he did in the General Election of 1892).

Charles Bradlaugh (1833-91) was a rationalist free-thinker and 'advanced' Liberal who was at the centre of a dispute about taking the oath in Parliament, resulting in his exclusion though MP for Northampton from 1880; see Palmer 1986: 54-5. Stuart Glennie was a London barrister who was on the executive of the Highland Land Law Reform Association; see MacPhail 1989: 138, 230.

1-6 For notes on the politicians mentioned in this poem, see Index 2.

37 **Dòmhnall Adhairc MacPhàrlain:** The poet cleverly translates MacFarlane's middle name *Horne* as if it were *horn*, thus making him seem rather grotesque.

39-40 MacFarlane's Irish wife was Mary Isabella Bagshawe, whom he married in 1857 (*Who Was Who*, I: 451). For his career in Ireland, see the entry in Index 2.

33. Oran air Bill nan Croitearan

Iain MacRatha

'S gun deachaidh an crann chur air an fharadh,
 'S talamh an arain a chur fàs;
Siud an rud tha uainn air aiseag
 Bh' aig ar n-athraichean air mhàl;   4
'S nam faigheamaid a-rìs air ais e,
 Cha bhiodh ar gearan ris an stàit
Airson gach cunnart agus mearachd
 Rinn fir an fhearainn air na Gàidheil.   8

Cuiridh sinn air falbh gach geamair,
 'S gach fiadh tha 'g ithe fearann àir,
Gan ruagadh suas a-rìs dhan fhireach,
 Agus thig na *Nimrods* bhàn;   12
Thèid na Sasannaich a thilleadh
 O bhith tighinn idir chun an àit',
Bhon rinn iad gu tur ar milleadh
 Le fèidh na beinne bhith cur fàs.   16

Is gu robh a' chaora fhèin co-ionnan
 Ga ar sgioladh chun a' chnàimh;
Chuir i 'n imrich air na h-iomadh,
 Sìos gan iomain chun na tràigh;   20
'S iomadh uair a phian e m' innibh
 A bhith cho minig 'na mo thràill,
Is caor' is fiadh bhith air an innis
 A bheireadh biadh dha iomadh Gàidheal.   24

Ach thèid an crann a thoirt dhen fharadh
 'S thèid na gearrain chur an sàs,
Is treabhar sìos leo talamh an arain,
 'S gheibh na h-ainnisich an sàth;   28
'S gum bi crodh air sliabh gu bainne
 Anns gach baile mar bu ghnàth,
'S cha tèid sinn sìos gu iasgach Ghallaibh –
 Gheibh sinn aig a' bhaile màl.   32

153

'S cha bhi [sinn] strìochdte don a' Bhile
   Thug an *government* an àird;
Chan eil stiall ann airson criomaig
   Anns an cuireadh duine bàrr;   36
'S e tha sinne 'g iarraidh ionad
   Sam biodh ionaltradh nam bà,
'S an talamh ìosal airson mine
   Don a' ghinealaich tha fàs.   40

NOTES

Source: The *Oban Times*, 20 March 1886.
   Tune: This is not specified in the source.
   Date and Context: The *OT* text is preceded by the following Gaelic
note: 'Sheinn an t-ùghdar, Iain MacRatha, Loch Carrainn, Siorramachd
Rois, an t-òran a leanas aig coinneamh mhòr chroitearan air an aon-
latha-deug den Mhàrt, 1886.' ('The author, John MacRae, Lochcarron,
Ross-shire, sang the following song at a large meeting of crofters on the
11th of March, 1886.') As the same issue of the *OT* reports, the meeting
took place in Lochcarron Schoolhouse. At the meeting, Mr Neil
MacKay, Janetown, moved a resolution: 'That the Crofters' Bill now
before Parliament, is a totally inadequate measure of land reform,
particularly in that it totally ignores the clan rights of the Highland
people to the land; that it fails to provide for the restoration of arable
land as well as pasturage; that it is, to all intents and purposes, to
stereotype rather than terminate the present obnoxious state of things in
the Highlands of Scotland.'
   For the views of crofters and politicians on the Crofters' Holdings
(Scotland) Bill and the subsequent Act, see MacPhail 1989: 169-73. The
Bill received the Royal Assent on 25th June 1886.

   1 The line is based on a well-known Gaelic prophecy; see Poem 1, lines
11-12 n.
   12 Transl. 'and the Nimrods (i.e. huntsmen) will come down'. The
line may echo the popular contemporary slogan 'Down with the deer-
forests!', but the poet may mean only that, with the driving away of the
deer, the huntsmen will come down from the hill with nothing to show
for their efforts.

34. Oran nan Saighdearan

Cailean MacDhòmhnaill

Gur fad am thàmh gun labhairt mi,
   Gun dad a chur air àird
Mu staid ro-bhochd na dùthcha seo
   Tha cunntas oirr' an dràsd;   4
Tha meas ac' air na pàipearan
   Air Ghalldachd 's anns gach àit',
'S gur lìonmhor ceàrn san dèanar luaidh
   An cruas sa bheil sinn 'n sàs.   8

Nuair thàinig feachd de phoiliosmain,
   Bha othail anns an àit;
Bu mhagail iad, na ragairean,
   'S bu chabach ris a' bhàrd;   12
Bha misneach aig na gallain ud,
   'S an lagh bhith ac' 'nan làimh;
Ach cha do ghabh sinn giorrag romhp',
   Is thilleadh iad gun dàil.   16

'Nan dèidh-san thàinig saighdearan,
   'S b' e 'n loinn iad air a' bhlàr;
Bha coin romhpa gan iomain ac'
   Air laghainn anns gach àit';   20
Nuair liubhair iad na pàipearan,
   Mun gann gu robh e 'm làimh,
Gun tug mi dhaibh mar onair,
   "Chun an Donais len cuid stràic!"   24

Gun tug mi 'n tiotal cinnteach do
   Na dìoghaltaich gun ghràs,
Na diùlnaich ghrànda phoiliosman
   Nach obadh dol 'nar dàil   28
Nam faigheadh iad an cuireadh
   A bhith ullamh gu bhith 'n sàs,
Is armailt làidir, chùramach,
   On Chrùn orra 'na geàrd.   32

'S e Grianal seo bu toillteanach
　　Air saighdearan gun fheum
A chur do thìr nan Gàidheal seo
　　Gar sàrachadh 'nar n-èis;　　　　　　　　　36
Nan robh sinn air ar n-ullachadh
　　Le ar gunnachan air ghleus,
Chan fhaigheadh iadsan cìs oirnn
　　An strì nan lannan geur.　　　　　　　　　40

Na suinn as fhad' bhon chualas iad
　　Bhith cruadalach 's gach linn,
Na Gàidheil reachdmhor, chalma,
　　Gun chearbaich anns an strì,　　　　　　　44
Lem biodagan geur cruadhach
　　Thug buaidh air iomadh rìoghachd –
Gun d'fhuaireas cliù a mhaireas orr'
　　Am batail nach robh clì.　　　　　　　　　48

An Tiriodh, tha mi 'g innse dhuibh,
　　Tha milltearan gun chèill –
Na poiliosmain 's na saighdearan,
　　'S cha choibhneil iad ri chèil';　　　　　　52
Ach nuair thèid MacPhàrlain chur
　　Don Phàrlamaid dar rèir,
Bidh laghannan nam mealltairean
　　'Nan deann dol as a chèil'.　　　　　　　　56

Nis tha mi 'n dùil gun sguir mi dheth,
　　'S gun dèan mi ullamh e,
Ach cuimhnicheam 'nam òran air –
　　Tha còir dhomh chur am meud –　　　　　　60
An t-sàr dhuin'-uasal urramach,
　　MacGuaire, 'n duine treun,
A leig mu sgaoil na prìosanaich,
　　'S nach dìobair sinn 'nar n-èis.　　　　　　64

NOTES
Source: Cameron 1932: 357-9.
　　Tune: This is not specified in the source, but is likely to be 'Is tìm dhomh nis bhith tòiseachadh'.
　　Date and Context: The song refers to events in Tiree in July 1886,

when policemen and soldiers were dispatched to the island after crofters and cottars occupied the tack of Greenhill, in the west end of the island. The agitation was fuelled, in part, by the underhand involvement of the brothers Lachlan and Neil MacNeill, who held prominent positions in the local branch of the Land League. Unknown to the crofters and cottars who wished to obtain the tack for themselves, Lachlan MacNeill had submitted an offer, and had been successful. The crofters and cottars consequently set their animals to graze on the farm. Policemen arrived in the island on 21st July 1886 in an attempt to serve notices of interdict on those who had put their animals on the tack, and in the process a sheriff officer was deforced at Balephuil. As a result gunboats, carrying marines and policemen, were dispatched to the island at the end of July. A number of islanders were arrested at different stages during the period of military presence, and they later stood trial in Edinburgh (MacPhail 1989: 166-92; Meek 1980). See further Poem 35.

61-64 For MacQuarrie's role, see Poem 35, line 37 n.

35. Oran nam Prìosanach

Iain MacIlleathain, Bàrd Bhaile Mhàrtainn

'S ro fhada tha mi gu tosdach, sàmhach,
Mun eilean ghràdhach a dh'àraich òg mi,
Bhon chaidh a' Bhànrighinn 's an Diùc le chèile
A chur 'na h-èiginn tìr rèidh an eòrna.   4

An t-eilean uaine tha torrach, snuadhmhor,
'S e 's balla-cuain dha na tonnan mòra;
'S cho fada siar e ri Barraidh 's Ile,
Làn lusan rìomhach, 's e ìosal còmhnard.   8

Sa mhadainn shamhraidh nuair chinneas seamrag,
'S i geal is dearg air a' mhachair chòmhnard,
Is lurach, blàthmhor a lusan sgiamhach,
Fo dhriùchd na h-iarmailt 's a' ghrian gan òradh.   12

Tha muran, luachair is biolair uaine
'Na lagain uaigneach far 'n goir an smeòrach;
Is tric a fhuair sinn a' mhil sna bruachan
Bho sheillean luaineach breac-ruadh a' chrònain.   16

Mun tàinig Diùc ann, no aon de shinnsir,
No Deòrsa rìoghail à rìoghachd Hanòbhair,
Bha 'n t-eilean ìosal, bu lìonmhor àirigh,
Aig clann nan Gàidheal 'na àite còmhnaidh.   20

Gach eilean ìosal no beanntan àrda,
'S gach gleann bha 'g àrach nan Gàidheal còire,
Tha mòran fàs dhiubh, gun duin' ach cìobair,
O Mhaol Chinntìre gu Taigh Iain Ghròta.   24

Tìr nan gaisgeach 's nam breacan rìomhach;
B' e uaill na rìoghachd iad ged chaidh am fògar;
Bu lìonmhor àirigh is bà air buaile,
Le ceòl nan gruagach mu bhruachaibh Mòirbheinn.   28

Chùm iad Cèasar as le chuid lèigion,
Fir Lochlainn ghèill iad do Chaledònia;
Aig blàr na Leirge chaidh ruaig air Hàcon;
'S e meud a thàmailt thug bàs ri bròn dha.   32

Is tha luchd-àiteachaidh an eilein ìosail
Fo ghrunnan millteach, gun àite còmhnaidh,
'S e 'n-diugh 'na fhàsach aig luchd am mìoruin
A chuir sa phrìosan ar gillean òga.   36

An Inbhir-aora, toll dubh a' chruadail,
Gun dhùnadh suas iad a Luan 's a Dhòmhnach;
Ach bha de dh' uaisle an com MhicGuaire
Nach biodh iad uair ann nam fuasgladh òr iad.   40

Theich na tràillean bho chùis na h-aimhreit
Mar nì an t-aingidh gun aon an tòir air;
Gun deach an tilleadh; cha robh ach breugan
An cùirt Dhun Eideann; bu lèir siud dhòmhsa.   44

B' iad sin na saighdearan smearail, lùthmhor,
A thighinn don dùthaich bho Chrùn Rìgh Deòrsa;
Gach fear ma seach dhiubh toirt eachdraidh ghàbhaidh
Air each MhicPhàidein bha 'n àite còirneil.   48

Chaidh sinne bhuaireadh le luchd an tuaileis,
Ach sheasadh suas leinn airson na còrach,
Gu fearail, cliùiteach, air chùl nan Gàidheal,
Mar rinn ar càirdean san Eilean Cheòthmhor.   52

NOTES
Source: Cameron 1932: 168-9.
   Tune: No tune is specified in the source, but the song was probably
sung to the tune of 'Och, och, mar tha mi 's mi 'n seo am ònar'.
   Date and Context: The song assumed its final form probably
towards the end of October 1886. On 18th October 1886, MacLean had
been present as a witness at the High Court in Edinburgh, where eight
Tiree men were tried and sentenced for their part in the agitation which
had reached a climax in the island in July.
   John MacLean participated fully in the meetings organised by the
Land League in Tiree in this period. After the first batch of 'prisoners'
had been sent to jail in Inveraray (see line 37 n.), a meeting of crofters
was held at Baugh. It was attended by MacLean, 'the bard of Tiree', and
a reporter noted that he was believed to be 'preparing a poem on the
present crisis' (*Oban Times*, 14 August 1886). This poem may well be
the present item, to which the poet would have added the reference to the
later trial in Edinburgh (lines 41-4).
   The defendants received heavy sentences in court. Five were given six

months' imprisonment, and three received four months. Popular opinion in Scotland was on the prisoners' side, and petitions poured in to the Scottish Office. The prisoners were released in the New Year. For general background, see MacPhail 1989: 186-92; for a detailed account of the Tiree agitation and its consequences, see Meek 1980.

6 Transl. 'The great waves form an ocean-wall around it'.

17 As a MacLean, the poet regarded the acquisition of Tiree by the Campbells as the end of an era of freedom and prosperity. His own family was, however, brought to the island in the later eighteenth century by the factor to the Duke of Argyll (Cameron 1932: 142).

28 **Mòirbheinn:** possibly an attempt at Gaelicising *Morve(r)n* (recte *a' Mhorairne*), but more probably a non-specific place-name constructed from the common elements *mòr* ('great') and *beann* ('mountain').

37 After the first batch of six 'prisoners' had been apprehended, they were subjected to judicial examination by Sheriff Irvine in Scarinish Hotel, and they left the island on board the steamship 'Nigel' on Friday 7th August. They were lodged in prison in Inveraray. The hardship to which the poet refers was alleviated by the kindness of sympathisers, who supplied them with meals in lieu of prison fare. They were released on bail on Wednesday 12th August. Their bail-money of £20 per head was paid by Lachlan MacQuarrie, 'residing at Cow Glen, proprietor of provision stores in Tiree' (*Oban Times*, 14 August 1886).

48 **each MhicPhàidein:** The reference is to the horse of Alan MacFadyen, the proprietor of Scarinish Hotel, who had accompanied the sheriff to Balephuil to serve the notices of interdict. The role of the horse was evidently a subject of controversy relating to the circumstances of the alleged deforcement. According to local opinion, the horse was among a crowd of children at the time of the deforcement, and men took hold of it to prevent an accident (*Oban Times*, 4 September 1886).

52 The line indicates that the Tiree people were well aware of what was happening in other parts of the Highlands and Islands, notably Skye. The grazing of cattle on the Greenhill tack resembled what had happened on the farm of Waterstein in 1882 (see Poems 20 and 21).

36. Cogadh Ghleann Dail

'Calum Posta'

'S e Ivory 'n duine gu strìochdadh gach buraidh;
'S beag feum a tha 'n-diugh aig air armachd;
An Cogadh Ghleann Dail thug e buaidh anns gach cath,
'S cha deach uiread is cailleach a mharbhadh.   4

Tha naidheachdan truagha mu na h-eileanan tuathach,
   Mar dh'èirich an sluagh ann an aimhreit;
Na croitearan iargalt' nach pàigheadh am fiachan,
   Cha robh iad ach riamh ann an ainfhiach.   8

Na fèidh tha neo-chronail an dèidh dol a dholaidh,
   'S nach faigh iad don choirce le pàircean,
'S na Sgiathanaich dhona gan ruagadh le coin
   Gus am bi iad an sloc air am bàthadh.   12

Ged chaill iad na srathan bu dàna leo talach,
   'S na h-uachdarain fhathast cho coibhneil;
An àit' an cur thairis gu dùthchannan fada,
   'S ann fhuair iad an cladach mar oighreachd.   16

Na baothairean tàireil, nach fhòghnadh dhaibh bàirnich,
   'S e meudachd an stràic a chuir gann iad,
'S na h-uaislean as àirde mun cuairt anns an àite,
   Gun gabh iad buntàta is annlan.   20

Bha 'n fhairge mun coinneamh ri fèath agus doineann,
   Sam faigheadh iad cosnadh is beòshlaint;
'S cha tigeadh am bàillidh bho Latha Fhèill Màrtainn
   A thogail a mhàil dhiubh – gu Bealltainn.   24

On fhuair iad bhith chòmhnaidh air leacaich 's air
   mòintich,
   Bha adhbhar gu leòr a bhith taingeil,
'S nan dèanadh iad feum dheth, bha solas na grèin' ac',
   Is gealach is reultan san anmoch.   28

161

Bha siud ac' an asgaidh bho uachdarain chneasda,
 Ged dh'fhaodadh e reic airson airgid;
'S a chòir air cho math 's a bha chòir air an fhearann –
 B' e òrdagh an Fhreasdail a dhealbh iad.   32

Nam biodh iad an làthair san linn san robh Phàraoh,
 'S iad aige 'nan tràillean gan ceannsach,
Bhiodh adhbhar no dhà air an iarradh iad fhàgail –
 'S e rabhadh do chàch bha san àm sin.   36

NOTES

Source: The *Oban Times*, 28 May 1887. The poem was published
under the pen-name 'Calum Posta', and dated 'Dara mìos a' Gheamh-
raidh, 1886' ('The second month of Winter, 1886'). Another text is found
in the Morison Manuscripts, lodged in the School of Scottish Studies.
The Morison MSS contain Gaelic poetry and other material written by
Counndullie Morison, Mull, and his relatives and correspondents. The
text is accompanied by the following note: 'The foregoing verses I have
just scribbled down. Do you consider them deserving of a corner in the
"Oban Times"? Sheriff Ivory deserves to have his name handed down to
all generations in rhyme. D. McN. "Colla Ciotach" '. The Morison
version was published in *Tocher*, xvii (1975), 22-4. This is very close to
the *OT* text. The latter, which is followed in the present edition, has a
few line readings which differ from those in *Tocher* (T). These are noted
below.

Tune: This is not specified in the sources.

Date and Context: The song was obviously inspired by the actions
of the military expedition (including a gunship, H.M.S. 'Humber')
which went to Skye in October 1886, with the aim of supporting an
attempt to enforce the payment of crofters' arrears in rents and rates.
The expedition was under the command of Sheriff William Ivory. The
actions of the sheriff officers under Ivory's control reached levels of
unprecedented absurdity, which brought widespread ridicule on Ivory.
'At Glasphein [in Glendale], on the estate of Dr Nicol Martin of
Husabost, a number of tenants had their ricks of corn and stacks of peats
poinded' (MacPhail 1989: 194). ['Poinding' is a Scots law term for a
legal process whereby goods of a debtor are valued by a sheriff officer or
messenger-at-arms, and put on an inventory for possible public auction
or adjudgement to the creditor.]

Although events in Glendale triggered the poem, the poet has
relatively little to say about Ivory. See, by contrast, Poems 38 and 39.

9 Na fèidh air bheag cron (T).
13 bu dàna dhoibh tathaich (T).
20 agus feòil leo (?) (T).
21 ri fachd agus doineann (T).
25 On fhuair iad cead chomhnuidh (T).

37. Oran Beinn Lì

Màiri Nic-a'-Phearsain

Thugaibh taing dhan a' mhuinntir
Tha fo riaghladh na Ban-righ,
Rinn an lagh dhuinn cho diongmhalt'
   'S nach caill sinn Beinn Lì.   4

Cuiribh beannachd le aiteas
Gu tuathanaich Bhaltois,
Bha air tùs anns a' bhatail,
   'S nach do mheataich san strì.   8

Thugaibh beannachd gu 'Pàrnell',
Thug a' bhuaidh air an 't-Sàtan',
Air chor 's nach faicear gu bràth e
   Tighinn air àrainn na tìr.   12

Nuair thàinig e chiad uair
'S leth-cheud 'aingeal' fo riaghladh,
Chuir e còignear an iarainn
   Ann an crìochan Beinn Lì.   16

'S na diùlnaich a b'uaisle,
'S nach robh riamh ann an tuasaid,
Chaidh na ruighich a shuaineadh
   Gu cruaidh air an dùirn.   20

Chaidh an giùlan leis na 'h-aingle',
'S an glasadh an gainntir;
'S a dh'aindeoin cumhachd an naimhdean,
   'S leo am fonn is Beinn Lì.   24

'S na mnathan bu shuairce
'S bu mhodhaile gluasad,
Chaidh an claiginn a spuaiceadh
   Ann am bruachan Beinn Lì.   28

'S ged bha 'n sealladh 'na uamhas,
'S an fhuil a' reothadh san luachair,
Le slacain nan truaghan,
   Cha d'fhuair iad Beinn Lì.   32

Siud a' bheinn a tha dealbhach,
'S dhan a' Bhan-righ bha sealbhach,
'S chan eil beinn ann an Albainn
    'N-diugh cho ainmeil 's Beinn Lì.   36

'S iomadh rosg a nì mùthadh,
Tighinn air bàta na smùide,
'S iad a' sealltainn len dùrachd
    Air bruthaichean Beinn Lì.   40

'S ged tha an Cuilthionn is Glàmaig
Measg nam beanntan as àille,
Cha bhi 'n eachdraidh air a fàgail
    Ach aig sàiltean Beinn Lì.   44

Nis *Albannaich* shuairce,
Cùl-taice na tuath-cheathairn,
Thoir an eachdraidh thar chuantan,
    Tha air luaidh ann ar tìr.   48

Cuiribh fios gu Dun Eideann,
Gu fear-tagraidh na h-eucoir,
Agus innsibh dha chlèirich
    Mun euchd rinn Beinn Lì.   52

Cuiribh litir le sòlas
Gu pàipear an Obain,
A bha riamh ga ar còmhnadh,
    Bhon là thòisich an strì.   56

Ghabh e bratach na tuath-cheathairn,
'S bha i paisgte mu ghuaillean,
'S nuair a thòisich an tuasaid,
    Chaidh i suas ris a' ghaoith.   60

Chaidh i suas ann ar fàbhar
Air na cnocan a b' àirde,
Chumail misnich sna Gàidheil,
    Mar nì gàirich nam pìob.   64

Cuiribh caismeachd a Ghlaschu,
Gu *Posta na Seachdain*,
'S bheir an Camshronach sgairteil
    Dhuibh le aiteas a brìogh.   68

Cuiribh fios gu na Dailich,
Dh'fhuiling eucoir sa charraid,
'S gu MacMhuirich, mo charaid,
    Nach do dh'fhannaich san strì.   72

'S math an colaisd am prìosan –
'S fhad o dh'aithnich mi fhìn sin –
Ach thig buaidh leis an fhìrinn,
    Dh'aindeoin innleachd nan daoi.   76

'S math an colaisd an Calton,
'S ceart a dh'fhòghlaim e 'm 'Martar',
Ged bha cuid thug as acaid
    Leis an rachd bha 'nan crìdh.   80

'S nis, a chroitearan ionmhainn,
Cumaibh cuimhn' air MacAonghais,
'S dèanaibh sòlas ri iomradh
    An duine shuilbhearra, ghrinn.   84

'S ged a dh'fhàg e ar sràidean,
Le bhanoglach bhàidheil,
Tha i son' ann a' Bhàlaidh,
    Dol gu àirigh cruidh-laoigh.   88

'S i athchuing is ùrnaigh
Gach bochd a bha dlùth dhi,
Gum bi toradh an dùrachd
    'Na cùrsan a-chaoidh.   92

NOTES

Source: Nic-a-Phearsoin 1891: 110-4.

    Tune: 'Bruthaichean Ghlinn Braoin'.

    Date and Context: The song was composed soon after the crofters of Braes, Skye, had received word from the Land Court in May 1887 that they were to be given back the grazings on Ben Lee, which they had lost in 1865 and which were the cause of the dispute leading to the 'Battle of the Braes' in April 1882 (see Poems 16 and 17).

    6 **tuathanaich Bhaltois:** The 'farmers' of Valtos were the first crofters in Skye who refused to pay increased rents for their crofts.

    9-12 **'Pàrnell':** This was the nickname of Norman Stewart of Valtos. He 'vanquished Satan', i.e. Sheriff William Ivory, in a case in the Court of Session in June 1887, and Ivory was compelled to pay him £25. The reason for the case was that 'Parnell' had been put in prison in Portree at the end of 1884 and the beginning of 1885 for his part in the agitation in Valtos when the district was visited by Ivory and his soldiers. When 'Parnell' was tried for this alleged offence in March 1885, he was proved innocent. A confidential report by Ivory which claimed that 'Parnell' was one of the ringleaders in the Valtos agitation had been published in newspapers, including the *Scotsman*. 'Parnell' therefore pursued Ivory for libel. See MacPhail 1989: 120-2.

15 **còignear:** The five arrested were Alexander Finlayson, Donald Nicolson, James Nicolson, Malcolm Finlayson and Peter MacDonald.

21 **'aingle':** the police under the command of Sheriff William Ivory, so called from his reference to himself and his contingent as 'Satan and his angels'.

45 **Albannaich:** the *Scottish Highlander*.

54 **pàipear an Obain:** the *Oban Times*.

66 **Posta na Seachdain:** the *Glasgow Weekly Mail*.

67 **an Camshronach:** Dr Charles Cameron, a Liberal M.P. in Glasgow, who owned the *North British Daily Mail* and the *Glasgow Weekly Mail*.

69 **Dailich:** the people of Glendale.

71 **MacMhuirich, mo charaid:** John MacPherson, the 'Glendale Martyr'. See Poem 22.

82 **MacAonghais:** This may be Miles MacInnes, who had a close link with the Portree branch of the Highland Land Law Reform Association, and was secretary to the Skye branch of the land League from 1886. It is not clear when he 'left our streets' (line 85), or why his wife went to Vallay (line 87).

38. Oran Cumha an Ibhirich

Màiri Nic-a'-Phearsain

Anns an linn a chaidh seachad, nuair bha tighearnas fearainn a' saltairt air gach duine, rinn neach àraidh dom b'ainm Sìochaire Mac Ibhiri e fhèin comharraichte air taobh an fhòirneirt, gu h-àraid an aghaidh bhantrach, dhìlleachdan agus naoidheanan. Thugadh an t-ainm air do bhrìgh gum b' eòl do gach duine gu robh e suarach on bhroinn agus ungte 'na thrusdair. Air dha a bhith air aithris gun deach an sìochaire gealtach seo a chur fodha an luba dhubh, beagan na bu doimhne na amhaich, le taod frìthir mu sprogan agus ceap air a mhullach, sa Mhòintich Mhòir, astar a tuath air Ceann Loch Chaluim Chille, sheinn Màiri nan Dàn, à Bràigh Thròtairnis, am marbhrann a leanas:

Chuala mi sgeul
'S ro-aighearach gleus;
Mur fìrinn, b' e 'm beud cruadalach,
Mun t-Sìochaire lom
A bhith dinnt' ann an toll,
'S e gun chlàr no chlobhd fuaight' uime.   6

Beannachd don làimh
A theannaich an t-snaim,
Toirt fùic air a' cheann chruaidh-ghreannach;
Chuir i 'n Sìochaire maol
Ann an gainntir gann caol,
'S cha toir earraid no maor fuasgladh dha.   12

'S uallach bhiodh ceum
Gach caillich 'na leum,
'S clann bheaga 'nan rèis luathghaireach;
Ga do shlaodadh à poll
Agus sùgan mud chom,
Dh'ionnsaigh tarraing nan lunn fuaidearnach.   18

Sguabar gu rèidh
Gach ùrlar fo chlèith,
Bidh torrann luchd-teud buaidh-cheòlach;
Chìtear danns air gach blàr,
Cluinntear fonn air gach àird
An robh an gealtair 'na ràp ruagarnach.   24

Saighdear, mas fhìor,
Chan fhacas a ghnìomh
Ach air siteig no liath òtraichean,
'S e 'na bhòcan air cloinn
'S air mnathan san oidhch',
Gus na sgreamhaich e 'n Roinn Eòrpachail.   30

Grunnas gach druaip
Is mallachd na tuath,
Chaidh ruith-lùb an dual còrcachail
Mun a' ghrèib amhaich chaoil,
Fon an smig a b'olc caoin,
An teannachadh fhaobhair sgòrnanaich.   36

Cuirear le cinnt
Clach ghlas os do chinn
A nochdas gach prìob dhòibheairteach,
'S mar a reic thu gach cliù
Airson beagan de spùill,
Tur, mar Iùdas, gud ghrunnd fòtusach.   42

NOTES

Source: The *Scottish Highlander*, 6 January 1887. This version is
very close to that of a broadsheet preserved in the MacKinnon Collection
(P. 44/53), Edinburgh University Library.

   Tune: No tune is specified in the sources.

   Date and Context: The poem was inspired by the actions of the
military expedition to Skye in the late autumn of 1886. The circumstances are described in Hunter 1976: 165-9 and MacPhail 1989: 192-99.
See also Poem 36.

   The poem is a mock elegy on Sheriff William Ivory, the leader of the
expedition. While there is ample evidence that Sheriff Ivory acted in a
high-handed and provocative manner, it needs to be noted that he
became something of a 'bogey-man' in the crofters' eyes. On this

expedition, at least, he was popularly held to blame for, and accused of, misdemeanours which were perpetrated by certain sheriff officers under his command. The most notorious of these was the poinding of a two-month-old baby belonging to Mrs MacRae of Peinness. The baby was poinded by Sheriff Officer Alexander MacDonald, whose action caused anger and embarrassment to Ivory's colleagues. Sheriff Patrick Blair of Inverness told Ivory in a letter that he thought that MacDonald had committed 'such an act of imprudence and heartlessness as tends to discredit his office and brings the law into disrepute' (SRO.GD. 1/36/1/45 (42)). MacDonald had already been reprimanded by Ivory for burning a Strathglass crofter's house after evicting him (ibid., 1/46), and he was subsequently suspended (MacPhail 1985: 550). The opprobrium due to MacDonald was transferred to Ivory, and is doubtless reflected in lines 25-30 of the present poem.

It is also apparent that Ivory did not lack supporters in Skye, although (understandably) these were not among the crofters. In a letter of 18 December 1886, the Rev. Donald MacKinnon of Broadford wrote to Ivory: 'We have all great cause of thankfulness who were not in sympathy with the land league at the marked change that your prompt action has had all over the country, in putting down the bad spirit which existed so long' (SRO.GD.1/36/1/47 (29)). Government officials and ministers, such as A. J. Balfour, likewise highly approved of Ivory's success in recovering most of the outstanding rates in Skye. (With respect to this poem and Poem 40, the Keeper of the Records of Scotland has kindly granted permission to quote documents held in the Scottish Record Office.)

34 Transl. 'about the thin scraggy neck'.

36 Transl. 'compressing the sharp edge of his gullet'. Perhaps we should read *An* as *A'* before *teannachadh*, but the line makes sense without emendation.

39. Ibhri agus na Croitearan

'Eisdealach'

Och mar tha mi, 's mi seo 'nam ònar;
Is truagh a tha mi an dèidh an sgeòil seo;
Mo chreach a dh'èirich nach robh Ibhri
 An tìr na dìochuimhn, e fhèin 's a sheòrsa.   4

Bha naidheachd bhrònach an *Tìm an Obain*
 A rinn mo leònadh, 's gu mòr a ghluais mi,
Mo cho-luchd-dùthcha bhith am prìosan dùnte,
 'S an cuid ga spùinneadh le ùghdarras uachdaran.   8

Nan robh na Gàidheil san uair mar b' àbhaist
 Nuair thàinig Teàrlach a-nall thar chuantan,
Bhiodh feachd na Bànrighinn 's an ruaig gun dàil orr',
 Is chaidleadh pàirt dhiubh gu bràth air chluaintean.   12

An Culodair dh'eug iad na dhèanadh feum dhaibh,
 Na gaisgich euchdail bha treun an cruadal;
Nan robh iad còmhl' riu 's an airm 'nan dòrnan,
 Bhiodh luchd an fhòirneirt gun deò san tuasaid.   16

'S gur e Ibhri am fear ceartais prìseil
 A rinn air m' fhìrinn an deagh ghnìomh a chualas;
Gach coileach dùnain, 's gach cearc nì crùban,
 'S gach ubh le cùram, gun d'chunnt e suas dhaibh.   20

Gach uan is caora, gach mart is laogh bh' ann,
 'S na daimh tha adharcach, gun d'rinn e 'n àireamh;
Bha beathaichean neòghlan a-measg a' chòrr aig',
 Is iomadh seòrsa a bha san àirce.   24

Gach caibe 's gràpa, gach creathaill 's pàisde,
 'S gach ball tha 'm fàrdaich gun do ghlac an treun-fhear;
Poitean cùbhraidh a bha sna cùiltean,
 Gun deach an sgùradh, is rinn e feum dhiubh.   28

Nach bochd da-rìribh tha lagh na rìoghachd
 A ghlacadh chìochran dhà mhìos mar thràillean;
'S nas lugha prìs dhaibh na 'n cù mun ghrìosaich –
 Seo ceartas Ibhri an tìr nan àrd-bheann.   32

170

NOTES

Source: The *Oban Times*, 12 March 1887.

   Tune: 'Och, och, mar tha mi 's mi 'n seo am ònar'.

   Date and Context: The song was inspired by the military expedition to Skye in the late autumn of 1886. It ridicules the process of poinding undertaken by Sheriff William Ivory and his subordinate officers. See Poems 36 and 38 for more detailed discussion of the context.

   29-31 The reference is to the poinding of a child belonging to Mrs MacRae of Peinness (see Poem 38). The child and cradle were valued at sixpence – half the value of her puppy! See Meek 1977c: 331.

40. 'S muladach mi 'n-diugh 's mi 'g èirigh

Uilleam Peuton

Sèisd:

'S muladach mi 'n-diugh 's mi 'g èirigh
Anns a' phrìosan an Dun Eideann;
'S muladach mi 'n-diugh 's mi 'g èirigh.

A Dhòmhnaill Ruaidh ud ann a Hàise,
Walkigeadh air feadh a' ghàrraidh,
'S olc a thig an deise bhàn dhut,
    Ged bu shràiceil air an fhèill thu.   7

Uilleam MacArtair 's e cho gòrach,
'S eagal aige roimh na bòcain;
Cha tig gin dhiubh tron a' chòmhlaidh,
    'S cha tèid bòrd dhith as a chèile.   11

Tha Iain Ceannaiche nas fheàrr dheth,
Pailteas aig' de Bheurla 's gràmar;
Nì e stòraidh ris a' *warder*
    Feuch an ann as fheàrr a ghrèidheadh.   15

Uilleam Peuton 's e cho seòlta,
Ged nach eil a Bheurla dòigheil;
Abraidh e 'Sir' riutha an còmhnaidh,
    Mar bu chòir a bhith sa Bheurla.   19

O, a Theàrlaich 'Ic-an-Tòisich,
'S mairg a chunnaic ort an còmhdach;
'S snasail rachadh tu 'nad fhòram,
    Dol Di-dòmhnaich don èisdeachd.   23

Facal beag mu bhean mo nàbaidh –
Thug iad i don chùirt as àirde;
Nuair a chunnaic iad a h-àilgheas,
    Cha bu dàna leo a h-èigheach.   27

Seonaidh MacAoidhein 's e cho brònach,
A' caoidh Anna Nic-an-Tòisich;
Chan fhaigh cìobair i no Nòrman
    Chaoidh ri bheò gu am faigh e fhèin i.   31

Ged a tha mo leabaidh fuar ann,
Ealag agam airson cluasaig,
Nuair a thilleas mi rim chuachaig,
   Cha bhi fuachd a' dèanamh èis dhomh.   35

Ged a chuir sibh mi 'n a' phrìosan,
A' seasamh còir airson mo sgìre,
Gheibh mi fhathast as ur h-ìngean,
   'S bidh mi sìnte ri mo chiad-ghràdh.   39

O, a Mhàiri Mhòr nan Oran,
'S math an drama thug thu dhòmhsa;
Ach ma thilleas mise beò as,
   Gheibh thu còig airson na tè ud.   43

NOTES

Source: The present text has been derived directly from oral transmission. It has been preserved by the family of Mr Donald Alick MacIntosh, a native of Herbusta, now living at Lianacro, Kilmuir, Skye, and a transcription was kindly provided by Mr MacIntosh's daughter, Mrs Mary Allan, Glasgow. The MacIntosh family, to whom I am deeply indebted, have supplied important information about the background to the song. The song alludes to two members of the family. These are Mr MacIntosh's father, Charles (line 20), and his aunt, Anna (line 29). A recording of the song being sung by Mr MacIntosh is lodged in the archives of the Gaelic Department, B.B.C. Scotland, Glasgow.

The composer of the song was William Beaton. The poet cleverly composed a verse about himself (line 16), and this conceals his identity in the text.

Tune: 'Chunna mi 'n damh donn 's na h-èildean'.

Date and Context: When attempting to serve writs at Herbusta, Kilmuir, during the second phase of Ivory's expedition to Skye (from 22nd October 1886) (see Poems 36 and 38), Sheriff Officer Alexander MacDonald was assaulted with clods by the crofters, and he claimed that he had been deforced. The first attempt to apprehend the Herbusta deforcers was undertaken on 27th October 1886. It resulted in the arrest of John Beaton, the Herbusta Herd (who later sued Sheriff Ivory unsuccessfully on the grounds of illegal arrest), and the 'wife of one of the principal offenders Alex MacMillan' (see line 24 n.). Those alleged to be chiefly responsible for the deforcement 'took to the hills', but eventually surrendered, following raids on their homes by police. The last of the suspects was arrested at the beginning of December. (SRO. GD. 1/36/1/44 (31); 1/45 (12), (20); 1/47 (7), 1/51; MacPhail 1985: 548-50).

Seven Herbusta men were tried at the High Court in Edinburgh on

3rd January 1887. They were given lenient sentences: two months' imprisonment to Donald Beaton (line 4), Alexander MacMillan (see line 24 n.) and John MacDonald (Seonaidh MacAoidhein, line 28); and one month each to William MacArthur (line 8), William Beaton (line 16), Charles MacIntosh (line 20) and John MacKenzie (Iain Ceannaiche, line 12) (SRO. High Court Record: Index No. 4, 8 January 1844-10 December 1888).

24 The reference is to the wife of Alexander MacMillan. 'She was the worst of the women who deforced the Sheriff Officer & urged on the men. & she concealed herself all day under her bed, but was forced out by the Police shortly before we left Herbusta, which we did about 4. O'clock...We thought it right to capture Mrs MacMillan to shew that women who are the most prominent offenders in these deforcements will not get off with impunity, but this being the first offence of the kind she will probably be tried summarily at Portree, & get a slight punishment' (Copy of Telegrams from Sheriff Ivory to the Secretary for Scotland, SRO.GD.1/36/1/44 (31)). Ivory's achievement in arresting Mrs Mac-Millan was warmly endorsed by A. J. Balfour, the Secretary for Scotland, who stated in a letter to the Sheriff that he was 'quite right to arrest the good lady who made herself so conspicuous in deforcing the Police' (Balfour to Ivory, ibid., (28)).

However, natural causes intervened, and Balfour and Ivory were unable to secure a prosecution. As this quatrain deftly indicates, and as Herbusta tradition asserts, Mrs MacMillan was evidently taken to court for committal proceedings (line 25), but she was found to be pregnant, and the case had to be dropped (lines 26-7). This was, no doubt, another embarrassment for the Ivory expedition.

41. Caoidh a' Chroiteir sa Phrìosan

Gilleasbaig MacAoidh

Rìgh, gur mise tha dheth cràiteach
Bhon a chàraich iad fo ghlais mi;

Bhon a chàraich iad fo chìs mi,
'S nach fhaigh mi mo rìbhinn fhaicinn;   4

Far nach fhaic mi mo chaomh chuachag,
Caileag shuairceil an fhuilt chleachdail;

Nan robh mi gun dol don Chaol-bheinn,
Cha robh mi bho mo dhaoine 'n ceart-uair;   8

Mi air m' uilinn anns a' phrìosan,
Mi leam fhìn 's mi dhìth tombaca.

An taobh a-staigh de gheata iarainn –
Seo a' bhliadhna cha b' iarraidh faicinn.   12

Mo bheannachd ortsa, Fhir a' Chàrnain,
Dhèanainn gàirdeachas rid fhaicinn.

'S ann air moch-thràth Diardaoin
Chunna mi d' aogas, 's ghabh mi beachd ort; 16

Do dhà ghruaidh cho geal 's an fhaoileann,
B' àbhaist bhith mar chaorann dathte.

Ach thèid sinn dhachaigh, 's nì sinn fhàgail,
'S cha till sinn gu bràth don Chalton.   20

NOTES

Source: The *Oban Times*, 8 October 1887.
 Tune: 'Dhèanainn sùgradh ris an nighinn duibh'.
 Date and Context: This poem was composed by Archibald
MacKay, Oban Seil, Easdale, when he was imprisoned in the Calton
Jail, Edinburgh, in connection with a case of eviction at Caolvin, near
Easdale. The eviction of Sam MacDougall, who had farmed at Caolvin
for about thirty years, was carried out early in September 1886 by
George Nicholson, a sheriff officer from Edinburgh, following a long-
running dispute about the reassignment of the lease. MacDougall had

refused to leave the farm after the expiry of his lease. A neighbouring farmer, Angus MacCalman, had tendered successfully for the lease, and it was claimed that, on the day of the eviction, he provided a horse and cart 'to help the officers to remove the goods and gear of Mr MacDougall'. Leaving in some haste halfway through the removal, Nicholson and his party were met by a hostile crowd of local people, who pelted them with mud. When the officers had departed, the people held a meeting at Ardincaple, at which MacCalman was denounced to his face. The principal speaker was Sam MacDougall, farmer at Carnan, who was a kinsman of the Caolvin tenant (*OT*, 11 September 1886). Although it was claimed in the first reports that there was no violence, the poet and Sam MacDougall of Carnan, together with Donald MacKay, Donald Clark, and four others, were charged at the Sheriff Court, Inveraray, with committing a breach of the peace, conducting themselves in an 'outrageous manner' and using threatening language. Archibald MacKay and Sam MacDougall were given sixty days' imprisonment, and Donald MacKay and Clark were given thirty days. Donald MacKay was released on appeal before the end of his sentence, but the others served their times. The poet and Sam MacDougall of Carnan were released from jail on 31st March 1887, and treated to a celebratory breakfast, chaired by Duncan Cameron, editor of the *Oban Times*, who claimed that MacDougall had exercised a restraining influence on the day. of the eviction (ibid., 26 February 1887, 2 April 1887).

42. Do Dhòmhnall MacCaluim

Murchadh MacIlleathain

Sèisd:
'S e Dòmhnall MacCaluim
An t-urramach còir;
Tha d' ainm an-diugh measail
    Air feadh na Roinn Eòrp'.   4

Nì mi teannadh ri luinneag
An seòmar nan uinneag
Don mhinistear lurach
    Tha 'n Dùthaich MhicLeòid.   8

Nach duilich gum facas
Thu riamh ann am Bhatairnis,
Measg dhaoine gun tapadh
    Nach seasadh a' chòir.   12

Ged thug dhaibh misneach
Tha 'n cridh' air a chlisgeadh;
Chaidh eagal a' Chaiptin
    Cho fada 'nam feòil.   16

'S na ministearan Saora,
Cha ghabh iad ar taobh-ne;
Ma gheibh iad cuid dhaoine,
    Tha iad sona gu leòr.   20

'S e comann nan uachdaran
Ni sònraicht' tha uapa;
Chan iarradh iad truaghan
    Bhith air uachdar an fheòir.   24

'S beag orr' na bochdan,
Gam faicinn le pocan
Dol dh'ionnsaigh an dorsan
    A shireadh an lòin.   28

Ach beannachd don ghaisgeach
A chleachd a bhith tapaidh,
A rachadh do Shasainn,
   'S a thagradh ar còir.   32

'S ged bhiodh tu san talamh
Is deanntag roimhd leabaidh,
Bhiodh cuimhn' air do thapadh –
   'S chan eil thu ro-mhòr.   36

'S an t-urramach fìnealt'
Tha mach Sròn an t-Sìthein,
Tha esan cho dìleas
   Ri neach a tha beò.   40

'S mo bheannachd le dùrachd
Le chèile gur n-ionnsaigh,
Fhir threuna na dùthcha
   'S nach diùltadh dhomh lòn.   44

NOTES

Source: The *Oban Times*, 5 November 1887.

   Tune: No tune is specified in the source.

   Date and Context: The subject of the poem, the Rev. Donald MacCallum, was one of the staunchest supporters and leaders of the crofters' movement in the 1880s; for his career, see Index 2. The poem was composed when MacCallum was minister of the parish of Hallin, in Waternish, Skye. It may have been composed before October 1886 (see line 37 n.), and published later as a tribute to MacCallum when it was known that he was leaving the parish. He moved to Heylipol, Tiree, in December 1887.

   15 **eagal a' Chaiptin:** Captain Allan MacDonald was the proprietor of the Waternish estate. Although he was regarded as a 'good landlord' (MacPhail 1989: 26), he was involved in disputes with local crofters. Early in 1885 fourteen men were committed for trial for deforcing a sheriff officer when he attempted to serve writs on Waternish crofters. MacDonald's relations with MacCallum were distinctly unfriendly; by June 1885 he had lodged a suit for libel against MacCallum, and MacCallum responded in like manner (Meek 1977a). Nevertheless, there was relatively little agitation on the Waternish estate, but it is not clear whether this owed more to 'fear of the Captain' than to his 'good' estate policy.

   17-24 The role of Free Church ministers in the Land Agitation was ambivalent. In Skye itself, the extent of their support for the crofters' movement varied according to individual perspectives. Some ministers allowed their buildings to be used for crofters' meetings, while others refused; some took part in meetings of the Highland Land Law Reform Association, while others avoided them. Generally, the active role of Free Church ministers in the movement aimed 'to induce the crofters to eschew violence and act on constitutional lines'. By 1886 Free Church ministers were unwilling to be identified with disruptive tactics; 'although there were certain exceptions like Dr Gustavus Aird of Creich, the Sutherland ministers and many other ministers throughout the country were becoming cooler in their support of the crofters, because of the contacts of some land law reformers with socialists' (MacPhail 1989: 104).

The accusation that Free Church ministers preferred 'the company of landlords' may reflect the popular perception of the unwillingness of the ministers in Snizort and Kilmuir to resort to outright criticism of Fraser, the landlord of Kilmuir, because they owed church sites to his generosity (ibid., 104).

31-2 MacCallum was in London on more than one occasion in order to plead the crofters' cause; see Poem 5.

37 **an t-urramach finealt':** Donald MacCallum's brother, Malcolm, was another Church of Scotland minister who supported the crofters. He was minister of Strontian, Ardnamurchan, from September 1882 to October 1886 (Scott 1866-: IV, 101, 139).

43. Bodach Isgein

An t-Urr. Domhnall MacCaluim

'Tha mise rìoghachadh
Cho fad' 's a chì mi,'
Thuirt Bodach Isgein,
    'Thar mòna 's cruach.'   4
'S gun duirt e 'n fhìrinn
'S e bhris mo chrìdh'-sa,
'S a dh'fhàg an tìr seo
    Air chrith le fuachd.   8

'A-mach on àirigh
San robh na h-àrmainn
A' gabhail tràth air
    Mo bhradain 's m' fhèidh,   12
Gu ruig a' Chàbaig
Tha tìr na Pàirce
Fom chois 'na fàsaich
    Lem iuchair glèidht'.   16

'Tha mise rìoghachadh
Cho fad' 's a chì mi
O thaobh Loch Sìothphort
    A h-uile ceum,   20
Gu ruig na crìochan
Bheir muir a-rìs dhut
Taobh thall an t-Sìthein,
    Gach ploc is leug.   24

'Do mhac a' Ghàidheil
Chuir mis' as àite
Le tuilleadh pàighidh
    A thoirt don triath,   28
Gur dìomhain àrdan
Gam chur thar sàile,
Is feachd na Bànrighinn
    Gur e mo sgiath.   32

'Tha mise rìoghachadh
Cho fad' 's a chì mi
San fhearann rìomhach
   As grinne snuadh,   36
'S gun ann ach sìthichean,
A' chuideachd chrìon sin,
Gun chron, gun mhìothlachd
   Nach cuir 's nach buain.   40

'Na beanntan bòidheach
Len uillt a' dòrtadh,
Roimh choir' is còmhnard,
   Gu fallain, caoin,   44
Len cinn sna neòilibh
'S mum mal' an còmhnaidh
An coron glòrmhor
   Nach caith an aois.   48

'Tha mise rìoghachadh
Cho fad' 's a chì mi
Le gillean lìonmhor
   A nì mo mhiann,   52
'S a bheir don phrìosan
Gach neach a dhìreas
Gun chead aig' sgrìobhte
   Ri aghaidh sliabh.   56

''S na fir an tràth seo
A ghabh de dhànachd
Bhith dol air àrainn
   An ionad naoimh,   60
Gum bi gun fhàrdaich
Ri fad an làithean,
Fo chomharr' Chàin,
   A h-uile aon.   64

'Tha mise rìoghachadh
Cho fad' 's a chì mi,
'S gach anail dìobraidh
   Nuair 's e mo rùn,   68

'S mur faic na daoine
A thèid air faondradh
Mo shanas, faodaidh
   Gum bi iad ciùrrt'.   72

'Mur eil gu leòr leo
Na ròidean mòra
Gun dol air mòintich
   Chur dragh air fèidh;   76
Gur e mo chòir-sa
Bhith faicinn cròic orr',
'S am fuil ma dhòirtear
   Biodh orra fèin.   80

'Tha mise rìoghachadh
Cho fad' 's a chì mi,
'S gun teagaisg m' innleachd
   Don uile shluagh   84
Gu dè cho dìomhain
'S a tha bhith strì rium
A cheannaich trì-fillt'
   Na beanntan fuar.   88

'Na fir gun nàire,
Gu ladarn', dàna,
A thug am bàs do
   Na gràidhean ruadh,   92
Cha chuir buntàta
Sna coirean sàmhach,
Is crodh chan àraich
   Sna lagain uain'.   96

'Tha mise rìoghachadh
Cho fad' 's a chì mi,'
Thuirt Bodach Isgein,
   'Thar mòna 's cruach.   100
'S airson na nìthear
Le sluagh na tìr seo
Gu leagail fhrìthean
   A dh'fhàg iad truagh.'   104

POEM 43 183

Cho fad' 's as beò e
Gun cumar còir ris
Mar iodhal òirdheirc
    Gan gleidheil suas,   108
Ach tha againn òlaich
Gun fhios don chòrr dhiubh
Nach crom mu stòl-san
    'S nach dèan as uaill.   112

NOTES

Source: MacCallum 1912: 149-51.
   Tune: No tune is specified in the source.
   Date and Context: The poem is a skilful satire on Joseph Arthur
Platt, to whom the deer forest of Park, in Lewis, was leased by Lady
Matheson in 1886 (Orr 1982: 136). Platt resided at Eishken Lodge; thus
his appellation 'Bodach Isgein' ('The Old Man of Eishken') in the poem.
   Lines 9-12 and 57-60 suggest that the poem was composed sometime
after the Park Deer Raid in November 1887. See further Poem 44.

105-8 As they stand, these lines can be translated:

   'As long as he lives
   his right will be maintained,
   like a beautiful idol
   keeping them up...'

Thus understood, line 108 would seem to refer to the deer forests or
possibly to Platt's flunkeys. However, this breaks the specific focus on
Platt, and it may be that we should emend the line to *Ga ghleidheil suas*,
'keeping him up', with reference to Platt himself.

44. Ruaig an Fhèidh

Gur moch a rinn sinn èirigh –
'S cha b' ann gun adhbhar èiginn –
A thoirt a-nuas le geur-chuims'
   Na fèidh as na mullaichean.   4

Di-màirt a-mach gun d'fhalbh sinn
Le brataichean 's le armachd;
Bha 'n latha soilleir, sealbhach,
   Mar dhearbhas sinn uile dhuibh.   8

Gach fear le ghunna làn-dheas
Ri aghaidh nam beann àrda,
'S nuair chìte fear na bàirich,
   Gu làr bheirte buille dha.   12

Mharbh sinn iad 'nan ceudan,
Dh'fheann sinn iad gu brèagha;
Dh'ith sinn iad gu rianail,
   Gu fialaidh 's gu cuireideach.   16

Chan eil sinn 'nar luchd-reubainn,
Mar theirear leis na breugan;
'S e th' annainn daoine treuna
   Gar lèireadh le uireasbhaidh.   20

'S iomadh latha 's bliadhna
Le bochdainn air ar riasladh
A dh'fhuirich sinn gu rianail
   Fo sheumarlain 's bhuraidhean.   24

Taing nan con cha d'fhuair sinn;
Bu thràillean sinn gun bhuannachd;
'S ann dh'fheumadh iad ar fuadach
   Mar ruadh-mhadaidh buileach as.   28

Ar mnathan agus pàisdean
Tha nise fulang ànraidh,
An t-aodach chan eil slàn orr',
   Gach tràth iad an uireasbhaidh.   32

Ar dùthaich tha 'na fàsach
Aig fèidh is caoraich bhàna,
'S chan fhaigh sinn dhith air mhàla
    Na shàsaicheas duin' againn.   36

Ach moladh do an Ard-rìgh
A thìodhlaic oirnn an t-àrmann –
'S e Dòmhnall MacRath à Alness
    Am martarach urramach.   40

'S e Dòmhnall MacRath an sàr-laoch
Nach strìochdadh do na gàrlaich,
Ged dh'fheuch iad ris, gu cràiteach,
    'S gach àite mar b'urrainn iad.   44

A chailleach bheag na mòrchuis
A their gur leatsa Leòdhas,
'S ann bhuineas i le còir-cheart
    Don mhòr-chuid tha fuireach innt'.   48

'S on fhuair sinn nis ceann-feadhna,
Cha stad sinn latha no oidhche,
Gus am buannaich sinn an oighreachd
    Gu h-aoibhneach 's gu h-urramach.   52

NOTES

Source: The *Scottish Highlander*, 22 December 1887. The place and date of composition are given at the foot as 'Lochs, December 1887', but the poet is not known.

Tune: 'An Dòmhnallach Urramach'.

Date and Context: The event which this poem commemorates took place on 22nd November 1887. The action involved destitute cottars from the parish of Lochs, Lewis, who raided the Park deer forest, then on lease to Joseph Arthur Platt. The cottars, whose plans were master-minded by the Balallan schoolmaster, Donald MacRae, spent three days in the forest, and may have killed 200 deer. The cottars claimed that the raid was mounted because they and their families were starving.

Through the evidence of one of the raiders who panicked, six men (including Donald MacRae, Balallan) were brought to trial at the High Court in Edinburgh on 16-17th January 1888, but were acquitted. See further MacPhail 1989: 202-6, and MacLeòid 1980: 32-43. For Donald MacRae, see Index 2.

45-6 **A chailleach bheag:** The reference is to Lady Jane Matheson, who became proprietrix of Lewis after the death of her husband, Sir James Matheson, in 1878 (MacPhail 1989: 201).

TRANSLATIONS

1. Song to the Lowland Shepherds

Allan MacDougall

A calamity has befallen us in Scotland;
poor folk are starkly exposed before it,
without food, without clothes, without shelter;
the north has been devastated;   4
only sheep and lambs are visible,
Lowlanders surrounding them on every slope;
all the lands have gone to waste,
chickweed has grown over Highlanders' heads.   8

Cows with calves are not seen in a glen,
or horses, hardly, being harnessed;
it was the essence of the prophecy
that the plough would become redundant;   12
hunters are under constraint,
every gun is bent, without capacity to fire;
neither roe nor kid can be killed,
and Lowlanders' screeching has banished the deer.   16

There is no mirth among the mountains,
hunters have been reined in sharply;
the antlered one has vanished,
every hind and fawn has gone;   20
the red-buck of the streams cannot be found
to be chased down to the strath with a hound;
as compensation for all that once existed,
the whistling of Lowlanders sounds in every hollow.   24

186

One cannot hear cattle lowing in a fold,
nobody cares now for white-shouldered cows;
one cannot hear a brown-haired maiden
singing ditty or song as she milks the cow;   28
since our cattle-tending has declined,
we have frequently been oppressed by thirst;
instead of the many close friends we had,
we find a grey sluggard at the foot of each hillock.   32

As if they had fallen from the tree,
blasted nuts are dying in the brushwood;
that too is how old folk are,
and little children for lack of milk;   36
they have been flung to the fringe of privilege,
away from the patrimony of their grandfathers;
we would love the French to come
to chop the heads off the Lowlanders.   40

Marriages have vanished – weddings have gone;
the songsters have stopped singing;
you have often heard it said that
'Cadgers make their living from creels';   44
that is exactly what has happened to me;
they do not ask for me at a market;
where I once was full of happiness,
they prefer a dog to set to cattle.   48

All who got the upper hand
have cleared out every person
who would advance to face the strife
if the foray should come in force;   52
if a war should break out in the kingdom,
the shepherds would be in distress;
that's the news we would love to hear –
that they were all going to be finished off.   56

They rise early on a Sabbath day,
and they meet with one another;
when they start to tell a story,
their conversation consists of talk about grass;   60

every one asks of his neighbour,
'How, then, did you leave the flock?
What price did the wedders make?
Have you sent them off to market?'   64

'There is no reason to complain this year;
they made sixteen (pence) and more;
if you want to know about it,
I bought the meal with the wool;   68
the crocks have been sold on credit,
and if I keep the young ones,
even if a third of them should die,
I will pay the rent with those that stay alive.'   72

When one of them climbs up a mountain,
after he has risen early,
a Lowland screech will come from his chest,
calling for his pack of dogs;   76
his yell would be no sweet music to us —
there is a load of braxy on his body,
wrapped in his grey plaid;
lice are in his hair and forelock.   80

When he comes upon us upwind,
pity help the person in his lee;
he cannot possibly have a sweet odour
when he is carrying home the paunches,   84
often soaked in entrail juice
from his waist down to his feet,
and whoever should go drinking with him
must screw up his nose.   88

When two or three sit down
to be chummy in the hostelry,
at the head of the table can be seen
a shepherd and a dog at heel;   92
he should be thrown into a corner,
and a knee thrust into his chest;
he should be chased out to the midden,
and allowed to tar himself.   96

Poor company he is for others,
this man whose custom is not cleanliness;
no companion for worthy folk is he
who uses his teeth to remove testicles,   100
on his knees in the slimy sheep-dirt,
sucking them out with his jaws;
and if you let him have a drink,
don't dare taste it after him.   104

Boot out the clumsy claw-handlers of wool,
if you want decent company!
Close the door firmly against them,
and don't let their nose inside,   108
since you can hear them tell no story
except the selling of hides and wool,
giving account of the weather, and at every chance
buying lambs before they are born.   112

We will sit around the table joyfully,
with music and harpstrings, without sorrow,
kind and jovial towards one another,
and don't let one of that flock come near us;   116
drink the health of MacKenzie,
and the fine Colonel of Glengarry,
since they have no time for sheep
or for those who raise the land-rent.   120

Fill up the glasses,
and do not forget the Laird of Erracht,
since he wishes us to survive
without that bad lot crossing our path;   124
if all the nobles of the kingdom
maintained kinship as faithfully as Allan,
the people would not be dispersed
and made to live on charity, regardless.   128

2.   Satire on Patrick Sellar

Donald Baillie

Refrain:
>   Hò the black rogue, hè the black rogue;
>   Hò the black rogue, who raised the land-rent.

I saw a dream,
and I would not mind seeing it again;
if I were to see it while awake,
it would make me merry all day.   6

A big fire was ready
and Roy was right in its middle,
Young was incarcerated,
and there was iron about Sellar's bones.   10

Sellar is in Culmailly,
left there like a wolf,
catching and oppressing
everything that comes within his range.   14

His nose is like an iron plough-share
or the tooth of the long-beaked porpoise;
he has a grey head like a seal
and his lower abdomen resembles that of a male ass.   18

His long neck is like that of the crane,
and his face has no appearance of gentleness;
his long, sharp-shinned legs
resemble ropes of large sea-tangle.   22

What a pity that you were not in prison
for years, existing on bread and water,
with a hard shackle of iron,
strong and immovable, about your thigh.   26

If I could get at you on an open field,
with people tying you down,
I would pull with my fists
three inches [of flesh] out of your lungs.   30

You yourself and your party
went up to the braes of Rosal,
and you set fire to your brother's house,
so that it burned to ashes.   34

When death comes upon you,
you will not be placed in the ground,
but your dung-like carcase will be spread
like manure on a field's surface.   38

Sellar and Roy
were guided by the very Devil,
when they commanded that the compass
and the chain be set to [measure] the land.   42

The Simpson man behaved like a dog
as befitted the nature of a seaman,
wearing a blue jacket from a shop
and trousers of thin cloth.   46

It was the black packet of the oil
that brought them to this land,
but they will yet be seen drowned
[and thrown up] on seaweed on the Banff shore.   50

3. Climbing up towards Ben Shiant

Dr John MacLachlan

As I climb up towards Ben Shiant,
my thoughts are filled with sadness,

seeing the mountain as a wilderness,
with no cultivation on its surface.   4

As I look down over the pass,
what a chilling view I have!

So many poor cottages in disarray,
in green ruins on each side,   8

and houses without a roof,
in heaps by the water-spring!

Where the fire and children once were,
that's where the rushes have grown tallest.   12

Where the heroes used to gather,
behold the white sheep and her lamb there!

But, covetous perpetrator of the evil deed,
[consider] how many families you have removed;   16

there are many orphans in hardship
and widows in poverty because of you;

the blind, the old, and the deranged
heap their curses on your trouble-making.   20

Just consider, when you pass from us,
how the King of All will reward you.

Better that you should remember it early,
before death takes you to the grave.   24

Will you purchase mercy with wealth?
Gold will never buy it for you.

Do you think you will win deliverance
because of your sheep and all your folds?   28

You'd be better with the blessings of the beggar
to whom you would give alms in secret.

Better to have his blessings with goodwill,
offered to you by a bruised heart.   32

Wherever they can find land,
a thousand blessings be on those you evicted.

The mist has thickened on Ben Shiant,
the sun has descended into the sea;   36

the sky has darkened,
and I shall now conclude my little poem.

4. Song in Dispraise of Riddell of Ardnamurchan

In the calm May morning
as I would rise to my work,
the thrush on a branch
would be earnestly tuning its base notes;   4
that was the joyful music
which would awaken my desire,
and cause me to spend time listening
before the sun rose.   8

Now it is not worth my effort
although I rise early,
with my turf-spade, and toil in my shirt-sleeves
to tear the hills apart;   12
I will not earn an alms
for myself or for the poor,
when three rents are yelling out at me,
imposed by the wicked rascal.   16

Thus speaks the ancient owl
which lives in Creag Aodainn down here;
it is imprecating and crying,
'May your work come to a bad end!'   20
The Clan Cameron of Strath Lochy,
who would raise a banner on every flagstaff –
that man Riddell would take the gold
from their pockets with his way of talking.   24

Although our [old] army leaders have gone,
it would be a sinful turn of events
if we were allowed to be plundered
at the will of the Crown,   28
under masters of the land
whose fame would not last,
and by a lad with no wax seal
who will never be proclaimed a duke.   32

194

5. Malcolm is a Wicked Man

Refrain:

> Malcolm is a wicked man,
> and for ever will I say it of him.   2

When the Frenchmen come over
to put him to flight,
who will stand up for Malcolm
and the rabble that surrounds him?   6

Every one of them will be fierce
in their desire to strike him,
and I myself will be there,
blowing the flames of the conflict.   10

Behind me, behind me,
behind me is this township;
behind me is the place
where I long spent my growing years.   14

Cattle can no longer be seen in a fold,
nor can the milkmaid's song be heard;
where there once were people,
there are now yellow-coloured sheep.   18

6. [Satire on Kenneth of Gesto]

I saw while I was sleeping
a dream that caused me to marvel,
the Fenians coming over the sea
to take the heads off the sheep;   4
not one skull will be left attached to a body,
they will be lopped from each one of them;
they will be exterminated from shore to hill;
then peace will come to the world.   8

I saw Kenneth of Gesto,
being pursued by a great crowd,
making his way out by the Bràighe Buidhe,
with flames of fire surrounding him;   12
he was crying and shouting,
'You will get what is fated for you and all
        that surrounds me,
and, if you spare my life,
you will get my houses and my stacks.'   16

7. The 'Venus' of the Gaels

I am here on a hillock,
at the foot of a hill, all alone,
thinking about my friends
and how I have been left behind;   4
my father and mother have gone
and all my brothers,
and although my laughter can be heard,
it breaks through the desire to shed tears.   8

When the 'Venus' departed,
that was a very great number of people;
there were four hundred and two of them
packed into her hull;   12
if only the breeze had favoured them
by carrying them over unharmed,
and the King of All had conveyed them safely
across the wave-tossed ocean!   16

But the wind was against them,
and the ocean rose in fury;
when the showers thickened,
their appearance was like a grey crow;   20
the head sails were torn
and the great masts bent down;
every one of them was in agony –
they had a tale of hardship to tell.   24

News came to the land
that the full complement had not survived;
that left me sorrowful,
my heart heavy with grief;   28
they had lost their way
and mist had come down thick upon them,
the slender masts were stripped,
and the helmsman was injured.   32

With firm land under [their] feet,
the sadness and weariness departed;
every one who had means
put self-esteem into effect;   36
they left me alone
on a lovely knoll in the heather;
in a dream I began [to talk],
and my conversation went like the wind.   40

The dream that I saw in my sleep
was that you were with me, my love;
when I woke in the morning,
that was a vain thought;   44
although I have been for a while
lying in the heather,
I have a great desire to go over
to the land of the trees.   48

8.   A Message for the Poet

William Livingston

The morning is clear and sunny
and the west wind gently blows;
the firth shimmers peacefully,
with the strife of skies now calm;   4
the ship is beautifully rigged,
and weariness will not make her seek rest,
just as I found and as I saw,
taking this message to the Poet.   8

This is the crowning beauty of the month
when herds of cattle go to the wilderness,
to the glens of lonely hollows
where the seed will not be sown or reaped,   12
the grazing-bed of lowing beasts –
my portion was not with the others yesterday;
just as I found and as I saw,
take this message to the Poet.   16

There are thousands of cattle on fields
and white sheep on heathery upper slopes,
and the deer on desolate tops
where the wind's base is unpolluted;   20
their wild, powerful offspring
are wet with the dew of the gentle breeze;
just as I found and as I saw,
take this message to the Poet.   24

The level plain and rough-land corries,
the ocean shoreline and every smooth cornfield
are reacting to the effects of the skies' warmth
as we would all desire;   28
the wild shamrock and the daisy
are in flower on fields of grass;
just as I found and as I saw,
take this message to the Poet.   32

The swift streams of pure water
descend from behind the rounded hills,
from lochs that are clean and scumless
on the eminences far from the shore;   36
where the deer will drink his fill,
beautiful flocks of wild duck swim;
just as I found and as I saw,
take this message to the Poet.   40

The great bow of the ocean
remains as before by an eternal decree,
in the majestic greatness of nature's beauty,
with its head high towards the waves;   44
its white arc extends seven miles,
its sands swept smooth from the tide's mouth;
just as I found and as I saw,
take this message to the Poet.   48

The elements, the foundation of creation,
warmth and streams and breath of clouds,
nurture fresh vegetation
on which the dew lies gently   52
as the shadow of night falls,
as if it were mourning what has gone;
just as I found and as I saw,
take this message to the Poet.   56

Although the shafts of sunlight impart
the gentleness of the skies to the meadows' hue,
and the cattle can be seen on the shieling,
and its folds are full of cattle's offspring,   60
Islay is today devoid of people;
the sheep has laid waste its townships;
just as I found and as I saw,
take this message to the Poet.   64

Although a poor lost wretch should come
to the harbour in a mist,
he will see no glimmer from a hearth
on this shore for ever more;   68

the bad feeling of the Foreigners has banished
those who have left us and will never return;
just as I found and as I saw,
take this message to the Poet.   72

Although the army of Scotland should be raised,
with its great reputation on the battlefield,
the heather banner of the Islaymen
will not advance to protect it with the others;   76
ill-will has scattered them over the sea,
and only dumb beasts have replaced them;
just as I found and as I saw,
take this message to the Poet.   80

The houses once owned by those who have left us
lie in cold heaps throughout the land;
the Gaels have gone, and they will never return;
cultivation, sowing and reaping have ceased;   84
the foundations of the sad ruins
bear witness to this and say,
'Just as I found and as I saw,
let the Poet have this message.'   88

The spirited ditty of maidens will not be heard,
with a chorus of songs at the waulking-board,
and strong fellows will not be seen as before
driving home a goal on a smooth field;   92
the oppression of eviction has taken them from us;
the strangers have won, just as they wanted;
with all that I have found and seen,
let the Poet have this message.   96

The beggar will not find shelter
nor will the traveller get rest from his weariness,
nor will a gospel preacher find an audience;
injustice, Foreigners and taxes have triumphed;   100

the speckled adder is lying in coils
on the floors where once there grew
the big men that I saw there;
take this message to the Poet.   104

The district of the Oa has been stripped bare,
the beautiful Lanndaidh and MacKay's Rinns;
sunny Largie with its many hollows
has a pathetic remnant on its slope;   108
the Glen has become a green wilderness,
owned by men of hatred without tenants or crops;
just as I found and as I saw,
take this message to the Poet.   112

9. Song on One who was Evicting Highlanders

When death comes upon you,
I will think it fine.
We will put you on a deal plank
in your speckled shirt.   4
We will lift you happily
on men's shoulders.
Nothing will go on top of you
except cow dung.   8
And never will a daisy grow on you
or the clean blade of grass.
But thistles and nettles will grow
at your feet.   12
When a spadeful of earth is put on top of you,
the country will be put to rights.
Every poor person and weakling
will be clapping their hands.   16
If you were found on the shore
instead of kelp,
there would be one or two people
who would laugh out loud.   20
No coffin or shroud would be put on you
but a speckled shirt.
There is a miserly heart
inside your chest.   24
Your face resembles a thimble,
made of pock-marked lean meat.
The gold that is in the calf-skin
is what dispossessed the people;   28
the gold of the red hide,
and its influence is not so good.
If you lost the efficacious stone,
your lambs would be very scarce.   32
My own curse be on you beyond others
for ever more.

10. Lament for the Factor Mòr

Eugene Rose (or Ross)

There is news in the land that we rejoice to hear –
that the Factor is laid out without a stitch on him but a
    shroud,
without the ability to speak, and unable to read or write;
the champion of the Islay folk is laid low, and will never rise
    again.   4

When they go to the boat we will laugh with glee,
and when we gather together, we will drink toasts to one
    another
with good Highland whisky, with strong wine and cider,
and we will not be worried any longer, since that beast has
    been vanquished.   8

The Factor will have the pre-eminence in Satan's pit,
and Big Angus will be right behind him, with a flame of fire
    about his buttocks,
because of all the oppression that you inflicted on women
    and children,
and the people of the country that you drove mercilessly
    overseas.   12

When they heard in Canada that that beast had expired,
bonfires were lit and banners were attached to branches;
people were cock-a-hoop with joy, as they met one another,
and they all got down on their knees and praised God that
    you had died.   16

11. Manitoba

John MacLean, the Balemartin Bard

Refrain:

How sad I am without a single companion
who can raise, or understand, or sing a song with me;
with all the goodwill of my heart, I bid a fond farewell to
    the lads
who sailed over the ocean to Manitoba.   4

How sunny was our morning when we were young laddies,
without anxiety, complaint, or the screwing of rent;
with music and fullest fun, no gloom would descend
on the companionship we had in the Town of the Bards.   8

I now sit in isolation on these green hillocks,
being disturbed by matters of which others have not heard;
I am lamenting the spirited fellows who were kind and
    highly esteemed,
who left their native island, forsaking it for ever.   12

When that morning came when they were to go to a strange
    land,
and every friend in the place had gathered,
I cannot express the sorrow that weighed me down
as they turned their backs on the township on that Tuesday
    morning.   16

The people are mere shadows; how fickle the world is!
It is ever its nature to change day by day;
we are strangers upon its face, we are fleeting and transient,
with thousands of poor wretches being driven overseas.   20

The free-holders of land at this time are obsessed
with dragging the world's riches away from the rest;
and foolish devices will always be tried in the Highlands
to disperse the people and put sheep in their place.   24

I can see nothing at present except sheep on the hillsides;
only a couple of Lowlanders can be found in a glen;
and the few who have remained on the ocean's headlands
are being driven down to the shoreline and flayed by
    rent.   28

Today the fine, light-hearted youngsters are banished;
to north and south houses lie empty and cold;
I don't see a maiden going to the cattle-fold in the evening,
nor do I hear her ditty as she herds the calves.   32

The wearers of kilts and hose and cocked bonnets
who were always extolled in the battle's front line –
they are being sent overseas to a place that's unhealthy,
and the perpetrators are concerned only to lay waste the
    land.   36

I shall say no more about the feats of the brave men
who won renown for Britain in every struggle and fray;
the raising of land-rent is what has thinned our number –
with no remembrance of Sebastopol and Balaclava.   40

12. The Paupers of the Kingdom

Calum Campbell MacPhail

The paupers of the kingdom
are under a hard sentence,
inflicted by the landlords,
and exploited by the tenants;   4
they cannot ask for poor-relief,
and work is very rare;
there is no alternative to the poorhouse –
and better be hanged than there.   8

The Highlands of Scotland
are a truly pitiful place,
where once there were thousands
of fine, young lads,   12
worthy old people,
generous women with warm hearts,
and girls who were more fragrant
than the dew-drops on the field.   16

Where are those people now
who were once on the hillsides,
with a few sheep and cattle
on the plain as was the way,   20
who would not refuse alms
to the needy in his plight,
and who would provide a night's quarter
with kindness and warmth?   24

The rulers of the country
are like a helm in the enemy's grip,
banishing the stalwarts
and replacing them with sheep;   28
the English-speaking Saxons
will get everything their way,
and the Highlanders will be driven
to barren lands to stay.   32

When the conflict begins
the paupers will be needed then,
and gentlemen will summon them
down from the slopes of bens;   36
the Echo will reply,
'Have no fear in your hard time,
since you have plenty hornless sheep
for use in the front line!'   40

Commanders will drive them
down to the Lowlands,
with their long, thin legs
and short, weak bodies,   44
eyes that cannot endure hardship,
and a useless shoulder;
if you have banished the Gaels,
you've put real trashes in their place!   48

Great houses will be reduced to ashes
and proud people will have no roof;
their families will be chased
off the shoulders of the hills;   52
let them drink their fill
of every bitter well
that they opened for the pauper –
they can drink from it themselves.   56

There was once a garden in Eden
and it was regal beyond others,
until the writhing serpent came
with covenants of death;   60
its fences then fell down,
and its sweet fruit became tart,
and that same serpent is presently
ripping the Highlanders apart.   64

If you say that I am hard
on the noble class today,
put them into the measuring-scale,
and observe what they weigh;   68
if injustice is not swimming
over justice and drowning it in waves,
I will allow myself to be driven
from the land of the Gaels.   72

13. Song to the People of Bernera

Murdo MacLeod, Glasgow

A hundred salutes to the folk of Bernera
from a poet of the people of Lewis;
you would really make fine heroes
who would be effective in the fight;   4
it would cause sorrow and pain
if Parliament were to see the like of you
being driven out of your houses
and your places given over to ewes.   8

My dear folk, what a pity
that I was not with you, when the dogs
began to scatter you, hoping to banish you
over the ocean away from your familiar haunts;   12
you did not think it worth injuring
the one who came with the eviction notices
at the whim of Donald,
but you tore his coat off him.   16

How happy I was when I read
about your rising together,
shoulder to shoulder, and it helped your cause;
you kept the grip you had every right to hold,   20
since Sir James offered you the grass
that your cattle had on the moor;
not one of you will be banished again
without the blood of their body being spilt.   24

You went splendidly into marching order
on the moorland early on Friday;
as they marched to upper Stornoway,
my dear people were a fine sight;   28
the drone-pipes provided you with music
while a good lad filled them with air,
and the echo in the rocks
answered them on every side.   32

210

Every officer and sheriff
and the lawyers in the place
shook with fear when they saw
the heroes on the march;   36
you kindly gave them an invitation
so that they could hear
how you were oppressed through the tyranny
of one of Satan's black angels.   40

When you had informed the sheriff
of all the oppression you had endured,
and he had interrogated each of you
about the messenger and the coat,   44
you made your way to Matheson
in the castle where he lived,
and there you gave a great shout
which he heard inside his chamber.   48

When he saw through the window
those who were seeking him –
all those heavy warriors who could crush bones
if they had an evil intent –   52
he came and listened to you,
and in English you gave him your account
of how you had been oppressed
under the hand of the bad administrator.   56

That dirty chick from the eagle's nest,
with his vicious, destructive beak,
tore a hole in many a lamb
and their blood was often on his talons;   60
but I will tell him of his danger,
if he does not stop his pecking –
he will be thrown down by the gun
into a pit from which he will not rise.   64

Wicked, big-bellied, brutal Donald,
scowling, dark-grey Donald,
of the miserly Munros of Tain –
they were evil in deed and reputation –   68

until you came to Lewis
you never had a shoe on your foot;
long wings on a rag of a coat
covered each of your thighs.   72

I will stop pursuing him,
and I will say no more meantime;
the voice of all the Lewismen in Glasgow –
and we are no small number – states: 76
If he does not give up his practice
of plundering the local people,
sixty of us will head for home
and we will stone him to death.   80

14.   The Spirit of Kindliness

John Smith

O Spirit clear, most beautiful,
so gracious and so kind,
who rules in that palatial place
which love completely fills;   4
if we accepted you with friendliness,
and welcomed you with grace,
surely that would elevate
the nature of our race.   8

If we knew you in your beauty,
and could appreciate your worth,
that would surely raise our mind
above this piteous earth;   12
how happy those who know you,
with whom you ever dwell;
through you come all the joys
of Glory's Land above.   16

You would effectively impart to us
the nature of heaven's realm;
you would replace the frown of injustice
with the beauteous sheen of grace;   20
you would destroy corruption's nature,
and renew our true desire;
you would lift us to the heavens
with the strong pull of your love.   24

O gentle Spirit of graciousness!
If you lived in our midst,
you would give healing and release
to people withering with wounds;   28
you would inspire the hearts of widows
to sing with joyful strain,
and you would not leave them heartlessly
in the dark prison of their pain.   32

You would extinguish the fire of enmity
in the eye of wildest gaze;
you would pacify and quieten
the dark and brutal brow;   36
you would remove the look of wickedness
from the barbaric tyrants' face,
take their greed for wealth from them
and cast treachery from its place.   40

You would provide for people
true views of heaven's realm;
you would give us a pure gospel,
as told in pristine state;   44
you would not leave us tossing
on the wretched frames of lies,
fashioned through the deviousness
of creed-makers' spiteful minds.   48

If only this world of evil deeds
would come to know you well,
that would give to all its peoples
a joy that would excel;   52
deceit and oppression then would stop
and sharp contentious strife;
cunning tricks would be removed
and lies' dark clouds dispelled.   56

But I fear that you have left us
and fled to heaven above;
our people have grown in wickedness
without the presence of your love;   60
the skin of surly selfishness
encloaks them all around;
nothing I know can pierce it
but the arrow of the Lord.   64

O World, you have gone far off course
from that hour when you lost
your kindliness and honour,
and took to Lies and Hate;   68

like a discordant instrument,
without a string in proper tone,
you will not play an ordered note,
and you refuse to go in tune.   72

The kindly man is oppressed by you,
while the wicked wins the day;
the well-to-do is stroked in ease,
while the starving man is flayed;   76
you are generous to the wealthy,
and stingey to the poor;
you make the well-clad warmer,
and you freeze the naked's bones.   80

You have nothing that is natural
that heaven would call grace;
you will never produce an action
that will win the High King's praise;   84
you contain every form of idleness
and pain that's in its wake,
of distresses and of horrors –
too many to relate.   88

To you belong oppressors' strength
and the shackles of the slaves;
you own the shout of tyrants
and the whimper of the pained;   92
you claim the spite and terror
of the people who rank grand,
who regard us as no better
than flotsam on the sand.   96

The loathsome battle is your lot,
with its roar that splits the ear;
the cries of death and pain therein
rise up to heaven's door,   100
when the oppressive princes
whose sport is brutal war,
set off to win unjust reward
in exchange for blood of poor.   104

To you belong the treacherous lusts
and the fiery, mad desires,
that take us from the proper path
and make us stray aside;   108
which make us love corruption
and loath all holy things;
from which, with speed and certainty,
mankind's damnation springs.   112

Yours too is that contentious creed
that rouses hate and ire,
the creed that will not make us kind,
and represses not our pride;   116
the creed beloved by those divines
who love the sharpest strife;
through them, Christianity has become
like the monster of many heads.   120

That preachy sermoniser claims –
who shouts aloud with strength –
that we are cursed if we heed not
his creed – the one that's best;   124
instead of ever reminding us
of our duty in all things,
which would make us sensible
before the King of Kings.   128

That surly, gloomy Christian
who meditates with zeal,
who assumes a holy countenance
like a prophet in a trance,   132
who makes a terrible slaughter
of all horror in his breast –
from his dealings you would never know
that Apollyon now was dead.   136

The gentle man who will ascend
to heaven on love's wing
is no contender about creeds,
nor will others feel his sting;   140

he is not Episcopal,
Presbyterian, Greek, or Pape,
but a man of humane heart
whose life by love is shaped.   144

O Kindliness, you are beautiful –
the grace of highest worth!
Yet many will never give you
a place in their hard heart.   148
If the Muses now would grant me
my verbal powers awhile,
I would relate some actions
of those beasts who gave you bile.   152

Poor Donald knew nothing of your way,
that man of grimmest frown,
who expected that each Lewisman
would be exiled to the woods;   156
but he paid for part of his misdeeds,
and his remaining dues he'll pay;
he will realise too painfully
that justice wins the day.   160

Your quality did not hold sway
in that hard, iron-breasted band,
the factors and the landlords
who oppressed the northern land;   164
the houses that were warm and snug
were once filled with kindly ways,
but now that land of kindly folk
is a poor, empty, desert waste.   168

They filled brim-full with snipe
the land of happy folk;
they dealt in harshest manner
with the very kindest souls;   172
because they could not drown them,
they sent them fleeing overseas;
worse than Babylon's captivity
was the plight that came to these.   176

They reckoned as mere threads
those cords of love that held
the hearts of those fine heroes
to the lofty land of bens;   180
their grief resulted in their death,
after no lack of godly fear,
and the cold world oppressed them
with no warm shelter near.   184

Is anyone presently alive
who recollects that awful day,
on which was fought the fearful fight –
Waterloo of bloody plains?   188
A fine victory was won by Gaels
when they rose in battle-arms;
faced with the blade of bravest men,
our fierce foes yielded fast.   192

What joy came to the fathers
of those who won the fray?
The warm homes of kindliness
towered round their ears in flames.   196
Their sons were on the battlefield
to save a heartless land;
their mothers were in the saddest plight,
and their homes reduced to ash.   200

As Britain was rejoicing,
they were lamenting sore;
in the land that reared them,
they had no shelter from the wind;   204
each grey hair was being tossed
by the cold breeze of the glen;
there were tears on their cheeks,
and cold dew upon their heads.   208

O Britain, it is a disgrace
should we recount your tale,
relating how hard you dealt
with your own and truest race.   212

The land that those heroes had,
who saved you in your straits,
has now become a field of sports
for those wasters without morals.   216

How base the fame of our big shots,
these men of strangest sort!
Why should they stand so very high,
when they live on senseless sport?   220
If the grouse, with dung and droppings,
should cover all the heather,
that is what they would prefer
to golden streets in heaven.   224

O tremble midst your pleasures,
you oppressor, hard and strong!
What pain or death can justly be
your reward for people's wrongs?   228
The sorrowful sighs of widows
are what inflates your wealth;
every cup of wine you drink
is filled with tears of dearth.   232

Though your estate should be so great,
and peoples yield to you,
death has the very firmest laws,
and you will accept its rule.   236
That landlord will surely give
fair dealing to all men;
your inheritance will be a shroud
and two paces of green earth.   240

That will be your lowly end,
you man of great disdain,
with your notices and summonses,
keeping others in their pain;   244
when you receive that quiet estate,
your pride will be cut down;
no factor there will make a row,
nor will a vile officer frown.   248

Then the crawling worm will praise you,
for the tastiness of your flesh,
when it finds you stretched straight out
on its board without a breath;   252
it will say, 'This one is plump,
just right for creepy beast,
since he made many hundreds thin
to make for me a feast.'   256

15. Song on Sportsmen

John Smith

How sad am I that I cannot
speak a good word about you, Scotland;
your morals are base to relate,
you behaved in such a mean, uncharacteristic
    manner.   4
Although you produced a very fine brood,
alas! you were a mother without pity;
you flung your children off your breast,
to make room for the churls who abused you.   8

Churls who abused you greatly,
because their pockets were full of gold;
you chose the old men with money,
and banished the men with a right to you.   12

You banished the men who had a right to you –
God! it was not a right but a wrong;
between them and the land that they knew,
great oceans are now roaring;   16
people who, to save you from oppression,
would go willingly into the battle;
people who, standing between you and incursions,
would fight and win stout conflicts.   20

People who, frequently in battles,
spilt their branching blood to the ground;
you rewarded them in a despicable manner,
you banished them from you for ever.   24

Who now will go boldly in your cause?
The heroic Gaels have been routed;
if they had stood shoulder to shoulder,
who under the sun could have put them to flight?   28
Now since you have sent them to foreign lands,
you are no longer 'the land of the brave';
you are the land of the English rascals,
the land of the hounds and the grouse.   32

221

When battle and slaughter arise,
and the handlers of the hounds go to war,
I fear greatly that they will yield in the strife,
though they can quickly cause pain to a hare.   36

The Highlanders have now been driven out
without cause from the land that reared them,
bearing the penalty of malefactors,
although they were of high repute;   40
they are lost in dark wastelands
among the barbarous strangers of the wild wood,
who shoot their arrows destructively
into your heart with lethal precision...   44

It was once the joy of the chieftains
to have the people living close by them;
they were pleased to see on each side
the hospitable homes in the glens;   48
everything has taken a rather treacherous turn for us,
a change for the worse has now come over us;
our glens have been made cold and desolate,
we have felt the hands of the oppressors.   52

The hands of the wretched oppressors
who ejected the people from the land;
in the place of heroes have come dwarfs,
who have flourished through making cold houses.   56

The noble chieftains have left us,
in whom were kindness and honesty;
in their place impostors have arrived;
they have had an evil influence on this land.   60
The fermenters of barley have come,
the singed distillers of the worm-pipes,
who made a fortune by plundering drunkards,
making thousands utterly miserable.   64

These are the wretches who are
in the place of those who once
were ruling the Highlands of Scotland;
good fortune cannot possibly be in store for us.   68

Some of them traded in opium;
they amassed much wealth;
the Chinamen experienced their treachery;
they destroyed hosts with that poison;   72
people without kindness, without mercy,
hard to wound in the conscience;
in requital for all their robbery,
they deserved to be stabbed with a whinger.   76

Pitiful is the wealthy man who is also foolish,
ignorant of the plight of humanity,
though he should send thousands to perdition
to enjoy one hour of mad sport.   80

That man who swells up like a monster,
growing great on terrible piles of wealth,
is a cause of fear among people.
if his movements are not well controlled.   84
Like the wild leviathan of the oceans,
he is a real source of terror when sporting;
one blow of his tail may bring
injury and death to many...   88

The One who established the foundation of the world,
and brought the wild sea to order,
the One who established the foundation of the mountains,
and lifted them up to the clouds: 92
the One who put soil on the deep,
and laid it with a beautiful carpet of grass,
when he saw that this world had been completed,
he asked that it should be filled with people.   96

The ruler of the elements will arise,
and he will yet plead the cause;
and the terrible pride of the possessors of grey charters
will be swept headlong over the edge of the abyss.   100

16. The Skye Crofters

Neil MacLeod

How sad is the story
tonight from my homeland,
my kinsfolk being battered
   by daft Lowland men;   4
with batons bared fully,
being walloped like bullocks,
like slaves that are useless,
   being cooped in a pen.   8

The folk who were friendly,
so warm and so kindly,
the arrogant landlords
   so hard oppressed them,   12
that their freedom has left them,
their fields are deserted,
and sheep have ejected
   the great men from the glen.   16

Forgotten those heroes
who protected our country,
with their weapons bared ready,
   who taught tyrants to heed;   20
who would yield not to thralldom,
but maintained the just causes,
and bequeathed their fine morals
   unspoilt to their seed.   24

Those men who were stalwarts,
how glad they went forward
beneath the banner of Scotland
   and showed their strong hand;   28
little wonder our chagrin
and the extent of our anger,
that their sons are forgotten
   and tossed off the land.   32

At one time our fathers
lived under fine landlords,
with minds that were noble
   with truth and with grace;   36
they loved their sweet language
and gave kinship such value
that in peace and in battle
   they held fast to their race.   40

They lived with their clansfolk,
as was always their practice;
they were fully informed
   of their plight at each time;   44
when they would foregather
at church on the Sabbath,
so concerned was their asking,
   so warm and so kind.   48

They and their people
so firm and united,
like a family so loving
   only death could them part;   52
neither sheep nor high profits
were desired by their honours,
but heroes unbending
   who could fend with their hearts.   56

Neither water nor moorland
was banned or excluded,
and freedom and goodness
   filled the youth of the land;   60
no mischievous factors
oppressed them with hardship,
or cut off their sustenance
   with merciless hand.   64

But, waken, my kinsfolk,
your land don't relinquish,
but, determined to win it,
   put up a strong stand;   68

your fathers bequeathed it
to you for your keeping,
and you must defend it
   for the unborn of your band.   72

Not at all with disorder,
but with sense and wise caution,
without bending or warping
   in word or in will;   76
hundreds and thousands
will rise to support you,
until you get all you wanted
   of the high ground of the hill.   80

All oppression will crumble,
there will be food and abundance,
peace and great solace
   will clothe the whole land;   84
there will be songs and fine music
on the lips of the young folk
and beautiful maidens
   will tend the cows and their calves.   88

Each heir and each factor
will shed their pomp and their malice,
they will show love to their land-folk,
   as was their original aim;   92
and the Gaels, in number unbounded,
will fill the land of the mountains,
adorning its glories,
   and growing greater in fame.   96

17. [The Challenge of the Men of Braes]

Neil the Merchant

If an official comes upon us from Portree
without the king's act in his hand,
we will show you that it is not peace
that we will offer you at the present time;   4
rather, we will give battle in earnest;
our leader will be faithful,
and the highest stone in the prison
will have its head laid low.   8

We will have Fair-haired Donald in addition,
we will have Charles and Red-haired Donald;
Kenneth will follow close on their heels,
and Black-haired John – he has a tempestuous nature;   12
notice will be sent to Donald son of Ranald
on the street, where he practises military drill;
he will excel all in soldiering,
and Roderick will be at their head.   16

The royal blood of old John Stewart will be there, –
he was found participating in many a feat –
and although age is robbing him of his strength,
he is enthusiastic in the fray,   20
protecting the man behind,
and keeping an eye on him over his shoulder;
O, he will receive honour in my country,
because the Prince's blood is flowing in his body.   24

18. Satire on the Eviction Notice

Calum Campbell MacPhail

I sing a satire on the greedy Notice
which has frequently spiked the heart of the Gael;
she has left the land of the Gaels unhappy,
the edict of the Devil and his friends;   4
she came this year to the Isle of Skye
to request that part of the population leave it,
issuing a hard, unloving order
to be ready to quit on St Brendan's Day.   8

She did not ask whether there was another person
who would give them shelter in their house;
if they were all as she was,
there would be nothing to expect but death;   12
she did not listen to the complaint of the Aged,
nor at all to the crying of children;
she threw their anchor out of its ground,
and left them tossing on the waves of pomposity.   16

She cast them adrift like a boat without a rudder,
without compass, without sails, without oars,
tossing on the ocean of injustice,
oppressed by the whirlwind generated by the wealthy;   20
those of you who are safe in harbour,
will you not draw alongside your friends;
make your stand in firm, manly, faithful fashion –
why should we yield like slaves?   24

Stand firmly, as one Society,
hold meetings in every place;
be astute, every warrior of you
in whom there is a drop of the blood of the Gael;   28
if they do not make a law to help you,
Donald will be no worse off than Patrick;
justice requires scope and speed,
and a blade that can never be overcome by treachery.   32

19. Song between a Tenant and a Landlord

Calum Campbell MacPhail

Tenant

It would almost be better to be dead under the turf
than to suffer the evicting which landlords impose upon us;
officers and eviction notices now pursue us
in ways to which we were not accustomed;   4
the crooked leg of the law gives them support,
and they will strike us in every possible way;
if our friends do not stand up for us in our plight,
our enemy will overcome us.   8

Landlord

If you were obedient to my will,
I would control you in a noble fashion,
but since you have staged a rebellion,
you will be given a fight which you will not win;   12
I will get soldiers from the Crown
who will send you fleeing over the seas;
and your land will be laid waste –
with white sheep and a large farm.   16

Tenant

When did we not give his due
to the landlord in every way?
Have we not always paid the rent
and the tax, although it was hard for us?   20
Since you would not change your way,
but tried underhand methods,
not one of us will yield in the struggle,
as long as we have a hand attached to a shoulder.   24

229

Landlord

When I take you to court,
you will have time to think;
you will be placed in prison
without doubt, and you will not be released;   28
you will then see that it is no joke
to despise my noble standing;
when your noses are put behind bars,
you will appreciate the control of the landlords.   32

20. Word Came to our Township

Alexander MacLean

Word came to our township
that the police were coming to catch us,
coming into the Glen at full speed,
and that checked our high spirits.   4

The Great Horn was sounded,
the pipers began to tune their drones,
and I heard an old woman shouting,
'The Children of the Gaels, Oh, they won't retreat!'   8

Although it was frightening, we had to move
and to hold our ground with hard courage;
there was one with a stick, one with a flail,
and one with a club made from a sooty rafter.   12

What a beautiful sight that was,
advancing up the brae of Fasach,
banners fluttering from high staffs
and waving gently in the wind.   16

Brave heroes came to our assistance,
all of one mind to accompany us –
the men of Skinidin and Colbost,
as fully armed as ourselves.   20

We drove them off as they deserved,
sending them over the boundary of the estate;
when we reached the public house,
night had come upon us, and we were tired.   24

231

21. MacTavish of the Summonsing

'The Great Rock'

MacTavish of the summonsing
will never again serve us with a notice;
he almost met his death
when we left him in Brunigil.   4

It was the hostess in the Dunvegan change-house
who provided you with a means of transport;
King above, I was amazed
that it wasn't smashed to dust.   8

I saw you with a scowl on your face
going out along the slope,
while the lads were shouting,
'James is wearing a cape.'   12

The cape which was no beautiful thing
and had been lying since Martinmas
in a former potato patch –
it was put on a real scoundrel.   16

You earned your pay dearly,
even though you took to drink;
you would have been better gathering shellfish
than be engaged in such dangerous officership.   20

When they beat the retreat,
and they set about James,
everyone was shouting,
'What a pity you should suffer at our hands!'   24

When they came to meet him,
and they came in sight of the group,
some said, 'Let him be caught alive,
so that we can put him in a peat-bog.'   28

But they employed a better method:
he was very nearly drowned;
the black bag was made into a plaster
to be put around his neck.   32

Black Angus from Roag
was seeking mercy from Norman,
and when the pursuers came,
they were all pacified.   36

Norman said, shouting aloud,
'How sad I am;
the lads of Marion, Patrick's daughter,
are the ones who have humiliated me completely.   40

'One after the other of them
was employed by myself,
but when they became rebels,
they would not listen to me any longer.'   44

22. A Poem to the three Highlanders who are in the Edinburgh Prison

Alexander MacLean

Do not be displeased with me
though I should compose this poem in sorrowful mood,
concerning the recent news we have received
which has caused us dejection and hurt –   4
that our dear and kind kinsmen
are in a grim, comfortless prison.
I sing the praise of those heroes
who have left the Isle of the Mist.   8

Although I should begin to tell you about it,
my faculties are not in good form;
there are many things troubling me;
my spirit is considerably distressed;   12
but I would stand with you in the face of hardship
and death, even if it were to confront us.
I sing the praise of those heroes
who have left the Isle of the Mist.   16

You are the heroes who would not bend,
and you are justly worthy of such reputation;
lively, good-humoured men,
who would climb hills and high mountains;   20
you struck a blow against the pundits
although the trial went against you;
I sing the praise of those heroes
who have left the Isle of the Mist.   24

Many a day in your country
you spent a great deal of time,
filled with concern
about the state of your land and the people,   28
because the arable ground of your fathers
is currently deer-forest and pasture
throughout other districts
and throughout the Isle of Mist.   32

234

O, how deep is our anxiety!
We miss you so greatly;
some of the people of our own district
are locked up in a court-house,   36
in the Calton prison,
because of the inhibiting judgement of the Lords –
and those who would accept their defence
are tonight in the Isle of the Mist.   40

But it is a cause of encouragement for each of us
that nobles and heroes throughout the population,
and high-ranking lawyers too, are to be found
in the kind company of our supporters;   44
those people have proved that they are faithful
in everything, as is proper;
they are full of unflinching enthusiasm
for the folk of the Isle of the Mist.   48

The factor, as hard as he can,
is employing cunning tactics;
he sometimes comes in humble guise
to impose bonds of peace upon us,   52
in the hope that we will pay him the rent,
and that we will be sufficiently kindly disposed,
and that we will forget everything else
that has happened in the Isle of the Mist.   56

But listen, factor, my man:
you have not properly understood
the temperament of the people of the district,
although you hoped to act cunningly;   60
for, when they are disposed to move,
they are united in every matter,
and no coward will bring confusion upon
the people of the Isle of the Mist.   64

You obtained a law in writing –
that is sure enough –
that no man or animal
could take a step in your pasture;   68

you deprived us of the rights of way
that the kindreds had from the beginning,
and every generation too, though I should stress it,
that was in the Isle of the Mist.   72

We will not forsake the law that we had,
and we will not let it lapse willingly,
in spite of whatever threat is breathed against us
or comes in our pursuit;   76
we will walk in the rights of way,
just as our needs require us to do,
right down to the last person
who will be in the Isle of the Mist.   80

The overlords of the land
enjoyed merriment and music,
spending every day happily,
with their giddy ladies in their satin dresses,   84
piling up wealth and riches
for their children who would survive them –
the fruit of the labour of others
who were in the Isle of the Mist.   88

When the nobles came to us
and the young landlord,
they did not leave a house without scrutiny –
O, it was a despicable way to act!   92
They said to us dismissively –
as if we would believe idle talk –
'You are in fine circumstances
in the Isle of the Mist.'   96

I shall conclude this poem,
though I consider it rather premature;
many things are troubling me
among the predicaments that are upon us;   100
but if I remain in the area,
and those others return to us alive,
I shall compose another small poem
for the people of the Isle of the Mist.   104

23. [Welcome to the Commission]

Charles MacKinnon

Ho-rò, we will not be sorrowful,
no longer will we be in need;
a Commission is coming to the district
in the hope of doing us good.   4

Then everything will be set in order,
and our rights will be proclaimed;
they have maps folded away,
and plans of all the crofts.   8

We will get Heall and Greallainn,
Feall and Druim Shlèite,
Oismaigearaidh and Sgor,
and we will live there without poverty.   12

See for yourselves Cnoc Oth yonder,
and every fine, smooth wall there;
we will yet see roofs on them,
and I would love to be in one.   16

We will give up fishing lobsters,
since our shirts are often soaked;
it is far better to be farming,
and digging a sedgy field.   20

24. The Queen's Commissioners

John MacLean, the Balemartin Bard

O, sing the praise of the Commissioners
beginning from the seventh day of that month;
a hundred greetings go over the seas
to that noble, royal Commission.   4

May the Queen have a long life,
since she gave the Commission a royal mandate
to come to this remote island
which lies low on the ocean's breast.   8

The Land below Sea-level, surrounded by rough waves,
the famous, valuable island;
the sea resounds constantly as it pounds it;
it is now known as Tiree.   12

We gave them an account as was proper;
most of it was in writing,
with a firm, particularised complaint
concerning the prettier side of the truth.   16

We have good hope and expectation
that the Duke will make peace with us,
and that the sun of a new morning will arise
which will climb above every dark cloud.   20

Although this famous island
now pays taxes to the Duke,
it was not by right dealing or by hard blades
that it was acquired by his ancestors;   24

It was by wily tricks and deviousness,
by smooth talk in court and rubbing the right way,
and he replaced the reign of our own rulers
with a destructive regime.   28

Like a ship battered by every squall
we were being tossed on the ocean,
but she will yet find a safe haven
if Highlanders remain loyal.   32

When they deliver their Report,
the landowners will be condemned,
and the *Oban Times* will be highly esteemed
in every city in the kingdom.   36

25. [In Praise of Henry George]

We will praise Henry George;
we will sing a song about him, and give him honour;
we will, and we ought to;
we will praise him gladly, in manly fashion.   4

He wrote a book about rights
called *Progress and Poverty*;
he caused the great men to tremble
throughout Europe and America.   8

Labour and land and management [he states]
are in the hands of surly, cruel men;
contempt for the pauper and the Christian
is increasing continually everywhere.   12

He put advance warning in words for them;
he told them of their impending loss and danger;
he conveyed a statement like a lad at great speed –
'The abundance that exists is not yours.'   16

He taught a rule to every rebel –
'Treat your neighbour like yourself';
love in relation to every creature –
that should be as the law of God and man to us.   20

They have had their own way with us for so long
that they will find it difficult to yield totally to us;
they will hear more from Henry
and [other] orators before we finish with them.   24

The population of the world has arisen;
hardship has taught them understanding;
there should be an end to every war and injustice,
because we are all brothers as we were at birth.   28

The societies of Glasgow and Edinburgh,
the societies of Ireland and London support us;
town and country stand together,
along with the people of foreign lands – and results
    will follow.   32

26. Song on the Crofters' Plight

Donald MacKinnon, Glasgow

We are disconsolate in the Lowlands;
my eyes are moist with tears, and little wonder,
when every paper in the country presently gives an account
of the plight of my people in the land of the bens.   4

From the Butt of Lewis to the Mull of Kintyre,
in the islands, the straths and the glens,
the folk are being flayed by rents, while the land is
    worthless,
and the patches are thin, although their price is fat.   8

Much soil that is good is in the possession of Lowlanders,
and there is no place for the descendants of the Gaels;
if they ask for land, they will be rewarded at present
by having 'Englishmen's' hounds sent speedily there.   12

Their children are being fleeced and sent packing without
    pity,
while a factor endlessly gives them a hard time with his lean
    dogs,
to maintain the landlords over yonder in France –
the noble beggars, who have lost their nobleness.   16

There are still plenty of antlered stags to be had,
the salmon can still be found, lively and steep-turning in
    the river,
to provide sport for the 'Englishmen' who come thick in
    pursuit,
but if we ourselves touch them, we are thrown into
    prison.   20

If it constitutes law, this ordinance made by themselves is
    not at all just;
the One who created all things under the sun
did not ordain that they should lay claim to everything,
every salmon and deer and the birds of the skies.   24

241

It is my sincere desire for the land of the mountains
that its children may succeed now that they have been
    roused;
history, whose evidence speaks for itself, indicates
that they are heroes to the core when they unsheath their
    swords.   28

Although the Gaels have few friends in the struggle,
there is a small but significant number in Parliament itself;
although the sky is overcast, and the weather foul,
the clouds will be dispersed, and the sun will shine
    through.   32

27.   The Crofters' Banner

Donald MacDonald, Greenock

The banner of the brave crofters,
who were not afraid to raise it aloft,
health to the hand that wove it in the loom
– it was waulked into a fine, thick cloth.   4

Its motto is 'The Land Question' –
come and follow it with firm resolve;
rise from every glen and harbour,
and no trickery will take it from you.   8

Welcome to MacCallum, the hero,
who is carrying it over the waves;
he can be seen in camp and pulpit
like a guiding star leading the people.   12

The unfaithful landlords have stolen
our ancestors' rights from us,
and they have left us bare, with nothing –
we had no way of rising up.   16

But we will get a strong leader
who will go to Parliament very soon;
the good MacFarlane will carry our banner,
and no enemy will overcome it.   20

And now he will not be alone
standing up for the people's rights;
Mackintosh will be at his shoulder,
and, along with him, will tackle the enemy.   24

28. The Lewis Crofters

Murdo MacLeod, Bru, Barvas

The most amazing wonder
that has ever been in Lewis
is that the poor people are now ruling there
and the landlords trampled down;   4
today they are coming generously
to ask us for our votes,
but they will not get them this year,
however fine their tales.   8

Children of the Gaels, please help me
so that we can begin to discriminate,
and say to the landlords
that they stay away from us for ever;   12
and we will stand as we were accustomed
with our shoulders close together,
and we will all defeat them
by means of the smooth-haired fellow.   16

Was not Doctor MacDonald
the hero at their head?
He is the one who knows the ways
of bringing justice into effect;   20
and I am putting my hope
in the people of this brown island,
that they will give him their votes,
and that he will assert their children's rights.   24

But now he has got all the votes,
and I myself have hope
that he will assert our rights for us
against the sharp oppressors;   28
and I pray that you'll get mercy
if you yourself are willing
not to go back to those ones
who always tell us lies.   32

You know that fellow Novar,
with the very handsome, young face;
he will not be seen in Parliament
ever representing this place;   36
we do not want the landlords
to be ruling in the court,
and we will not trust their words
till we see action first.   40

That Novar has an estate
and it does him no good now;
the poor are being oppressed,
they have no food for their families;   44
and he will not give them a drill of potatoes
to round off their meal –
and he wants into Parliament
to stand up for us!   48

Some of my friends
have stood for Novar's cause,
but that was a wasted effort for them
and has done them no good at all;   52
they could not entice their neighbours
to stand on their side,
and they are now humiliated,
miscalling them far and wide.   56

Today, how proud I am
of the people to whom I belong,
every family and kindred –
they were not found to yield;   60
and although selfish individuals
are winning a prize for themselves,
Ross-shire is triumphing,
although the landlords will not submit.   64

The landlords were humiliated
when they heard the news
that the poor were triumphing
whom they themselves despised;   68

and that caused the landlords,
who were proud of themselves,
to promise a reward to us
if we would elect them.   72

Although we are poor, we were found
to be noble compared with them,
and let them give their bribes
to the people who are in their own pocket;   76
we will not fight for a bribe,
but we will triumph mightily;
justice will be our watchword,
and we will not accept the reward of lies.   80

A terrible judgement follows
as a reward for untruthfulness;
even Judas put his curse on it,
although his character was frightening;   84
and the man who sold the land
got a penalty after that –
he fell dead as an example,
and his sweetheart after him.   88

How sad is the plight of our divines,
if one is permitted to say so,
as they supported the landlords
who were killing off the people!   92
They did not release the prisoners,
as they were told in God's command,
but they followed the shepherds
who were laying waste the land.   96

Will you not tell me, divines,
the thoughts you had yourselves,
when in the early days of innocence,
you gave assent to a lie?   100
Did you not make enquiry
about all that you proclaimed?
If you did not, why should you condemn
that which the truth maintains?   104

But there was one noble man
who adhered to the people in every step –
Greenfield, the gentleman,
who would not be deceived by bribes;   108
honesty was his watchword,
and he did not yield to toffs;
he would not take one reward from them,
as he looked up to heaven.   112

But what has sent you to this place,
Novar, who has no concern,
since you banished your tenants,
and left them small in number?   116
You have deer and white sheep,
and you can have my hand as a pledge
that if they do not elect you to Parliament,
I will never send you there.   120

29. I would Sing the Heroes' Praise

John MacLean, Mulbuiè

Refrain:

Regardless, I would sing the heroes' praise
wherever I would drink a dram;
regardless, I would sing the heroes' praise.   3

This Dr MacDonald of whom I speak
is undeniably a crofter's son;
he defeated the laird of Novar –
he kept him out of Parliament House.   7

I have the greatest affection for that fine man
who stood faithfully in the struggle;
he has now defeated them all,
and he has been returned regardless.   11

The rags were always ready
to circulate their empty propaganda,
telling us in every way
that young Novar would bring us justice.   15

I truly admire that hero
who won the great esteem of Highlanders;
he has defeated his enemy,
and he will reduce the land-rent for us.   19

Dr MacDonald is full of valour;
Lewis in the north rose to support him
and Ross-shire of the hardy men;
it was the Black Isle that kept the flag flying.   23

All my esteem goes to Roderick,
who has been honoured by this northern district;
he has now been placed among the nobility
so that he can uphold justice.   27

Macdonald Cameron was there from the outset;
he has the care of many towns;
if he gets the goodwill of everyone,
we need not have any fear for justice.   31

Dr Clark is a truly fine gentleman,
and we would have been much the worse without him;
he defeated Sinclair,
and he will rid us of cold and hunger.   35

Jesse Collings is behind us
to support us in the courts,
and there is no factor under the crown
who will extract a double rent from us next year.   39

The Sutherland folk who did not stand
as firmly as they ought in the struggle
could have had the gentle Sutherland,
who would have brought gloom to Duke and Marquis.   43

How proud we can be –
with Dr MacDonald and MacFarlane,
and Fraser-Mackintosh, the hero;
the people of Sutherland are a disgrace.   47

30. To Donald MacFarlane

John MacLean, the Balemartin Bard

Refrain:

> The land of the bens, glens and tartans,
> the land of the bens, glens and heroes;
> a hearty welcome to Donald MacFarlane
> in the land of the high bens and tartans.   4

We wish you long life, full of success and good order,
so that you may proceed forthwith to govern
the beautiful country of the generous men,
of the roes and deer and salmon.   8

The people have honourably shown their esteem for you,
in spite of those who spread malicious untruth,
and they have made ready a seat for you
in St Stephen's in England.   12

Early on Wednesday we were of a mind
to be faithful to you in the battle;
the best ship that was ever sailed
would not have come near the harbour.   16

We carried a boat on our shoulders
to the head of Gott Bay – a port full of difficulty –
to go to Mull of the cold hills
in spite of ocean's storm and tempest.   20

The 'Hebridean' took her course,
cleaving the grey-black waves into white;
I mistook the Dutchman's Cap
for the coastline of Mull close to Staffa.   24

We found the Highlanders of the Ross of Mull
hearty, kindly, courteous, noble;
they are the descendants of those long renowned
for routing an enemy and pursuing intently.   28

That truly was the day of hard struggle;
the whole of Argyll was involved in the battle;
in the twentieth fray you won the victory,
and you went in pursuit with the tartan-clad men.   32

The following Monday a joyful story
spread throughout the Highland people;
and Highland hills and eminences
were ablaze with overflowing love.   36

There were great bonfires on green hills;
pipers were playing proudly;
and the cheering of the people
made a noise which moved the Echo.   40

The bards will compose songs;
in every wood the thrushes will sing;
nobody has any claim to that music
except those who held out for land-rights.   44

Your friends are with you to help you,
and to stand on the side of justice;
Charles Fraser-Mackintosh
and the young Reverend MacCallum.   48

There are many treacherous, bold Ahabs
today in the Highlands of Scotland;
I would wish to see the blood of every rogue
and his chariot being consumed by dogs.   52

May the *Oban Times* come safely
like Noah's dove to the ark,
with the news that the flood has subsided,
although it has devastated the land.   56

This is truly the New Year for the Queen,
Gladstone and Donald MacFarlane,
to begin the process of giving Highlanders
strong security in their land.   60

I wish success to Donald MacFarlane –
a man of good leadership at the head of Highlanders,
just like Moses of old in the wilderness
bringing those others to the Promised Land.   64

31. A Health to Donald MacFarlane

John MacLean, the Balemartin Bard

Here's a health to Donald MacFarlane;
you are a kindly, friendly gentleman;
the good wishes of the Children of the Gaels go with you
every day, although we have parted.   4

It will be drunk in a multitude of places
in the land of the glens and lofty mountains,
the health-drink of the noble gentleman –
gold will be spent buying it in his honour.   8

We will drink it with enthusiasm
in the land of heather in our native fashion,
since it was a great honour to our country
that you were sent to the English court.   12

[You are] a highly esteemed, far-famed gentleman,
like a clean fountain flowing endlessly,
although so much antipathy was stirred up
against you by MacKinnon and Poltalloch.   16

Argyll has forgotten about you
because of all the turncoats living there;
that is what has made Scarinish today
as famous as Sebastopol.   20

In the storm and gale of winter,
although Argyll made him its leader,
the damage was done by the deceivers
and all the boot-lickers who entered it.   24

The heroes who are long renowned
for their valour on sea and on land
reside in this low-lying, green island,
the customary residence of their forefathers.   28

That friend who was always loyal to us,
and who obtained the prisoners' release,
will receive honour throughout every generation –
this sandy island bids him a farewell blessing.   32

32.   Song on the Election

'The Lame Tailor'

May success and prosperity for ever attend
Argyllshire of the [many] heroes;
they turned their backs on MacFarlane,
on the Pope and on Gladstone;   4
they turned their backs on the wretches –
Parnell's lads – and their habits;
the constituency is now as was customary
raising high the blue banner –   8
    the Union Jack.

Long live the gentleman
who won the victory in the tussle;
long live, in like manner,   12
those who supported him in it;
the high praise of Argyll is heard
today throughout the world;
it stood closely and faithfully   16
on the side of truth and the Union –
    and is that not good?

Pass over the bottle, Mary,
and fill each glass to its brim,   20
so that we can drink the health
of my hearty fellow, the Laird of Poltalloch;
he is the very essence of the gentleman;
skulduggery is not his intention;   24
he dislikes strife and contention;
peace and kindness would be the desire
    of the good man.

He is honoured and highly regarded   28
throughout the land as a person;
he is merciful and sympathetic
to the tenantry who are in poverty;
he is humble, warm-hearted,   32

253

kind, friendly, most genial,
towards the high and the low;
he is my own choice of all menfolk,
    my fine fellow.   36

Donald 'of the Horn' MacFarlane
is the brave lad who likes some fun;
he found a wife in Ireland,
and he esteemed her for her gold;   40
he has wholly rejected
the custom of his country since he married;
he preferred to become a Paddy
so that he could go fighting and boxing   44
    at Donnybrook.

When Donald was a young man,
he was a character of great piety;
he would be in the company of the 'men',   48
and the Free Church was his place of rest;
but godly Donny liked better
to be under the wings of the Pope;
he left the 'men' in the lurch   52
and the Free Church, and he followed Parnell –
    and it was not advantageous.

In Ardnamurchan of the gurnet,
in Lismore with its sheep-stock,   56
in Mull of the high mountains
and in level Tiree of the sand,
in Coll and in Cowal,
in beautiful Islay and in Morvern,   60
in Lorn and in Oban,
Donald was highly regarded until he proved
    that he was no good.

Although the people should request   64
all the wealth in the world,
Donald would say that they could have it
all to their heart's content;
he promised them plenty of land,   68

cattle and store in the autumn;
but 'I promise but I do not deliver'
was my kind Donny's policy –
     my fine laddie.   72

Although Donald is so plausible,
sweet and loquacious with people,
pretending to be generous,
he never gave them any of his treasure;   76
although thousands of gold pieces
go into his pocket every year,
the poor of the country do not get
what would buy as much as a pound of soap   80
     from the good man.

There is many a fellow who will cut chunks
and thongs that are very long
from other people's leather   84
in order to entice his friends;
that is Donald's policy;
he is kind-natured like Gladstone;
he is every bit as generous as   88
Iain mac Eachainn's grey cockerel
     in scattering the horse's food.

33. Song about the Crofters' Bill

John MacRae

The plough has indeed been placed on the cross-beam,
and the arable land has been laid waste;
what has been taken from us is precisely
what our forefathers had on rent;   4
and if we were able to recover it,
we would not make our complaint to the state
about every danger and injustice
that the landowners have inflicted on the Gaels.   8

We will drive away every gamekeeper,
and every deer that consumes arable land,
chasing them up again to the deer-forest,
and the Nimrods will be brought low;   12
the English will be repulsed
from coming near the place at all,
since they have ruined us completely
by laying waste [our land] with the deer of the hill.   16

The sheep itself was just as bad
in nibbling us down to the bone;
it caused many to migrate,
driving them down to the shore;   20
many a time it pained my guts
to be so frequently a slave,
while sheep and deer were on the pasture
that would have fed many Gaels.   24

But the plough will [yet] be taken off the cross-beam,
and the garrons set in harness;
the arable land will be ploughed by them,
and the poor folk will get their fill;   28
the cows for milking will be on the hill
in every township as was customary,
and we will not go down to the Caithness fishing –
we will get rent-money at home.   32

We will not submit to the Bill
that the government has introduced;
it says nothing about a patch
where a man could plant a crop;   36
what we want is a place
where cows could find grazing
and the low land to produce meal
for the growing generation.   40

34. Song about the Soldiers

Colin MacDonald

Too long have 1 been quiet and silent
without making any public sound
about the very poor state of this country
which is being described now;   4
they are fond of newspapers
in the Lowlands and elsewhere,
and in many places there is mention
of the hard strait that we now bear.   8

When a posse of policemen came,
there was excitement in the place;
they were contemptuous, the villains,
and spoke curtly to the bard;   12
these fellows were full of courage
because the law was in their hand,
but they gave us no quick fright,
and were repulsed without a stand.   16

After them came the soldiers,
and they were a fine sight on the field;
they had dogs which went before them
in every place on leash;   20
when they served the papers,
mine was hardly in my hand,
when I gave them as an honour –
'To the Devil with their pride!'   24

I gave the fitting appellation to
the avengers without grace,
these ugly lumps of policemen
who would not have refused to charge,   28
if they had been given the invitation
to be ready to engage,
with a strong and careful army
from the Crown to be their guard.   32

It was Greenhill here that caused
useless soldiers to be sent
to this land of Highlanders
to oppress us in our plight;   36
if we had been prepared
with our guns primed to fire,
they would not have won the upper hand
in the fight with blades so fine.   40

Those heroes who are long renowned
for hardihood at every time,
the strong, robust Highlanders
who did not act foolishly in the fray,   44
with their hard and steely daggers,
that brought many kingdoms into line –
they won enduring fame
in a battle that was dire.   48

In Tiree, I'm telling you,
there are plunderers without sense,
the policemen and the soldiers,
and they are not kind to one another;   52
but when MacFarlane is returned
to Parliament as we desire,
the laws of the deceivers
will be rescinded in short time.   56

I now think that I'll conclude,
and that I'll complete my song,
but let me remember as I do –
I ought to sing his praise –   60
that fine, honourable gentleman,
MacQuarrie, the brave fellow,
who liberated the prisoners
and will not forsake us in distress.   64

35. Song about the Prisoners

John MacLean, the Balemartin Bard

For too long I have been quiet and silent
about the much-loved island which reared me,
since the Queen and the Duke have collaborated
to reduce to desperation the level-surfaced land of barley.   4

This green, productive, pleasant island
is surrounded by an ocean-wall formed by great breakers;
it lies as far west as Barra and Islay,
and is full of pretty flowers – a low-lying expanse.   8

On a summer morning when the shamrock grows
white and red on the level machair,
its beautiful flowers are many-coloured and attractive
under the dew of the sky, as the sun gilds them.   12

Marram-grass, rushes and green water-cress
adorn its secluded hollows where the thrush sings;
frequently we discovered honey in the banks,
deposited by the restless, brown-speckled,
        humming bee.   16

Before the Duke arrived there or any of his ancestors,
or royal George of the family of Hanover,
the low-lying island with its many shielings
belonged to Highlanders as a dwelling-place.   20

All low-lying islands and high mountains
and every glen which reared the hospitable Highlanders
are, in most cases, deserted, with nobody but a shepherd,
from the Mull of Kintyre to John O' Groats.   24

This is the land of fine tartans and heroes
who were the pride of the nation, though now exiled;
it had many shielings and cows in cattle-folds,
with maidens' songs around the banks of Morven.   28

They kept out Caesar and all his legions,
the Norsemen surrendered to Caledonia;
at the Battle of Largs Haakon was routed;
he was so deeply humiliated that he died in grief.   32

The inhabitants of the low-lying island,
in subjection to a destructive minority, have no
    place to live;
today it has been laid waste by those who despise us,
who have put in prison our young lads.   36

In Inveraray, that black hole of hardship,
they were incarcerated Monday and Sabbath;
but there was sufficient nobleness in MacQuarrie's breast
to ensure that they would not be there one hour, if gold
    could release them.   40

The wretches fled from the scene of the confrontation,
as the wicked flees when no man pursues him;
they were driven back; there was nothing but lies
in the Edinburgh court; that was clear to me.   44

What clever, strong soldiers those were
to come to the island by order of the Crown of King George;
every one in turn was telling a terrifying story
about MacFadyen's horse, that took the place
    of a colonel.   48

We have been troubled by scandal-mongers,
but we stood up for what was just,
in a manly, honourable manner, supporting our
    fellow Highlanders,
as did our kinspeople in the Misty Isle.   52

36. The Battle of Glendale

'Calum the Post'

Ivory is just the fellow to quash every daftie,
he has little need of weapons today;
in the Glendale battle he won every fight,
and not even one old wifie was slain.   4

There is sad news about the northerly isles,
telling how the people have risen in riot;
the boorish crofters who would not pay their arrears
have always been deep in bad debts.   8

The harmless deer have gone into decay
since enclosures prevent their access to oats,
and naughty Skyemen keep chasing them with dogs
until they will be drowned in a pit.   12

Though they lost the straths, they had the
        neck to complain,
when the landlords were being so generous;
instead of sending them overseas to distant lands,
they received the shore as their estate.   16

These disdainful fools, not content with limpets,
were impoverished by the extent of their arrogance,
when the highest nobles to be found in the place
will live on potatoes and scraps.   20

The ocean lay before them in calm and in storm,
where they could get employment and livelihood;
and the factor would not come from Martinmas
to extract his rents from them – until May Day.   24

Since they were allowed to live on the rocks and moss
there was plenty of reason for gratitude,
and if they could use it, they had the light of the sun,
and the moon and the stars in late evening.   28

They got all of that free from the kindly landlord,
although he could have sold it for money,
since he had as much right to it as he had to the land –
it was the order of Providence that created them.   32

If they had been alive in Pharaoh's time
and had been in subjection to him as slaves,
they might have had a reason or two for leaving him –
those days were meant as a warning to others.   36

37. Song on Ben Lee

Mary MacPherson

Give thanks to the people
under the rule of the Queen,
who made the law so secure
that we will not lose Ben Lee.   4

Bear greetings with gladness
to the farmers of Valtos,
who were first in the battle
and did not flinch in the fray.   8

Take a blessing to 'Parnell'
who vanquished the 'Satan',
so that he will never be seen
coming near to the land.   12

When he came the first time
with fifty 'angels' beside him,
he put five folk in irons
by the sides of Ben Lee.   16

Those heroes most noble
who were never in a fracas
had their wrists put in handcuffs,
wrapped hard round their fists.   20

They were carried by the 'angels'
and cast into a dungeon,
and despite their enemies' power,
they own the land and Ben Lee.   24

And the kindliest women
of the most mannerly bearing,
their skulls were split open
on the banks of Ben Lee.   28

Though the sight was horrifying,
with blood congealing on rushes
because of the batons of the wretches –
they did not get Ben Lee.   32

That is the truly attractive mountain
which gave the Queen a happy outcome,
and there is no mountain in Scotland
today as famed as Ben Lee.   36

Many an eye will moisten,
travelling over by steamship,
as people look with affection
on the braes of Ben Lee.   40

And although the Cuillin and Glamaig
are among the loveliest mountains,
their history will rank no higher
than the foot-slopes of Ben Lee.   44

Now, kindly *Highlander*,
the pillar of the tenants,
bear overseas the story
that is told in our land.   48

Send a message to Edinburgh,
to the opponent of injustice,
and tell all his penmen
of the feat done by Ben Lee.   52

Send a letter with solace
to the paper in Oban,
which supported us always,
since the first day of the fray.   56

It took up the tenants' banner,
and bore it on its shoulders,
and when the struggle began,
it was raised in the wind.   60

It was raised in our favour
on the hills that were highest,
to maintain the Gaels' morale
as does the skirl of the pipes.   64

Send a reveille to Glasgow
to the *Weekly Post*,

and the energetic Cameron
will gladly give you its substance.   68

Send word to the Glendale folk
who suffered injustice in the battle,
and to my friend, MacPherson,
who did not weaken in the fight.   72

Prison is a fine college –
I have long had such knowledge –
but truth will always triumph,
despite the devices of fools.   76

The Calton is a fine college;
it gave the Martyr good schooling,
although some have caused him anguish
because of the pain in their hearts.   80

Now, my dear crofters,
be mindful of MacInnes,
and be glad to hear mention
of that genial, fine man.   84

Although he has left our streets
with his warm-hearted wife,
she is happy in Vallay
going to the shieling with the calves.   88

It is the petition and prayer
of each poor person near her
that the fulfilment of their desire
may accompany her for ever.   92

38. Elegy-Song on Ivory

Mary MacPherson

In the century gone past, when landlordism trampled on every man, a certain person named the Coward Ivory distinguished himself on the side of the oppression, especially against widows, orphans and infants. He was named thus because everyone knew that he was despicable from the womb and anointed as a rogue. When it was reported that this timid coward had been immersed in a black pool, a little deeper than his neck, with a forester's (?) halter round his gullet and a turf on top of him, in the Mòinteach Mhòr, some distance north of Ceann Loch Chaluim Chille, Mary of the Songs from the Braes of Trotternish sang the following elegy:

I heard a story
on a very happy note,
and were it not true, it would be a hard blow,
that the mean Coward
had been stuffed in a hole
without a board or a rag fixed round him.   6

Blessed be the hand
that tightened the knot,
pressing down the hard, surly head;
it put the bald-pated Coward
in a scanty narrow cage,
and no official or officer will free him.   12

Every old woman would hasten
with a light step,
and children would go in a rapturous race
to pull you from the mud
with a straw rope around your body,
to be dragged away on swift bier-poles.   18

Every floor under roof-trees
will be swept smoothly;
musicians will make a joyful noise;
dancing will be seen on every field,
and music will be heard on every height
where the coward acted as a worthless pursuer.   24

A soldier, supposedly;
he was to be seen in action
only on a dung-hill or on grey muck-heaps;
he was a spectre haunting children
and women at night,
until he disgusted Europe.   30

He was the dregs of every sediment
and the curse of the people;
a noose on a hempen rope
was placed about the scraggy, thin neck,
under the wicked-looking chin,
and tightened about his sharp gullet.   36

A grey stone will certainly be placed above you
which will record every one of your iniquitous bribes,
and how you sold your entire reputation
for a little booty,
for the sake of your corrupt ground,
exactly like Judas.   42

39. Ivory and the Crofters

'Easdale Native'

Alas for my plight, here all alone;
how sad I am having heard this news;
what a pity that it has not transpired that Ivory
has been consigned to oblivion, himself and his kind.　　4

There was a sad story in the *Oban Times*
which pained me and moved me greatly,
that my fellow countrymen are locked up in prison,
while their possessions are being plundered by
　　landlords' authority.　　8

If the Gaels were now as they used to be
when Charles came over the oceans,
the Queen's army would promptly be put to flight,
and some of them would sleep for ever on open fields.　　12

Those who would have helped them died at Culloden,
the heroic stalwarts who were brave in hardship;
if they were with them, with their weapons in their fists,
the oppressors would be lifeless in the tussle.　　16

Ivory is the priceless man of justice,
who, in truth, did the fine deed we heard about;
every dunghill cock, and every hen that crouches,
and every egg, he carefully tallied up for the authorities.　　20

Every lamb and sheep, every cow and calf,
and the horned bullocks, he counted them too;
he included unclean beasts along with the rest,
and many kinds that were in the ark.　　24

The brave lad seized every spade and grape,
every cradle and child, and every article in the house;
fragrant pots that were in the corners
were scoured, and he put them to use.　　28

Is the law of the land not truly pitiful,
when it would seize, like slaves, infants two months old,
and value them at less than the dog at the fireside?
That is Ivory's justice in the land of the mountains.　　32

269

40. Sad am I as I Rise Today

William Beaton

Refrain:

Sad am I as I rise today
in the prison in Edinburgh;
sad am I as I rise today.   3

Red-haired Donald who hails from Haise,
walking there throughout the garden,
the white suit befits you badly,
although you were pompous at the market.   7

William MacArthur is such a silly fellow –
he is afraid of ghosts;
none of them can come through the door,
and not one board of it will break.   11

Iain the Merchant is better off –
he has an abundance of English and grammar;
he will tell the warder a story
to see if he'll get better attention.   15

William Beaton is such a cunning man;
although his English is not up to much,
he will always say 'Sir' to them
just as it should be said in English.   19

O Charles MacIntosh,
pity the one who saw you in such attire!
You would go splendidly in top dress
on your way to church on Sunday.   23

A brief word now about my neighbour's wife,
whom they took to the highest court;
when they observed her proud condition,
they did not dare to summon her.   27

Johnnie MacAoidhein is so sorrowful
since he misses Anna MacIntosh;
neither a shepherd nor Norman will get her;
he will have her all the days of his life.   31

Although my bed is cold in prison,
with a block acting as my pillow,
when I return to my dear one,
the cold will not be troubling me.   35

Although you have put me in prison
for standing up for the rights of my district,
I shall yet escape from your talons,
and I shall lie beside my first love.   39

O Big Màiri of the Songs,
what a splendid dram you gave me!
But if I return alive,
you will get five in return for that one.   43

41. The Crofter's Lament in Prison

Archibald MacKay

Great King, how sorely pained I am
since they put me under lock;

since they put me under sentence,
so that I cannot see my sweetheart;   4

where I will not see my dear darling,
the kindly girl of the curling hair.

If I had not gone to Caolvin,
I would not now be separated from my people.   8

I am resting on my elbow in prison;
I am alone, and I lack tobacco;

on the inside of an iron gate –
this is the year I had no desire to see.   12

My blessings upon you, Laird of Carnan;
I would be overjoyed to see you.

It was early on Thursday
that I saw your appearance, and observed you closely;   16

your two cheeks as white as a seagull
that were once like the bright-red rowan.

But we will leave prison and go home,
and we will never return to the Calton.   20

42. To Donald MacCallum

Murdo MacLean

Refrain:

> Donald MacCallum is
> the worthy reverend man;
> your name is now cherished
> > throughout Europe's land.   4

I will make a start on a ditty
in the house with the windows,
to the lovely minister
> who is in the Land of MacLeod.   8

What a pity you came to
the region of Waternish,
among weak-kneed people
> who would not stand up for justice.   12

Although you gave them more courage,
their heart has been frightened;
fear of the Captain
> has deeply entered their flesh.   16

And the Free Church ministers
will not take our side;
if they get people's possessions,
> they are happy enough.   20

To keep company with landlords
is all that they aim for;
they would not put up with a pauper
> on the face of the earth.   24

They care not for poor folk,
seeing them with their sacks,
going up to their doors
> to look for their food.   28

But a blessing on the hero
who made bravery his custom,
who would go down to England
    and plead for our rights.   32

Though you should be buried
with a nettle before your grave,
your bravery would be remembered –
    and you are not a large man.   36

And that refined clergyman
who is out by Strontian,
he is as loyal
    as any man who has life.   40

My blessing goes heartily
to the two of you jointly,
brave men of the country
    who would not refuse me my food.   44

43. The Old Man of Eishken

Rev. Donald MacCallum

'My rule extends
over all that I see,'
said the Old Man of Eishken,
  'both peatland and hill'.   4
That he spoke the truth
has broken my heart,
and has caused this country
  to shiver with chill.   8

'Out from the Shieling
where there were those heroes
who made a meal
  of my trout and deer,   12
as far as Kebbock
I control the Park
which is now a wasteland
  kept by my key.   16

'My rule extends
over all that I see,
from the side of Loch Seaforth,
  every single pace,   20
as far as the limits
imposed by the ocean,
on the far side of the Sìthean,
  every sod and space.   24

'For the son of the Gael
whom I have displaced
by giving more payment
  to the lord of the field,   28
it is futile arrogance
to try to expel me,
when the Queen's own army
  is my sturdy shield.   32

'My rule extends
as far as I see
in the lovely land
    of fairest shape;   36
no one lives there
but little fairies
without guile or hatred
    who neither plant nor reap.   40

'[I rule] those beautiful mountains
with their rivers pouring
down plain and corrie
    in healthy spate;   44
their peaks are clouded
but their brows bear proudly
the crown of glory
    that age cannot efface.   48

'My rule extends
over all that I see,
with lads aplenty
    to do my will,   52
and who consign to prison
each one who ventures
without written permission
    up the face of the hill.   56

'As for those fellows
who were so feckless
as to come in range
    of the holy place,   60
they will have no homesteads
for all their lifetimes,
and will bear Cain's marking
    on every face.   64

'My rule extends
over all that I see,
and every breath ceases
    whenever I say;   68

if these vagrants
whose ways are aimless
do not see my notice,
    they may suffer pain.   72

'If the main highways
will not suffice them
without invading the moorland
    to trouble the deer,   76
as it is my privilege
to observe their antlers,
if their blood is spilt,
    on their heads let it be.   80

'My rule extends
as far as I see,
and my devices
    will teach all men   84
what a waste of effort
it is to fight me,
who gave a three-fold rental
    for these cold bens.   88

'These shameless rascals
who went without asking
to kill off harshly
    the red-coated deer,   92
will plant no potatoes
in the quiet corries
nor rear any cattle
    in green-grassed fields.   96

'My rule extends
over all that I see',
said the Old Man of Eishken,
    'both peatland and moor;   100
and I give good reason
to this land's people
to destroy the deer forests
    that have made them poor.'   104

Throughout his lifetime
he will be established,
like a glittering idol,
    in splendid style;　　　　　　　　　　108
but we have stalwarts
who will not falter,
or bend their knee
    before his pomp and pride.　　　　　　112

44. The Deer Drive

We rose early in the morning –
driven by some desperation –
to bring down, with sharp aim,
the deer from the mountain tops.   4

We set out on Tuesday
with banners and with weapons;
the day was bright and favourable,
as we can tell you readily.   8

Each man with his gun loaded ready
climbed the high hills,
and when a bellowing stag was seen,
it was struck down forcibly.   12

We killed them in their hundreds,
we flayed them splendidly,
and we ate them in orderly fashion,
with generous portions, deftly.   16

We are certainly not robbers,
as lying statements claim;
we are, in truth, brave people
being ruined by poverty.   20

Many days and many years,
harrassed by poverty,
we have waited without disorder,
under fools and chamberlains.   24

We got no thanks whatever;
we were thralls who had gained nothing;
they were set on banishing us
like foxes off the land totally.   28

Our wives and children
now suffer hardship;
their clothes are tattered,
and they are in need at every mealtime.   32

279

Our country is a wilderness
because of deer and white sheep,
and we cannot get sufficient on rent
to satisfy any of us.   36

But praise to the High King
who bestowed on us the hero –
Donald MacRae from Alness
is the honourable martyr.   40

Donald MacRae was the stalwart
who would not yield to the villains,
although they tested him painfully
everywhere, to the extent of their abilities.   44

You haughty little wifie
who say that you own Lewis,
it really belongs by proper right
to the majority who live there.   48

And since we have now found a leader,
we will not cease by day or night
until we win possession of the estate
joyfully and honourably.   52

GLOSSARY

Note: **The system of referencing provides, first, the number of the poem, followed, after the colon, by the line number(s) in each case.**

The following abbreviations are used in the Glossary:

adj. = adjective
adv. = adverb
compar. = comparative
conj. = conjunction
constr. = construction
dat. = dative
f. = feminine
fut. = future
gen. = genitive
impv. = imperative
lit. = literally
m. = masculine

n. = noun; or note (after line numbers)
nom. = nominative
part. = participle
pass. = passive
pl. = plural
prep. = preposition
q.v. = look under that word
sg. = singular
superl. = superlative
vb = verb
vb n. = verbal noun

àbhachd, f., sport, hilarity, good humour, 1: 17

àbhaist, f., custom; in idioms of the type *is àbhaist (dhomh)*, it is (my) custom, 1: 47, 98; 12: 20

a-bhàn, adv., down, 29: 19; 33: 12 n.

ablach, m., carcase; untidy thing, rag, 13: 71

acaid, f., pain, 37: 79

acain, f., moan, sob, sigh, 7: 23

acair, f., anchor, 18: 15

achadh, m., field, 2: 38

Achd, m., Act (of Parliament or sovereign), 17: 2

a-chaoidh, adv., ever, 9: 9; 28: 12

adharcach, adj., horned, 39: 22

adhbhar, m., reason, 1: 65; 12: 10; 13: 5 etc.; cause, 15: 25

àgh, m., virtue, 14: 82

aghaidh, f., face; *ri aghaidh*, in the face of, 1: 51; in sense of 'up', 43: 56; 44: 10

àicheadh, vb n. of *àich*, vb, deny, 29: 5

aigeal, m., depths of the ocean, the deep, 15: 93

aigeannach, adj., spirited, 22: 19

aighear, m., merriment, joyfulness, 10: 15; 11: 7; 22: 82

aighearach, adj., joyful, happy; with intensive prefix *ro-*, 38: 2

aigne, f., spirit, mind, 22: 12

àilgheas, m., pride, desire, will; unstable emotion, 7: 8; whim, 13: 14; proud condition (of being pregnant), 40: 26

àill, adj., pleasing, pleasant, 1: 106; 37: 42; *mar as àill*, just as one wishes, 8: 94; 12: 30

aimhleas, m., harm, misfortune, 14: 40

aimhleasach, adj., harmful, 14: 105

aimhreit, f., agitation, 32: 25; 35: 41; 36: 6

aimsir, f., weather, 1: 111

aindeoin, in phrase *a dh'aindeoin*, in spite of; against one's will, willy-nilly, 1: 128; *a dheòin no dh'aindeoin*, willy-nilly, come what may, 29: 11

aois, f., old age, 18: 13

aom, vb, incline, yield, 16: 56; but also applied to mental process, 'incline to a particular view', 22: 61

Aonadh, m., Union (of Great Britain and Ireland), 32: 17

aonta, f., agreement, 28: 100

aontach, adj., of one mind, united, 16: 50

aontaichte, adj., of one mind, united, 20: 18

aosmhor, adj., old, ancient, 4: 17

àr, m., tillage; *fearann àir*, arable land, 33: 10

àr, m., slaughter, 15: 33; *faich' an àir*, field of slaughter, battlefield, 8: 74

àrach, f., battlefield, 14: 197

àraich, vb, rear, 43: 95; be brought up, 5: 14; 35: 2; vb n. *àrach*, means of upbringing, rearing, 28: 44; *tìr/dùthaich an àraich*, their native land, 14: 203; 15: 38

àrainn, f., district, area; *air àrainn*, in the vicinity of, 37: 12

aramach, m., rebellion, insurrection, 19: 11

aran, m., bread; *talamh an arain*, land that produces bread, 33: 2

àrdachadh (vb n. of *àrdaich*), m., uplift, elevation, 14: 7

àrdaich, vb, raise up, lift, 15: 92; elect to Parliament, 28: 120

àrdan, m., pride, 14: 246; 16: 90; 18: 16

àrdan, m., small hill; pl., 30: 35

Ard-rìgh, m., high king, i.e. God, 42: 37

arm, m., weapon; pl., 14: 190; *arm-cogaidh*, weapon of war; pl., 16: 19

armachd, f., weapons, arms, 36: 2; 44: 6

armaichte, adj., armed, equipped with weapons, 20: 20

armailt, f., army, 34: 31

àrmann, m., hero; pl., 13: 3; 43: 10; gen. pl., 14: 179; 15: 55 etc.

àros, m., dwelling, palace, 14: 3

asal, f., ass, 2: 18

asgaidh, f., gift; *an asgaidh*, as a gift, free, 36: 29

a-sìos, adv., down; with vb, *thoir*, and directional object, 'make one's way

to', as in 3: 36, 'the sun made her way down into the ocean'

astar, m., distance, space, 18: 31; 38: intro.; speed, 20: 3

at, vb, swell, 15: 81

atharnach, f., ground from which potatoes or turnips have been lifted, 21: 15

athchuing, f., prayer, 37: 89

bà, used for the sake of internal rhyme in place of *bò*, the usual gen. pl. of *bò*, cow, 35: 27

bac, vb, prohibit, 22: 69

bacach, adj., causing delay or hindrance, 22: 38

bagradh, m., threat, 22: 75

baidealach, m., battlement, tower; used (perhaps ironically) of towers of ruin, pl., 14: 196

bàidheil, adj., kindly disposed, warmhearted, 16: 10; 31: 2; 32: 32 etc.

baigear, m., beggar, 26: 16

baile, m., village, township, 11: 16; pl., 8: 62

bàillidh, m., factor, bailiff, 10: 2; 14: 163; 22: 49 etc.

bàir, f., goal (in a game), 8: 92

bàirich, f., lowing, bellowing, 44: 11

bàirlig, vb, serve with an eviction notice, 21: 2

bàirlinn, f. (‹Eng. *warning*), eviction notice, 18: title, 1; 19: 3; pl., 14: 243

bàirneach, m., limpet; pl. *bàirnich*, 36: 17

bàirnigeadh, variant of *bàirligeadh* (vb n. of *bàirlig*, q.v.), m., eviction notice; pl., 13: 13

balbh, adj., silent, speechless, 8: 78

ball, m., item, article, 39: 26

balla-cuain, m., an ocean wall, a break-water, 35: 6 n.

banais, f., wedding, 1: 41

banarach, f., milkmaid, 5: 16

bann, f., bond, (legal) condition, pl. *bannan*, 22: 52

banoglach, f., young lady, 37: 86

ban-rìgh, f., queen, 37: 2; otherwise, *bànrighinn*, f., queen, 24: title, 5; 35: 3; 43: 31

bantrach, f., widow, 3: 18; 9: 15-16 n.; pl., 14: 29, 229; 38: intro.

baoghalta, adj., foolish, silly, 11: 23

baoth, adj., empty-headed, foolish, 15: 77

baothair, m., idiot, simpleton; pl., 36: 17

barail, f., opinion, notion, 7: 44

bàrr, m., top, point; in adv. phrase, *am bàrr*, upwards, 15: 92

bàrr, m., crops, harvest, 8: 110; 33: 36

barrach, m., brushwood, 1: 34

bàs, m., death, 1: 71; 2: 35; 3: 24 etc.

bas, f., palm of the hand; gen. pl., 9: 16

bàsmhor, adj., inflicting death; with intensive *ro-*, exceedingly lethal, 15: 44

bata, m., stick, 20: 11; pl. *bataichean*, 16: 5

bàta, m., ship; *bàta na smùide*, steamship, 37: 38

bata(i)l, m., battle, 14: 97; 17: 5; 37: 7; pl., 34: 48

bàth, vb, drown; vb n. *bàthadh*, 12: 70; 14: 173; past part. *bàthte*, 2: 49

beachd, f., opinion, observation; *gabh beachd air*, observe, look closely at, 41: 16

beag, adj., small; in idiom, *is beag orra*, they think little of, 1: 119

beag-chuis, f., disdain, 22: 93

beairt, f., loom, 27: 3

beairteach, see *beartach*

beairteas, m., wealth, 3: 25; 15: 63; 22: 85

bealach, m., pass between mountains, 3: 5

Bealltainn, f., Beltane, May Day, 17: 30; 36: 24

bean, vb, touch, 26: 20

beannachd, f., blessing, 3: 34; 37: 5, 9; 38: 7; pl., 3: 29, 31

beart, f., deed, work, activity, 14: 126

beartach, adj., rich; n., m., rich person, 18: 20

beatha, f., life, 6: 15

beic, f., courtesy, obsequious doffing, 10: 10 n.

bèist, f., beast, brute (in derogatory sense), 10: 13

beò, m., life, living; *ri bheò*, 28: 36

beòshlaint, f., living, livelihood, 36: 22

beuc, vb, cry, shout, roar; vb n.

beucadh, 15: 16

beud, m., injury, loss, 38: 3; in idiomatic sense, pity, 21: 24

beul, see *cliabh*

beum, vb, strike, injure; make cutting remarks about someone, vb n. 14: 140

beus, vb, sing the base parts (‹Eng. *base*); vb n. in pass. constr., 4: 4

beus, m., moral code, morals, 14: 216; pl., 15: 3

bhàn: see *a-bhàn*

bhòt, f., vote; pl. *bhòtaichean*, 28: 23, 25; gen. pl. *bhòts*, 28: 6

biadh, m., food, 1: 3; 16: 82

bialach, adj., talkative, plausible, 32: 73

biasd, f., beast, monster, 14: 120, 254; gen. pl., 14: 152

biath, vb, feed; vb n. *biathadh*, 14: 256

bìdeadh, m. (vb n. of *bìd*), biting, pecking, 13: 62

Bile, m., Bill (of Parliament), 33: 33

binn, f., sentence (in legal sense), 12: 2

binn, adj., sweet, 1: 55; 16: 37, 86

biodag, f., dagger; pl., 34: 45

biolair, f., water-cress, 35: 13

bior, m., skelf, spike, 18: 2

bithbhuan, adj., eternal, 8: 42

blàr, m., fight, battle, 12: 40; 30: 31; 35: 31; pl., *blàir*, 11: 34; 15: 21

blàr, m., field, open space, 34: 18; 38: 22; *blàr-spòrsa*, sports field, 14: 215

blàths, m., warmth, 8: 27, 49; 12: 24

blas, m., taste, 1: 104

blàth, m., blossom, 8: 30

blàthmhor, adj., rich in blossom, 35: 11

bleodhain, vb, milk, 1: 28

blianach, f., or possibly m., lean meat, 9: 26; cf. *blianas*, a lump of pale flesh; applied to a man with a large, fat, colourless face (Campbell 1958: 44)

bòcan, m., sprite, spectre, ghost, 38: 28; pl., 40: 9

bochd, adj., poor; used as n., m., poor person, pauper, 4: 14; 9: 15; 25: 11; pl. *bochdan*, 12: title, 1, etc.; *taigh nam bochd*, m., poor-house, 12: 7

bodach, m., old man, churl; pl., 15: 8, 9, 11

bòdhan, m., ham or thigh, part of the body below the navel, 2: 18

bogha, m., bow, crescent-shaped bay, 8: 41

bòidheach, adj., beautiful, 16: 87; 43: 41; superl., 24: 16

boil, f., rage, fury, 7: 18

bòilich, f., empty talk, 29: 13

bonaid, f., bonnet; gen. pl. in phrase, *bhonaidean cocte*, of cocked bonnets, 11: 33

borb, adj., violent, savage, cruel, 14: 38; 15: 42

bòrd, m., board, plank, 40: 11

botall, m., bottle, 32: 19

bothan, m., cottage, small house, 3: 7

bracsaidh, f., braxy; carcase of sheep killed by braxy, 1: 78

bradan, m., salmon, 26: 18; pl., 43: 12; gen. pl., 30: 8

bràighe, f., brae, upper slope, 2: 32; 13: 27; 21: 10

bras-charach, adj., swift-turning, 26: 18

brat, m., covering, carpet, 15: 94

bratach, f., banner, 8: 75; 10: 14; 16: 27 etc.; pl., *brataichean*, 20: 15; 44: 6

bràth, in adv. phrase *gu bràth(a)*, for ever, 3: 26; 5: 2; 9: 34 etc.

bràthair, m., brother; pl., *bràithrean*, 25: 28

breac, adj., speckled, 8: 101; dat. sg. f., *bhric*, 9: 4; perhaps in sense of 'pock-marked', 9: 26

breacan, m., tartan, 1: 79; gen. pl., 30: 1, 32; 35: 25

breac-ruadh, adj., red-speckled, 35: 16

breisleach, f., confusion, 22: 63

breith, f., judgement, 22: 38

breith, vb n. of *beir*, give birth; in pass. constr., 1: 112

breitheanas, m., judgement, retribution, 28: 81

breug, f., lie, 14: 46; 28: 32, 82; gen. sg. *brèig(e)*, 28: 80; pl., 44: 18; gen. pl., 35: 43

breun, adj., foul, 26: 31

briathrach, adj., loquacious, 32: 74

briathran, pl., words, 16: 76; gen. pl., 28: 39

brìogh, f., substance, 26: 9; 37: 68

broilleach, m., breast, chest, 14: 162; 15: 7

broinn (dat. sg. of *brù*, used as nom.), f., womb, 38: intro.

bròg, f., shoe, 13: 70

bròn, m., sorrow, 11: 15; 12: 10; 13: 5 etc.

bronnach, m., having a large stomach, big-bellied, 13: 65

bruach, f., bank, edge, 15: 100; pl., 35: 15; 37: 28; dat. pl., 35: 28

bruadar, m., dream, 2: 3; 7: 39, 41

brùchd, m., sudden rush, 15: 100

brùid, f., brute; pl., 16: 6

bruid, f., captivity, 14: 175

brùideil, adj., brutal, 13: 65; 14: 36

brùite, past part. of *brùth*, vb, bruise, 3: 32; 7: 28

bruthach, m. (but f. in Skye), hill, slope, 7: 2; 20: 14; pl., 37: 40

buachar, m., dung, 14: 222; *buachar mairt*, cow dung, 9: 8

buadhach, adj., efficacious; applied to stone with allegedly magical powers, 9: 31

buadhaich, vb, win, succeed, 14: 74; *buadhaich le*, work out successfully for someone/thing, 19: 12; *nam buadhaicht' e oirnn*, 'if it were won over us', i.e. if the worst came to the worst, 22: 14; vb n. *buadhach*, 28: 63, 67

buaidh, f., victory, 8: 94; 14: 189, 194; 16: 68 etc. *thoir buaidh air/anns*, win a victory over/in, 19: 8; 28: 15; 34: 46 etc.; influence, effect, 9: 30; see also *don-bhuaidh*; natural power, quality; pl. *buaidhean*, 8: 27; *buadhan*, mental powers, 22: 10

buaidh-cheòlach, adj., exultant, making victory-music, 38: 21

buail, vb, strike, strike a blow at, attack, 22: 21; vb n., 5: 8

buaile, f., fold for sheep or cattle, 1: 25; 5: 15; 11: 31 etc.; pl. *buailtean*, 3: 28; 8: 60

buailtean, m., flail (for threshing corn), 20: 11

buain, vb, reap, 21: 19; 28: 35; 43: 40; vb n., 8: 84; *'s na bhuaineadh iad*, from which they were taken, i.e.

from which they sprang, 28: 59

buaintich, probably a variant of *buannaich*, vb, win, obtain, 4: 30

buair, vb, trouble, cause worry to; vb n. *buaireadh*, in pass. constr., 35: 49; *gam/ga mo bhuaireadh*, causing me anxiety, 11: 10; 22: 11, 99; past part. *buairte*, 22: 12

buaireas, m., trouble-making, contention, 3: 20

buaireasach, adj., contentious, liable to cause trouble, 14: 113; 17: 12

buan, adj., long-lasting, 11: 19; 24: 5; 32: 10, 12; *gu buan*, for ever, 14: 14

buannachd, f., profit, gain: 44: 26

buannaich vb, win, obtain possession of, 44: 51; vb n. *buannachd*, 3: 26

buar, m., cattle, 8: 13

buidhe, adj., yellow; applied to sheep, perhaps because of effect of tarsmearing, 5: 18 n.

buil, f., effect; *bidh a' bhuil orra*, the effect will be seen on them, 25: 32

buileach, adv., completely, totally, 25: 22; 32: 41; 44: 28

buille, f., blow, 15: 87; 44: 12

buin, vb, belong to, have to do with, 25: 16; 28: 34; 30: 43 etc.; take to do with, deal with, 14: 211; 15: 4

bun, m., base; foot of a hill, 1: 32

bun-daingeann, m., foundation, 15: 89, 91

buntàta, m., potatoes, 28: 45; 43: 93

buraidh, m., fool, idiot, 36: 1; pl. *buraidhean*, fools, 44: 24

cabach, adj., giving short, curt answers, 34: 12

cabar-saoidh, m. (< *cabar*, beam of wood + *saoidh*, f., soot), sooty rafter of a black house, 20: 12

cabrach, adj., antlered, 26: 17

càch, the rest, the remainder, 1: 97; 30: 64; *thar chàcha/chàich*, beyond all others, 9: 33; 12: 58; *càch a chèil'*, one another, 1: 58

cagailt, f., hearth, 8: 67

caibe, m., spade with cutting edge, 4: 11; 39: 25

caidil, vb, sleep; die, 10: 13; vb. n. *cadal*, 6: 1

caidsear, m., cadger; pl., 1: 44 n.

caill, vb, lose, 7: 29; 9: 31; 37: 4

cailleach, f., old woman, 36: 4; 38: 14; 44: 45

càin, f., tax, surcharge, tribute, 19: 20

càin, vb, miscall, 28: 56

cainnt, f., language, talk, 4: 24

càirdean, m., possibly a diminutive form of *caraid* (see below), 1: 31 n.

càirdeas, m., friendship, 1: 126; 16: 38

càirdeil, adj., friendly, 14: 5; 16: 9, 91; 32: 33

càirear, see *càraich*

cairt, f., card, chart; possibly charter, in phrase *luchd nan cairt odhar*, 'the possessors of grey charters', 15: 99

cairt-iùil, f., sea-chart, compass; probably the latter in 18: 18

caismeachd, f., alarm, warning; loud message, 37: 65

caisteal, m., castle, 13: 46

caith, vb, spend, 22: 26; wear away, 43: 48

caladh, m., harbour, 8: 66; 18: 21; 24: 31 etc.

calaman, m., dove, 30: 54

call, m., loss, 25: 14; *air chall*, lost, 1: 39

callaid, f., wall, hedge; pl., 12: 61

calma, adj., brave, 16: 25; 18: 25; 20: 17 etc.

cam, adj., crooked, bent, 1: 14

camp, f., camp; probably in sense of 'military camp', 27: 11

can, vb, speak, say; in older sense of 'sing', 25: 2

cànain, f., language, 16: 37

caoch, adj., empty, blasted; *cnothan caoch*, blasted nuts, 1: 34

caoch, variant spelling of *cuthach*, m., madness, insanity; *spòrs chaoich*, insane sport, 15: 80

caochail, vb, change (for the worse); vb n. *caochladh*, 11: 18; 15: 50

caochan, m., streamlet; pl., 8: 33

caoidh, f., lamentation, lament, 41: title; as vb n., lamenting, missing the company of, 8: 54; 11: 11; 14: 202 etc.

caoin, adj., kind, gentle, 1: 83; 14: 2; 43: 44

caoin, f., exterior surface, appearance,

38: 35

caoineadh, m., crying, weeping, 18: 14

caol, adj., narrow, 38: 11, 34

caol-druim, m., small of the back, 1: 86

caomh, adj., gentle, kind, 14: 6, 137; 22: 5

caonnag, f., fight, struggle, 32: 11

caora, f., sheep, 3: 14; pl. *caoraich*, 3: 27; 8: 18; 11: 25 etc.; gen. pl. *chaorach*, 11: 24; 12: 19, 28; *caoraich-mhaola*, hornless sheep, i.e. non-Highland breeds, 12: 39

caorann, m., rowan berry, 41: 18

caothach, m., madness, 14: 106; see also *caoch*

carachd, f., trickery, cunning, 27: 8

càradh, m., plight, predicament, 14: 176; 15: 78

caraibh, dat. pl. of *car*, m., twist, turn, used in idiom *an caraibh*, in the vicinity of, come near to; *'na charaibh*, 2: 14; *'nar caraibh*, near us, 1: 116

càraich, vb, thrust, put (firmly), 41: 23; pres./fut. pass. *càirear*, 2: 36; vb n. *càradh*, 7: 12; 14: 251; 19: 27 etc.

caraid, m., friend, 37: 71; pl. *càirdean*, 7: 3; 18: 22; 19: 7 etc.

carbad, m., chariot, 30: 52

carcais, f., carcase, 2: 37

càrn, m., cairn, pile of stones; pl., 8: 82

càrn, vb, pile up; vb n. *càrnadh*, 22: 85

carraid, f., contention, quarrel, 37: 70

carthannach, carthantach, adj., kindly, compassionate, 1: 115; 14: 165

carthannas, m., kindliness, compassion, 14: title, 67, 145, 195

càs, m., plight, predicament, 12: 22, 38; 16: 44; 19: 7, 23

cas, vb, wrinkle up (of nose); vb n., 1: 88

cas-chrom, m., lit. 'crooked leg', the name given to the traditional foot-plough, because of its shape; used with implication of deviousness, in sense of 'crooked arm', in 19: 5

casgairt, f., slaughter, 14: 133

cath, m., battle, 14: 187; 36: 3

cead, m., permission, 43: 55

cealgair, m., deceiver, treacherous person, 30: 51; pl., 31: 18

ceanalta, adj., kind, amiable, 11: 11

ceangail, vb, tie, truss up; vb n., 2: 28

ceann, m., head; roof, 23: 15; *thoir gu ceann*, bring to an end, round off, 28: 46

ceannaich, vb, buy, 1: 68; 3: 25; 43: 87; vb n. *ceannach*, 1: 112; 31: 8

ceannard, m., leader, 27: 17; 31: 22; pl., 15: 57; *àrd-cheannard*, commander-in-chief, 17: 6

ceann-feachda, m., leader of an army, pl. *cinn-fheachda*, 4: 25

ceann-feadhna, m., head, leader, chieftain, 14: 49; gen. pl., 15: 45

ceannsaich, vb, subdue; vb n. *ceannsach*, 36: 34

ceap, m., divot, sod, 38: intro.

cearbaich, f., awkwardness, clumsiness, 34: 44

cearcall, m., ring-shaped fetter, 2: 25

ceàrd, m., tinker; in sense of rogue, 2: 1, 2

ceàrn, m., part of the country, district, region, 8: 105; 34: 7

ceart, f., right, 24: 23; *chearta*, adv., used to reinforce the equative *cho*, 32: 88

ceartas, m., justice, 12: 70; 16: 22; 18: 31 etc.

ceart-uair, preceded by *an*, adv., at this moment, 41: 8

ceasnaich, vb, question, interrogate, 13: 43

cèile, m./f., companion; *cuir as a chèil'*, take apart, break up, 12: 64; *dol as a chèil'*, going to pieces, 34: 56

ceilg, f., treachery, 18: 32

cèill, dat. sg. of *ciall*, f., sense; *cuir an cèill*, make clear to, give expression to, 25: 13; 28: 102; *gun chèill*, without sense, 14: 220; 34: 50

cèillidh, adj., wise, prudent, 14: 127

cèin (dat. sg. of *cian*), adj., distant, foreign, 25: 32; *bho chèin*, long ago, 14: 44; in idiom *cuir air chèin*, send into a distant land, 15: 29

cèireadh, m., waxing, i.e., a wax seal, 4: 31

ceist, f., term of endearment; dear one, 29: 8

Cèitean, m., month of May, 4: 1

ceò, m., mist, 7: 30

ceòl, m., music, 1: 77; 13: 29; 35: 28

ceòlach, adj., musical, 1: 114

ceòlraidh, f., the Muses, 14: 149

ceud, m., one hundred, 7: 11; pl., 14: 255; 16: 77; 44: 13

ceudna, adj., former; mar an ceudn', likewise, 28: 86

ceum, m., step, 28: 106; 38: 13; 43: 20; pace (in measurement), 14: 240

ceutach, adj., splendid, excellent, 15: 2

chaoidh, adv., ever, 28: 120; 40: 31; see also a-chaoidh

ciallach, adj., sensible, 16: 74

cianail, adj., sad, melancholy, 3: 2; 8: 108; 14: 199; pitiful, 15: 77

ciarghlas, adj., dark grey, 13: 66

cinn, vb, grow, 9: 9, 10; 35: 9; otherwise cinnich, in sense 'grow luxuriantly', 15: 56

cinn, variant of cionn, in phrase os do chinn, above you, 38: 38

cinnich, see cinn

cinnt, f., certainty, 15: 44; 38: 37

cinnteach, adj., certain, correct, 34: 25

ciobair, m., shepherd, 35: 23; 40: 30; pl., 1: 54; 28: 95; dat. pl., 1: title

ciochran, m., infant; gen. pl., 39: 30

cìs, f., rent, tribute, tax, 8: 100; fo chìs, in submission, under sentence, 12: 4; 41: 3; gen. pl. chìsean, 24: 22; faigh cìs air, bring into submission, 34: 39

ciste, f., coffin, 9: 21

ciùin, adj., calm, 4: 1

ciùinich, vb, quieten, 8: 4; 14: 35

ciùrr, vb, cause pain (to), 15: 36; past part. ciùrrte, injured, wounded, 43: 72

clach, f., stone, 17: 7; head-stone, 38: 38; testicle, gen. pl., 1: 100

clach, vb, stone, throw stones at, 13: 80

clachan, m., kirkton; kirk, church, 16: 46

cladach, m., shore, 8: 68; 11: 28; 36: 16

claigeann, m., skull, 6: 5; pl., 37: 27

clann, f., children, 38: 15; dat. sg., cloinn, 28: 44; pl., kindreds, 26: 10; clann daoin', humanity, 14: 112; 15: 78

claoidh, vb, exhaust, wear down, 14: 73; vb n., 1: 30

claon, adj., perverse, 15: 49; 14: 108

claonadh, m., deviation, 16: 55

clàr, m., board, 38: 6

cleachd, vb, use, employ; vb n. cleachdadh, 22: 50

cleachdadh, m., habit, 13: 77; 32: 6

cleachdail, adj., curly (of hair of head), 41: 6

clèibh, see cliabh

clèireach, m., clerk; pl., 37: 51

Clèireach, m., Presbyterian, 14: 141

clèith, see cliath

clì, adj., left-handed, awkward; ineffectual, 34: 48

cliabh, f., creel; pl., 1: 44; chest (of the body), 9: 24; 14: 134; beul a chlèibh, top part of his chest, 1: 75, 94

cliath, f., wooden frame, with meaning extended to apply to a variety of frames used on crofts, from waulking boards to harrows; fo chlèith, 38: 20, perhaps 'under the roof-frame'; air a' chlèith, on the waulking board, 8: 90

clisg, vb, jump with fear, be startled; vb n. in pass. constr., 42: 14

cliù, f., fame, reputation, 13: 68; 15: 2; 16: 96 etc.; praise, 10: 16

cliùiteach, adj., of good repute, 8: 74; 11: 11; 15: 40; praiseworthy, 35: 51; famous, 24: 21

clobhd, m., rag of cloth, 38: 6

clòimh, f., wool, 1: 68, 110

cluain, f., meadow, pasture; pl. cluaintean, 14: 188, 39: 12

cluain, f., shelter, 1: 3

cluasag, f., pillow, 40: 33

cnàmh, m., bone, 35: 18; pl., 2: 10

cnàmh vb n., withering, decaying, 14: 28

cneasda, adj., humane, kindly, 36: 29

cnoc, m., hill; gen. pl., 12: 36

cnòdan, m., gurnet (type of fish), 32: 55

cnothan, see caoch

cnuasaich, vb, consider, ponder, 14: 130; vb n. cnuasach, scrutinising, 22: 91

cnuimh, f., worm, 14: 249

co-dhàimh (< co, with + dàimh, f., relationship), close relationship, 25: 19

cog, vb, fight, contend, 28: 53

cogadh, m., battle, war, 1: 53; 15: 33; 16: 39; 36: 3

coibhneas, m., kindness, 12: 24; 15: 73

coibhneil, adj., kind, 1: 115; 16: 47; 30: 26; 32: 33 etc.

coigreach, m., stranger; pl. *coigrich*, 11: 19

coileach, m., cockerel, 32: 89

coill(e), f., wood, 14: 156; 30: 42

coimheach, m., stranger; pl. *coimhich*, 8: 94

coimhearsnach, m., neighbour, 25: 18

coimisean, m., commission (of enquiry), 23: 3

coinneamh, f., meeting; pl. *coinneamhan*, 18: 26

co-ionnan, adj., equal, 14: 238; 33: 17

còir, f., right, claim, 14: 160, 238; 15: 14; 19: 17 etc. gen. sg. *còir*, 107; 24: 13; 30: 46 etc.; pl. *còraichean*, 23: 6, 27: 14, 22; *còirean*, 25: 5; *còir-cheart*, proper right, 44: 47; *air chòir*, adv., properly, 22: 58; *seas a' chòir*, stand up for right, 28: 24, 27; 42: 12; *thoir a' chòir gu ceann*, bring justice into effect, 28: 20

còir (otherwise *comhair*), in phrase *a chòir*, close to, 30: 16

còir, adj., friendly, warm-hearted, 12: 14; 13: 30; 14: 167 etc.

coirce, m., oats, 36: 10

coire, m., hollow surrounded by hills, 43: 43; pl., 8: 25; 43: 94

còirneal, m., colonel, 1: 118; 35: 48

coisinn, vb, win, earn, 4: 13; 15: 20; 28: 69; vb n. *cosnadh*, 28: 62

colann, f., body, carcase, 6: 5

colaisd, m., college, 37: 73, 77

colg, m., rage, wrath, 14: 34

coltar, m., coulter of a plough, the blade that cuts the turf ahead of the share, 2: 15

co-luchd-dùthcha, m., fellow countrymen, 39: 7

com, m., trunk (of the body), cavity (of the chest), 35: 39; 38: 17; hull or hold of a ship, 7: 12; gen. sg. *cuim*, 13: 24

comann, m., company, society, 1: 106; 18: 25; 22: 44 etc.; conviviality, 11: 8; commission (of government), 24: 4, 6

comanndair, m., commander; pl., 12: 41

comas, m., capacity, power, 10: 3; 14: 150

comhachag, f., owl, 4: 17

comharradh, m., mark, 43: 63

comharraichte, adj., conspicuous, 38: intro.

còmhdach, m. covering concealment, 16: 58; clothing, 14: 79; used of prison clothes, 40: 21; vb n., 16: 84

còmhdaich, vb, cover, conceal, 14: 221; vb n. *còmhdachadh*, 13: 72

còmhdhail, f., meeting, *thig an còmhdhail*, come to meet, 21: 25

còmhla, f., board, plank, 9: notes; door-valve, 1: 107; dat. sg. *còmhlaidh*, 40: 10

còmhla, adv., together, 13: 17; 16: 45

còmhlan, m., company, group, 9: notes; 21: 26

còmhnadh, vb n. and n., help, 18: 29; 19: 5; 30: 45 etc.

còmhnaich, vb, favour, help, 28: 9

còmhnaich, vb, live, abide, 14: 14

còmhnaidh, vb n., living, dwelling, 13: 46; 15: 46; 16: 41; with lenition, 36: 25; *àite còmhnaidh*, dwelling place, 35: 20, 34

còmhnaidh, in adv. phrase, *an còmhnaidh*, always, 28: 32; 43: 46

còmhnard, adj., level, smooth, 32: 58; 35: 8; n., m., level plain, 8: 25; 43: 43

còmhradh, m., conversation, 1: 60; 7: 40

còmhrag, f., fight, contention, 13: 4

còmhraiteach, adj., conversing, engaging in conversation, 16: 48

còmhstri, f., strife, contention, battle, 14: 54, 118; 30: 14

compaist, f., compass, used for measuring land, 2: 41

companach, m., companion, 1: 99

cor, m., plight, condition, 28: 89

còrach, see *còir*

còrcachail, adj., made of hemp (rope), 38: 33

còrd, m., cord; pl., 14: 178

coron, m., crown, coronet, 43: 47

corp, m., body, 1: 78; pl. *cuirp*, 12: 44

corr-riabhach, f., speckled crane, 2: 19

còrs(a), m., coast, 8: 26

còs, m., crevice, hole; gen. pl., 14: 254

cos-cheum, otherwise *cas-cheum*, m., footpath, right of way; pl. *coscheuman*, 22: 69, 77

cosnadh, m., earning, means of living, 14: 103; 28: 38; 36: 22

còta, m., coat, 13: 16, 44

cothrom, m., opportunity, circumstances; *'S gasda 'n cothrom sa bheil sibh*, You are in fine circumstances, 22: 95

cràbhach, adj., religious, devoted to religion, 14: 131; 32: 47

cràbhadh, m., religious devotion, 14: 182

cràdh, m., sorrow, pain, 13: 5

craiceann, m., skin; of sheep, pl., 1: 110

cràiteach, adj., sorrowful, unhappy, painful, 41: 1; 44: 43

crann, m., mast, flagstaff, 4: 22; pl. *cruinn*, 7: 22; dat. pl. *crannaibh*, 20: 15

crann, m., plough, 1: 12; 33: 1

craobhach, adj., flowing, ramifying (of blood), 15: 22

craos, m., mouth of a beast, 1: 102

creach, vb, plunder; vb n. *creachadh*, 4: 27; 13: 78; 15: 63

creachann, m., upper slope of hill; pl., 8: 18

creathaill, f., cradle, 39: 25

creic, vb, dialectal variant of *reic*, sell, 1: 110

creid, vb, believe, 28: 79

creideamh, m., belief, religion, 14: 113, 117

creud, f., creed, 14: 48, 124; pl. 14: 139

creutair, m., creature, 25: 19

cridhe, m., heart, 3: 32; 9: 23; 11: 3 etc.

cridheil, adj., hearty, 30: 26

crìoch, f., end, boundary, 3: 38; 16: 81; 20: 22; pl., 37: 16; 43: 21; *cuir crìoch ri*, bring to an end, conclude, 3: 38

crìochnaich, vb, finish; past part. *crìochnaicht'*, 15: 95

criomag, f., a small piece of anything, 33: 35

crìon, adj., tiny, 43: 38

Crìosdaidh, m., Christian, 14: 129; 25: 11

Crìosdalachd, f., Christendom, 14: 119

criothnaich, vb, shake, tremble, 14: 225

crith, f., shaking, trembling, 25: 7; *air chrith*, in a state of shaking, trembling, 13: 35

crò, f., cattle-fold, pen, 16: 88

crochte (past part. of *croch*, vb), hanged, 12: 8

crodh, m., cows, 1: 26; 43: 95; gen. sg. *cruidh*, 12: 19

crodhan, m., hoof; presumably, hoofed animal, 17: 29

crodh-laoigh, m., cows with calves, 1: 9; 16: 88; 37: 88

crog, f., crock, old sheep; pl., 1: 69

cròic, f., antlers, 43: 78; *fear na cròice*, 'the antlered one', stag, 1: 19

crois, f., cross, calamity, 1: 1

croitear, m., crofter, 41: title; 37: 81

crom, vb, bend, bow, 43: 111

cron, m., harm, damage, 13: 52; 43: 39

crònan, m., croon, purr; hum of a bee, 35: 16

cruach, f., rounded hill, pinnacle, pl., 8: 36; stack (of peat or hay), pl., 6: 16; gen. pl., 43: 4, 100

cruadal, m., hardihood, toughness, 20: 10; 29: 20; struggle, 12: 45; 17: 20; 29: 9; 30: 18, 29 etc.; *ri aghaidh cruadail, ri uchd cruadail*, in the face of adversity, 1: 51; 22: 13

cruadalach, adj., hardy, 31: 26; 34: 42; hard to bear, 38: 3

cruadhach, see *cruaidh*, f.

cruaidh, adj., hard, 12: 3, 65; 29: 40; *cuir cruaidh ri*, give a hard time to someone, 26: 14

cruaidh, f., metal, steel; gen. sg., *cruadhach*, 34: 45

cruaidh-ghreannach, adj. (< *cruaidh*, q.v. + *greann*, q.v.), with a harsh surly look, 38: 9

cruas, m., hardship, 34: 8

crùbach, adj., lame, 32: ascription

crùban, m., crouching, 39: 19

cruinn, see *crann*

cruinne, f., the orb of the world, globe, 25: 25

cruinnich, adj., gather, 3: 13; 10: 6
cruitheachd, f., creation, 8: 49
crùn, m., crown, 35: 46; *an Crùn*, the Crown, 4: 28; 19: 13; 34: 32
crùnadh, m., crowning; *crùnadh mais a' mhìos*, crowning beauty of the month, 8: 9
cruthaich, vb, create, 26: 22
cuachag, f., neat young girl, girl with curly hair, 40: 34; 41: 5
cuaille, m., large staff or stick, 20: 12
cuallaich, vb, tend or herd cattle; vb n. *cuallach*, 1: 29; 11: 32
cuan, m., ocean, 3: 36; 7: 18; 18: 19; 30: 20; gen. pl. *c(h)uantan*, 15: 85; 24: 3; *cuan-luasgadh*, vb n., tossing on the ocean, 24: 29
cùbaid, f., pulpit, 27: 11
cùbhraidh, adj., fragrant, 12: 15; 39: 27
cuid, f., portion (of), 3: 28; 16: 49; 35: 29; *cuid na h-oidhche*, the night's portion, 'bed and breakfast', 12: 23; *cuid dhaoine*, people's possessions, 42: 19
cuideachd, f., company, 1: 97; body of people, 43: 38; group, society, pl., 25: 29; see also *teanga*
cùil, f., corner, nook, 1: 93; pl. *cùiltean*, 39: 27
cuilbhear, m., gun, musket, 1: 14
cuilbheart, f., trick; pl., 24: 25
cuim, see *com*
cuime, interrog., why, 28: 103
cuimhnich, vb, remember, 3: 23
cuinnsear, m., whinger, i.e. a kind of dagger, 15: 76
cuinnseas, m., conscience, 15: 74
cuir vb, put; plant, 8: 12; 43: 40, 93; vb n. *cur*, sowing, 8: 84; *cuir fo*, subjugate, as in phrase, *gan cur fodhp'*, 'being put under them', 28: 4; *cuir fodha*, submerge, 38: intro.; *cuir sìos*, subjugate, 14: 164; *cuir suas*, elect to Parliament, 28: 72
cuireadh, m., invitation, 13: 37; 34: 29
cuireideach, adj., cunning, 44: 16
cuirp, see *corp*
cùirt, f., court, 19: 25; 35: 44 etc.; Parliament, 28: 38; 31: 12; privilege, honour, 1: 37
cùis, f., circumstance(s), cause, source,

1: 23; 15: 98; 35: 41; matter, 28: 50; *thoir cùis de*, win a victory over, 16: 20; *an cùis*, with the intention of, 1: 90
cùl, m., back; *(cuir) cùl ri*, turn one's back on, 11: 16; 12: 47; 32: 5; in compound prep., *air chùl*, behind, 35: 51
cùlaibh, dat. pl. of *cùl*, m., back of someone/thing; used with adv. force in phrase *mo chùlaibh ris*, 'my back to', i.e. I turn my back on, 5: 11-12
culaidh, f., object (of something); *culaidh eagail*, object of fear, 15: 83; *culaidh uamhais*, object of horror, 15: 86
cù-lomhainn, m., dog on a leash (*lomhainn*), hound; pl., 26: 12
cùl-taice, m., support, prop; used of person in sense of supporter, 10: 4; 37: 46
cumasg, f., tumult, battle, 11: 38
cumha, f., lament, 10: title; 38: title
cumhachd, m., power, 37: 23
cùmhnant, m., covenant, contract; pl., 12: 60
cunnart, m., danger, 13: 61; 25: 14
cunnt, vb, count, 39: 20
cunntas, m., account, 1: 111; 16: 1; 25: 15 etc.; ship's complement, 7: 26
curag, m., head-dress or cape, 21: 12, 13
curaidh, m., hero, 18: 27; pl., 13: 36; 20: 17
cùram, m., care, worry, anxiety, 11: 6; 22: 27, 33
cùramach, adj., careful, watchful, 34: 31
curanta, adj., heroic, brave, 11: 37
currac, m., cap, 10: 10 n.
cùrsa, m., course of life; pl., 37: 92; ship's course, 7: 29; 30: 21
dachaigh, f., home, 16: 41
dàil, f., meeting; *rach an dàil*, go to meet; in military sense, 34: 28
dàil, f., delay; *gun dàil*, without delay, speedily, 30: 6; 34: 16; 39: 11; *air dàil*, on credit, 1: 69
dàimheachd, f., close relationship, bond, 30: 60
daingeann, adj., firm, 2: 26

dall, m., blind person, 3: 19

dalma, adj., bold, 30: 49

damh, m., stag, 26: 17; bullock, pl., 39: 22

dàn, m., fate; *an dàn*, fated, 15: 68; *na tha 'n dàn*, what is allotted, 6: 14

dàn, m., song, 11: 2

dàna, adj., bold, 15: 25; 43: 90; *bu dàna leo*, they had the audacity, 36: 13; with negative, 40: 27

dànachd, f., boldness, 43: 58

danns, vb, dance, 10: 10 n.

danns(a), m., dance, 38: 22

daoi, m., foolish person, blockhead; gen. pl., 37: 76

daoine, pl. of *duine*, the 'men' in Highland Presbyterianism, 32: 48, 52

daoiread, m., costliness; in sense of 'high rent', 11: 37-40 n.

daondachail, adj., humane, kindly, 14: 143

daonnan, adv., always, 11: 18, 23

daor, *daoraich*, vb, enslave; increase the rent (of land), 2: 2; vb. n. *daoradh*, 11: 39; see also *luchd-daorachaidh*

daorach, f., drunkenness, 21: 18

daormann, m., dwarf; pl., 15: 55

daorsa, f., thralldom, slavery, bondage, 16: 21

da-rìribh, adv., indeed, 39: 29; in earnest, 17: 5; 28: 101

dathte, adj., coloured, 41: 18

dealaich, vb, separate, part company, 31: 4

dealbh, f., picture; plan, 23: 8

dealbh, vb, design, plan, 14: 47; 36: 32

dealbhach, adj., beautiful, shapely, 37: 33

dealt, m., dew, 8: 22

Deamhan, m., Devil, 2: 40

deann, f., haste, speed, 34: 56; *deann-ruith*, running at full speed, 25: 15

deanntag, f., variant form of *feanntag*, q.v.

dearbh, in adv. *gu dearbh*, indeed, 12: 10

dearbh, vb , prove, demonstrate, 16: 28; 22: 45; 32: 62 etc.

dearg, adj., red, 35: 10

dearmad, m., act of forgetting, neglect, 16: 31; 31: 17

deas, adj., ready, 18: 8

deasbair, m., disputer, debater, 14: 139

deilbh, vb, warp or weave in a loom, 27: 3

dèilidh, f., deal plank, 9: 3

dèiliginn, f., dealing, 14: 135

dèirc, *dèirce*, f., alms, 3: 30; 4: 13; 12: 5, 21

dèirceach, m., beggar, 8: 97

dèistinneach, adj., horrid, disgusting, 14: 97

deò, f., breath, 39: 16

deoch-slàinte, f., toast to the health of a person, 1: 117; 30: title, 1, 7

deòin, f., will, desire; *cha deòin leat*, you have no desire (to), 14: 72; *dhar deòin*, of our own will, 22: 74; *a dheòin no dh'aindeoin*, see under *aindeoin*

deònach, adj., willing, 25: 4; 30: 13

deònaich, vb, grant, allow, 14: 149; 28: 30

deur, m., tear; pl. *deòir*, 14: 232; dat. pl. used as nom. pl., *deuraibh*, 14: 207

diadhaidh, adj., godly, 32: 50

diadhair, m., theologian; pl., 14: 117

dian, adj., intense, 14: 130, 139; 30: 28

dìblidh, adj., lowly, low, 14: 217; grovelling, obsequious, 22: 51

dìcheall, m., diligence, 22: 49

Di-dòmhnaich, Sunday; on Sunday, 16: 46; 40: 23

dìleab, f., legacy, 16: 70

dìleas, adj., faithful, loyal, 1: 126; 17: 6; 18: 23 etc.

dilleachdan, m., orphan, 3: 17; gen. pl., 38: intro.

dìlseachd, f., loyalty, 16: 40

di-moladh, vb n., dispraise, 4: title

dinn, vb, thrust, stuff; past part. *dinnt'*, stuffed, thrust, 38: 5

dìobair, vb, forsake, 34: 64; leave (the body), 43: 67

dìochuimhn, f., forgetfulness; *gun dìochuimhn air*, without forgetting, 1: 122; *tìr na dìochuimhn*, the land of forgetfulness, i.e. oblivion, 39: 4

dìoghaltach, m., vengeful person,

avenger; pl., 34: 26

dìomhain, adj., vain, useless, 43: 29, 85

dìomhanas, m., idleness, 14: 85

dìon, vb, protect, 16: 71; vb n., protecting, protection, 8: 76; 16: 18, 58, 78 etc.

dìonghmhalta, adj., stable, secure, 37: 3

dìrich, vb, climb, 43: 54; straighten, 1: 73; vb n. *dìreadh*, act of straightening, climbing, 3: 1; 20: 14; 22: 20 etc.; climb out of, 13: 64

dìt, vb, condemn, 28: 103; past part. *dìte*, condemned, 24: 34

dìth, f., lack; *(a) dhìth*, lacking, 16: 54; *gu dìth*, to destruction, perdition, 1: 56; *gun dìth*, unstinting, 16: 48

dithis, f., two persons, 1: 89

dìthreabh, m., desert, wilderness, 8: 10

diù, m., worth, value, 16: 7

diùc(a), m., duke, 4: 32; specifically, the Duke of Argyll, 24: 18, 22; 35: 3

diùlnach, otherwise *diùlannach*, m., brave man, hero, 27: 9; pl., 37: 17; used sarcastically, 34: 27

diùlt, vb, refuse, 12: 21; 16: 22; 42: 44

dleasdanas, m., duty, 14: 126

dlùth, adj., close, 32: 16; 37: 90

dòbhaidh, adj., stormy, terrible, 14: 168

do bhrìgh, conj., because, 38: intro.

dochann, m., injury, 15: 88

dòchas, m., hope, 24: 17; 28: 21

dòibheairt, f., wicked deed, 15: 71; pl., 14: 157

dòibheairteach, adj., wicked, vicious, treacherous, 14: 49; 38: 39

dòigh, m., way, manner, 19: 4, 6; 22: 92; circumstances, 16: 44; *air dòigh*, in proper order, 22: 10; *gun dòigh*, lacking proper amenities, 22: 6

dòigheil, adj., correct, proper, 40: 17

doineann, f., storm, 30: 20; 31: 21; 36: 21

dòirt, vb, pour, 43: 79; vb n. *dòrtadh*, 43: 42

dòite, adj., singed, burnt, 15: 62; thus, presumably, stingey, 14: 78

dolaidh, f., harm, loss; *rach a dholaidh*, go to waste/ruin, 36: 9

domha(i)n, m., earth, world, 15: 95; 32: 65

domhain, adj., deep, 15: 100

Donas, m., Devil, 18: 4; 34: 24

don-bhuaidh, f., bad influence, evil effect, 15: 60

dòrainn, f., pain, anguish; pl., 14: 87

dòrainneach, adj., painful, 14: 159

dòrn, f., fist; pl. *dùirn*, 37: 20; dat. pl. *dòrnaibh*, 2: 29

dòrnadh (from *dòrn*, above), vb n., boxing, 32: 44

dos, m., forelock, 1: 80; drone of a bagpipe, gen. pl., 13: 29

dragh, m., annoyance, bother, 43: 76

dream, f., company, group of people, 14: 28

drèin, f., grimace, scowl, 21: 9

driùchd, m., dew, 8: 52; 12: 16; 35: 12

droch-bheairt, f., evil deed, 3: 15

druaip, f., dregs, sediment, slops, 38: 31

druid, vb, close, 1: 107

duaichnidh, adj., gloomy, dismal, 22: 6

duais, f., reward, bribe, 3: 22; 15: 23; 28: 62, 71 etc.; pl., 28: 75, 108

dual, m., plait of a rope, 38: 33

dual, in phrase *is/bu dual*, is/was the hereditary property of, 31: 28; as was customary, 28: 13; 32: 7

dualach, adj., customary, 19: 4

duan, m., song, tune, 5: 16; 22: 2

duanag, f., little song, ditty, 1: 27; 3: 38; 11: 32; 22: title

dùbailte, adj., double, 29: 39

dubhach, adj., gloomy, 14: 129

dubh-dhòlas (< *dubh*, adj., black + *dòlas*, m., misery), utter misery, 15: 64

dùbh-ghlas, adj., grey-black, dark grey, 30: 22

dùbhlan, m., defiance, challenge to authority, 17: title; challenge to one's argument, 22: 22

dùdach, f., horn (for sounding), 20: 5

duibhre, f., darkness, 3: 37

dùil, f., element; pl., 8: 49

dùil, f., expectation, 23: 4; 24: 16

duilich, adj., sad, pitiful, 28: 89

dùin, vb, close; lock up, incarcerate; vb n. *dùnadh*, in pass. constr., 16: 8; past pass. *dhùnadh*, 35: 38

fàiltich, vb, welcome; vb n. fàilteach-
adh, 14: 6
fairge, f., sea, ocean, 8: 26, 77; 24: 11
fairich, vb, feel, notice (with the
senses); hear, 20: 7
fàisg, vb, press, squeeze; vb n.
fàsgadh, 16: 12
fàisinneachd, f., prophecy, 1: 11
fallain, adj., healthy, 43: 44
falt, m., hair, 1: 80
fa-near, in phrase fa-near do, in one's
intention, 32: 24
fang, m., fank for penning animals, 16:
8
fann, adj., weak, 12: 44; 14: 92, 116
fannaich, vb, weaken, 37: 72
faobhar, m., edge, blade; see 38: 36 n.
faoileann, f., seagull, 41: 17
faoilte, f., cheerfulness, welcome; used
adjectivally, 15: 48
faoin, adj., vain, empty, 7: 44
faondradh, m., wandering; rach air
faondradh, go astray, 43: 70
faradh, m., hen-roost, cross-beams of a
barn 33: 1
faraon, adv., individually, 22: 41
fàrdach, f., house, dwelling, 3: 9; 18:
10; 39: 26 etc.; pl. fàrdaichean, 13: 7;
14: 165, 200; 15: 48, 56
fàs, vb, grow; vb n., 16: 96
fàs, adj., deserted, overgrown, unculti-
vated, 1: 7; 11: 30; 12: 32; 35: 23; (of
effort), wasted, empty, 28: 51; cuir
fàs, lay waste, take out of cultivation, 8: 62; 11: 36; 28: 96 etc.
fàsach, m. or f., waste ground, wilderness, 3: 3; 14: 168; 16: 14 etc.; pl.,
15: 41; 16: 14
fàsail, adj., deserted, overgrown, 8: 19;
15: 51
fasan, m., fashion, 11: 18
fàs-choill, f., dense forest, 15: 42
fasgadh, m., shelter, 8: 97; 18: 10;
taobh an fhasgaidh, the sheltered
side, downwind, 1: 82
fastadh, m., employment, air fastadh,
employed, 21: 42
fàth, m., reason, 22: 41
feachd, m., army, 8: 73; 39: 11; 43: 31;
detachment of police, 34: 9
feadaireachd, f., whistling, 1: 24

feadhainn, f., collect. n., some, 28: 49
feàirrd, abstr. n. from feàrr, compar. of
math, good; in idiom chan fheàirrd,
is none the better of, 28: 42, 52
fealla-dhà, m., levity, make-believe, 19:
29
feann, vb, remove coat or skin (of
animal), flay, 44: 14; vb n.
feannadh, 11: 28; 16: 62; 26: 7 etc.
feannag, f., crow; feannag ghlas,
hoodie crow, 7: 20
feanntag, f., nettle, 9: 11
fearail, adj., manly, 18: 23; 35: 51
fearann, m., land, 1: 7, 120; 2: 42, 48; 3:
33; 7: 48 etc.; fir an fhearainn, men
of the land, i.e. landowners, 33: 8;
luchd an fhearainn, landowners, 24:
34; luchd fearainn shaoir, holders of
free land, i.e. landlords, those who
do not have to pay rent or burdens
for their land, 11: 21
fear an stiùiridh, m., the helmsman, 7:
32
fear-astair, m., traveller, 8: 98
fear-riaghlaidh, m., ruler; administrator, chamberlain, 13: 56; fear-
raighlaidh nan dùl, the ruler of the
elements, i.e. God, 15: 97
fearg, f., anger, 16: 30
fear-tagraidh, m., advocate, one who
pleads for or against, 37: 50
feart, m., power; Dia nam feart, God of
(all) powers, almighty, 14: 128
fèath, f., calm, 36: 21
fèidh, see fiadh
fèileadh, m., kilt; gen. pl. fhèileadh,
11: 33
fèill, f., market, 1: 46, 64; 40: 7; feast
day, thus Fèill Màrtainn, Martinmas, 21: 14
fèinealeachd, f., selfishness, 14: 61
feòir, see feur
feòirlinn, m., probably blade of grass,
9: 10
feòraich, vb, ask for, enquire about, 28:
101, 103; vb n., 1: 46; 16: 47
feuch, vb, behold, see; impv., 3: 14
feuch, fiach, vb, try, 1: 104; with ri, in
sense of 'make things difficult for',
44: 43; feuch nach, see that you are
not/do not, 22: 1

feudail, f., stock, cattle, 22: 67

feum, m., need, use, 1: 12; 12: 34; 22: 78; *dèan feum de*, make use of, 36: 27; *dèan feum do*, do good for, be of value to, 13: 19; *gun fheum*, useless, 12: 46; *is beag m' fheum*, it is of little use to me, 4: 9

feumnach, m., person in need, 3: 29; 12: 22

feur, m., grass, 1: 60; 13: 21; gen. sg. *feòir*, 8: 30; 22: 68

fiacail, f., tooth; pl. *fiaclan*, 1: 100

fiach, m., debt, 36: 7

fiach, m., value, worth; in phrase *as fiach*, having worth, worthy, 1: 99; *nach fhiach*, of no worth, 26: 7

fiachail, adj., valuable, precious, 12: 13; 24: 10

fiadh, m., deer, 26: 24; gen. sg. *fèidh*, 44: 1; pl., 1: 16; 28: 117; 43: 12, 76 etc.; gen. pl., 30: 8

fiadhaich, adj., angry, 5: 7; wild, untamed, 8: 21

fiadhain, adj., wild, 8: 29

fiadhair, m., lea land, 8: 109

fial, adj., generous, 12: 14; 14: 77

fialachd, f., generosity, 28: 5

fialaidh, adj., generous, 30: 7; 32: 75, 88; 44: 16

fianais, f., evidence, witness, 8: 86

fiaradh, m., deviating, twisting, 16: 75

fine, f., kindred, family, 28: 59

finealta, adj., gentle, fine, 42: 37

fion, m., wine, 10: 7

fìorghlan, adj., truly clean, pure, 14: 43

fior-shliochd, see *sliochd*

fios, m., notice, 17: 25; 37: 49; information, 1: 67; message, 8: 8, 16 etc.; *fios-fithich*, m., lit. 'a raven's information', i.e. supernatural knowledge or an advance warning, such as the raven appears to have about the availability of carrion, so that it arrives at the right time, 25: 13

fiosrach, adj., well informed, 16: 43

fireach, m., deer-forest, 33: 11

firean, m., righteous man, 28: 69

fireann, adj., male, 2: 18

firinn, f., truth, 16: 36; 24: 16; 28: 104, 109; 32: 17 etc.

fiù, m., worth, value, 32: 80

fiùran, m., hero; pl., 16: 17; gen. pl., 22: 7, 15, 23

flaitheas, m., kingdom, dominion; gen. pl., 14: 18

fliodh, m., chickweed; *fo fhliodh*, under chickweed, i.e. implying that the land has been over-run by the weed through lack of proper attention, 1: 8

fògair, vb, banish, 1: 50; 15: 24; *fògar*, *fògaradh*, see *fògradh*

foghainn (do), vb, suffice (to), 36: 17

foghanan, variant of *foghnan*, m., thistle, pl. *foghanain*, 9: 11

fòghlaim, vb, learn; teach, 37: 78

fòghlamaichte, adj., well educated, 22: 21

fògradh, vb n. of *fògair*, banish, evict, 11: 24; 12: 27; 14: 55, 156; also *fògar*, 35: 26; as n., m., banishment, eviction, 8: 93; 19: 2

fòid, f., turf, sod, 19: 1

foileadh, vb n. of *foil*, perhaps to be equated with *fail*, putrefy, but it appears to refer here to the absorption of putrefying liquids, 1: 85

foill, f., treachery, deceit, 14: 53, 160; 16: 90

foilleil, adj., treacherous, 30: 49

foirm, f., fashion, form; pl., 14: 46

fòirneart, m., oppression, 13: 42; 14: 53; 15:17 etc.; *fear-fòirneirt*, oppressor, pl., 14: 226

fòirneartach, adj., oppressive, 14: 101

fois, f., rest, 8: 98

fonn, m., land, 27: 15; 37: 24; gen. sg. *fuinn*, 8: 82

fonn, m., music, tune, 38: 23; pl. *fuinn*, 16: 85; *tog fonn*, vb, raise a tune in praise of, 29: 1; 30: 40

fòram (< Eng. *form*), m., form, probably used of 'top dress', 40: 22

fòsaig, m., pacify, quieten, 21: 36

fòtusach, adj., corrupt, blemished, 38: 42

fraoch, m., heather, 7: 42; 8: 18

fras, f., shower; pl., 7: 19

freagairt, f., answer, 13: 32

Freasdal, m., Fortune, Providence, 36: 32

frìth, f., deer-forest; pl., 22: 30; gen. pl.,

43: 103

frìthir, probably a variant of *frìthire*, m., forester, 38: intro.

fuachd, m., coldness, 29: 35; 40: 35; 43: 8

fuadaich, vb, banish, expel, 1: 16; 13: 23; 28: 115; vb n. *fuadach*, 11: 20, 29; 13: 11; 44: 27; *cuir air fuadach*, banish, 8: 69

fuadain, adj., strange, false; *luchd fuadain*, impostors, 15: 59

fuaidearnach, 38: 18, probably a variant of *fuadarach*, adj., hasty, in a hurry

fuaigh, vb, stitch, sew; past part. *fuaight'*, stitched, sewn, 38: 6

fuaraidh, adj., chilling, 3: 6

fuaran, m., well, spring, 3: 10

fuar-dhealt, m., cold dew, 14: 208

fuasgail, vb, release, set free, 14: 27; 28: 93; 35: 40

fuasgladh, m., release, 19: 28; 38: 12

fuath, m., hatred, 14: 68, 110, 152; see also *luchd-fuath*

fuathach, adj., hateful, terrifying, 2: 4

fùic, 38: 9, probably a strong, downward thrust; cf. *fùcadh*, waulking of cloth

fuidheall, m., remnant, 8: 108

fuil, f., blood, 13: 60

fuileachdach, adj., bloody, cruel, 25: 10

fuiling, vb, suffer, 13: 42; 28: 86; 37: 70; permit, allow, 12: 71; vb n. *fulang*, 21: 24

fuiltean, m., a single hair, 14: 205

fuinn, see *fonn*

fuirich, vb, live, remain, 44: 23; vb n. *fuireach*, 44: 48

furan, m., welcome, salutation, 30: 3

gabh, vb, take; *gabh le*, take to do with, 28: 111

gàbhadh, m., hard plight, predicament; pl., 14: 87

gàbhaidh, adj., terrible, terrifying, 35: 47

gadhar, m., hound, hunting dog; gen. pl., 15: 34

gailbheach, adj., stormy, 15: 90

gailleann, f., storm, tempest, 30: 20; 31: 21

gainmheach, gen. sg. *gainmhich*, 32:

58, variant of *gainneamh*, q.v.

gainne, f., lack, 32: 31

gainneamh, f., sand; *tìr na gainneimh*, 'the land of the sand', a poetic name for the island of Tiree, 31: 32; pl. *gainmhean*, 8: 46

gainntir, f., prison, cage, 14: 32; 37: 22; 38: 11

gàir, vb, laugh loudly, shout, 9: 20

gàirdeachas, m., joy, rejoicing, 14: 201; 30: 33; 41: 14

gàirdean, m., shoulder, 12: 46

gàire, m., a laugh, 7: 7; 10: 5

gàirich, f., shout, noise, 9: notes; 37: 64

gaiseadh, m., blemish, blight; used of 'failing' of the heart, 20: 4

gaisgeach, m., hero, 14: 29; pl., 14: 213; 16: 55; 22: 17; gen. pl., 14: 194; 29: 1; 30: 2 etc.

gaisgeil, adj., heroic, 26: 28

gal, m., weeping, crying, 9: notes

Gall, m., foreigner, Lowlander, gen. pl., 8: 69; dat. pl. *Gallaibh*, 1: 40; *dùthaich nan Gall*, Lowlands, 26: 1; *Gallda*, non-Gaelic, belonging to the Lowlands, 1: title, 75

gallan, m., young man; pl., 34: 13

gamhlas, m., ill-will, spite, 8: 69

gann, adj., short (of food etc.), 36: 18; with intensive *ro-*, 28: 116; restricted, with little room to spare, 38: 11; *ach gann*, hardly, scarcely, 1: 10; *nach bu ghann*, which was not in short supply, 14: 182

ganntar, m., poverty, scarcity, 3: 17

gaolach, adj., beloved, loving, 16: 51; with intensive *ro-*, exceedingly fond of, 11: 21

gaorr, m., guts, entrails; liquid contents of entrails, 1: 85

gaoth, f., wind, 7: 17; 8: 2; 13: 30 etc.; *sa ghaoithidh*, lit., 'in the wind', i.e. with his smell carried by the wind, 1: 81

garbhlach, f., rugged ground, 8: 25

garbh-lebhiàtan, see *lebhiàtan*

garbh-thonn, m., wild wave; gen. pl., 24: 9

garbhuaic, f., slimy sheep-dirt, 1: 101 n.

garg, adj., fierce, 14: 192

goir, vb, call, cry, 35: 14

goirid, adj., short, 12: 44

gorm-bratach, f., blue banner, 32: 8

gortach, adj., miserly, parsimonious, 13: 67

gortaich, vb, hurt; vb n. *gortachadh*, 13: 15

gràdh, m., love, 16: 36; *gràidhean ruadh*, red darlings, i.e. deer, 43: 92

gràdhach, adj., beloved, 35: 2

gràinnean, m., small quantity, 26: 30

gràinseach, f., grange, corn farm, 8: 26

gràisg, f., rabble, mob, 5: 6

gramail, adj., firm, with strong grip, 18: 23

gràmar, m., grammar, 40: 13

grànda, adj., ugly, horrid, 15: 3; 34: 27; superl., 14: 34

gràpa, m., farmyard grape, 39: 25

gràs, m., grace (in religious sense), 14: 146; gen. pl., 14: 20; *gun ghràs*, graceless, in the sense of being an infidel, 34: 26

gràsalachd, f., graciousness, kindness; gen. pl., 14: 25

gràsmhor, adj., gracious, 14: 2

greann, f., frown, 14: 19, 114

greannach, adj., surly, 14: 61

grèib, perhaps a variant of *grìob*, m., usually applied to a coastal precipice; it appears to form a compound noun with *amhach*; see 38: 34 n.

grèidh, vb, treat kindly or liberally; vb n. *grèidheadh*, 40: 15

grèim, m., grip, 13: 20; 18: 15

greis, f., short period of time, 4: 7

Greugach, m., member of the Greek Orthodox Church, 14: 142

grian, f., sun, 35: 12; gen. sg. *grèine*, 8: 56

grianach, adj., sunny, 8: 1

grinn, adj., neat, trim, well dressed, 11: 29; 12: 12; 37: 84 etc.; *sàr-ghrinn*, extremely pleasant, 15: 5

grìosach, f., fireside, 39: 31

gruag, f., hair of the head, 28: 16; *rach an gruaig*, take (a person) by the hair when fighting, 27: 24

gruagach, f., girl with long hair, maiden, 1: 28; 11: 31; gen. pl., 35: 28

gruaidh, f., cheek (of face), 41: 17

gruaim, f., scowl, surly look, 14: 114; 29: 43; *an gruaim ri*, angry with, ill disposed towards, 22: 1

gruamach, adj., surly, gloomy, 14: 129

grunnan, m., small group, clique, 35: 34

grunnas, m., dregs, sediment, 38: 31

grunnd, m., ground, 38: 42

guailfhionn, adj., white-shouldered, 1: 26

guaille, see *gualainn*

gual, m., charcoal, 14: 200

gualainn, *guaille*, f., shoulder, 17: 22; 19: 24; pl. *guaillean*, 28: 14; 37: 58; dat. pl., *guaillibh*, 9: 6; *an guaillibh a chèile*, shoulder to shoulder, 15: 27

guanach, adj., giddy, light-headed, 22: 84

guidh, vb, pray; *guidheam*, 1st sg. pres. indic., 'I pray', 30: 61; vb n. *guidhe*, 28: 29; in sense of 'cursing, swearing', 4: 19

guineach, adj., sharp-pointed, 13: 58

guth, m., voice, 14: 91; unanimous view, 13: 75

guth-gàirdeachais, m., cheer, jubilation (< *guth*, m., voice + *gàirdeachas*, q.v.), 30: 39

iall, f., strip of leather, thong; pl., 32: 83

iarann, m., iron, 2: 15, 25; fetters, 2: 10; pl., handcuffs, 37: 15

iargalta, adj., surly, 25: 10; 36: 7

iarmailt, f., sky, 3: 37; 8: 27; 26: 31 etc.

iasgach, m., fishing, 33: 31

imrich, f., flitting, removal (of house), 33: 19

ìngean, pl. of *ionga*, f., nail, talon, 13: 60; 40: 38

inneal, m., device; pl. *innealan*, 11: 23; *inneal-ciùil*, m., musical instrument, 14: 69

innibh, dat. pl. of *innidh*, f., bowels, intestines; used as nom., 33: 21

innis, f., pasture, 33: 23

innleachd, f., device, trick, 37: 76; pl., 22: 50; ingenuity, 43: 83

inntinn, f., mind, 16: 35; interest, 14: 11

iochdmhor, adj., merciful, 32: 30

iodhal, m., idol, 43: 107

ioghnadh, m., wonder, amazement, 16: 29; *gabh ioghnadh de*, be amazed at, 6: 2

iolach, m., shout, cry, 13: 47

iolair, f., eagle, 13: 57

iomaghaoth, f., whirlwind, 18: 20

iomain, vb, drive, 33: 20; vb n., 1: 95; 34: 19

iomall, m., edge, 1: 37

ìomhaigh, f., face, appearance, 2: 20

iomradh, m., mention, 37: 83

iomraiteach, adj., famous, renowned, 31: 13

ionad, m., place, 14: 94, 184; 15: 55; 33: 37 etc.

ionaltradh, m., grazing, pasturing, 33: 38

iongantas, m., wonder, 28: 1

ionmhainn, adj., beloved, 37: 81

ionnan, adj., same; *'s ionnan siud*, that is the equivalent of, 1: 45

ionndrainn, f., sense of loss or 'missing' absent people, 22: 34

ionntas, m., treasure, wealth, 15: 70

ionracas, m., righteousness, 28: 99

ioraghaill, f., contention, quarrel, 31: 15

ìosal, adj., low-lying, 31: 27; 33: 39; 35: 8, 21, 33; n., m., person of low estate, 32: 34

iriosal, adj., humble, 32: 32

isean, m., chick, 13: 57

ìslich, vb, lower, 17: 8

iuchair, f., key, 43: 16

iùl, f., guidance, steering, 30: 62

iùl-riaghlaidh, f., guide for ruling; government, 25: 9

là, see *latha*

labhair, vb, speak, 11: 37; vb n., speaking, 34: 1

lach, f., wild duck; gen. pl., 8: 38

ladarna, adj., bold, impudent, 43: 90

lag-tàimh, f., hollow of residence, resting-place, 32: 49

lagan, m., small hollow, 8: 11; pl. *lagain*, 35: 14; 43: 96; gen. pl., 8: 11

lagh, m., law, 34: 14; 37: 3; pl., 14: 235; 34: 55

laghach, adj., kind, nice, 32: 71

laghainn, probably a variant of *lomhainn*, f., leash for a dog, 34: 20

làmh-an-uachdair (< *làmh*, f., hand + *uachdar*, m., top part, surface), upper hand, 1: 49

làn, m., tide, 8: 46; full amount (of a glass), 32: 20

làn-dheas, adj., fully ready, loaded (of gun), 44: 9

lann, f., sword-blade, 18: 32; pl., 24: 23; gen. pl., 26: 28; 34: 40

laoch, m., hero; pl. *laoich*, 16: 55; 22: 42; 31: 25; gen. pl. 12: 27; *sàr-laoch*, 42: 41

laoighcionn, m., deerskin, 9: 27

làrach, f., site of building; ruin, commonly used in pl., as in 3: 8; gen. pl., 8: 85; site or 'ground' of a battle, 20: 10

las, vb, light, ignite, vb n. *lasadh*, 30: 36

lasair, f., flame, 2: 34; 10: 10; pl. *lasraichean*, 6: 12

latha, m., day; *Là Fheill Bhrèanainn*, St Brendan's Day, 18: 8 n.; *Latha Fhèill Màrtainn*, Martinmas, 36: 23

làthair in adv. phrase *an làthair*, present, in existence, 36: 33

leabaidh, f., bed, 40: 32; grave, 42: 34

leab-innse (< *leabaidh* + *innis*), f., pasture-bed, 8: 13

leacach, f., bare summit of hill, 36: 25

leag, vb, knock down; break up, abolish, 43: 103

lean, vb, follow, pursue enemies in a rout, 30: 28, 32; vb n. *leantainn*, pursuing a topic, 13: 73

leannan, m., sweetheart, 28: 88

leathair, m., leather, 32: 84

lebhiàtan, m., leviathan, monster; *garbh-lebhiàtan*, massive leviathan, 15: 85

leibideach, adj., shabby, contemptible, 15: 23

leig, vb, permit, allow, let; *leig do*, allow something to someone, 6: 15; *leig dheth*, let go, give up, 13: 77

lèigion, f., legion; gen. pl., 35: 29

lèine, f., shirt, pl., 23: 18; *as mo lèine*, lit. 'out of my shirt', i.e. with my jacket off, 4: 11; shroud, 9: 4; 10: 2; 14: 239

lèir, adj., visible, manifest, 35: 44; *gu*

lèir, completely, 25: 28

lèir, vb, torment, harass; vb n. *lèireadh*, 44: 20

leisgeul, m., excuse, defence; *ghabhadh an leisgeul*, here in legal sense of 'would accept their defence', 22: 39

lèith, gen. sg. of *liath*, q.v.

leòin, vb, wound; vb n. *leònadh*, 39: 6

leòn, m., wound, 7: 32; 14: 28; 15: 74

leth-bhreith, f., partial judgement, unfair decision, 22: 47

leud, m., breadth, scope, 18: 31

leug, f., small stone, 43: 24

leugh, vb, read; in sense of 'read out loud, proclaim', 23: 6

leum, vb n., leaping, jumping, 38: 14

liadhach, adj., ladle-like, or perhaps to be equated with *liaghach*, sharp-shinned, 2: 21

liath, adj., grey, 2: 17; 14: 205; 38: 27

linn, f., generation, 14: 185; 31: 31; 34: 42

linne, f., pool, ocean, 8: 3; 11: 4

lìon, vb, fill; vb n. *lìonadh*, 22: 27; *lìont'*, would be filled, 15: 96

lìonmhor, adj., plentiful, 3: 7; 14: 147; 34: 7 etc.; with intensive *ro-*, 31: 5

liubhair, vb, deliver; used of delivering legal papers, 34: 21

liuthad, adv., several, (how) many, 3: 16

loinn, f., fine sight, 34: 18

loinneil, adj., splendid, handsome, 1: 118

lom, adj., poverty-stricken, 27: 15; bare-headed, 38: 4

lom, vb, make bare, denude, 8: 105

lòn, m., meadow, 12: 16; pl. *lòin*, 22: 30, *lòintean*, 8: 30; gen. pl., 8: 58

lòn, m., food, sustenance, 16: 63; 42: 28, 44

long, f., ship; dat. sg. *luing*, 24: 29

luach, m., value, worth, 14: 10

luachair, f., rushes, 3: 12; 35: 13; 37: 30

luadh, otherwise *luadhadh*, vb n. of *luaidh*, vb, waulk cloth, 27: 4

luaidh, f., beloved person, dear one, 32: 35

luaidh, vb n., mentioning, telling, commonly used with auxiliary verbs, 15: 2; 22: 9; 34: 7; 37: 48

luaineach, adj., restless, 35: 16

luaisgean, m., tossing, 14: 205

luaithre, f., ashes, 12: 49

luasgadh, vb n., tossing, 14: 45

luathaich, vb, hasten, 14: 111

luathghaireach, adj., exultant, full of joy, 38: 15

lùb, vb, bend, 7: 22; give way in the face of adversity, 16: 21; 22: 17; vb n. *lùbadh*, 16: 75

lùb, f., bend, twist; *'na lùban*, in coils, 8: 101

luba, f., moorland pool, marsh, dub, 38: intro.

lùbach, adj., deceitful, crafty, 12: 59

lùbaireachd, f., craftiness, 24: 25

luchd, m., people, 13: 28; 28: 28

luchd-àiteachaidh, m., inhabitants, population, 35: 33

luchd-brachaidh, m., malters, 15: 61

luchd-cràgairt, m., awkward handlers, 1: 105

luchd-daorachaidh, m., raisers of the land-rent, 1: 120; see *daor*

luchd-ealaidh, m., musicians, 1: 42

luchd-èisdeachd, m., audience, 8: 99

luchd-fòir, m., assistants, helpers, 22: 44

luchd-fuath, m., people of hate, haters, 8: 110

luchd-lagh(a), m., lawyers, 13: 34; 22: 43

luchd-pòite, m., drinkers, carousers, 15: 63

luchd-reubainn, m., people of pillage, plunderers, 44: 17

luchd-tagair, m., those making a claim for or pleading the cause of, 30: 44; see also *fear-tagraidh*

luchd-teud, m., players of stringed instruments, harpers, 38: 21

luchd-tòrachd, m., pursuers, 21: 35

luchd-tuaileis, m., slanderers, defamers; used with *brèige*, gen. sg. of *breug*, f., lie, in sense of 'untruthful slanderers', 30: 10; see *tuaileas*

luchd-uilc, m., wrong-doers, 15: 39

luinneag, f., song, ditty, 1: 27; 8: 89; 42: 5

luinnseach, m., lounger, sluggard, 1: 32 (where it appears as f.)

lunn, m., pole for carrying a bier or

coffin; gen. pl., 38: 18

lurach, adj., beautiful, 35: 11; fine, 42: 7

lus, m., plant; pl., 8: 51; 35: 11; gen. pl., 35: 8

lùthmhor, adj., strong, agile, 35: 45

lùths, m., strength, 17: 19

mac, m., son; *macaibh*, dat. pl. used as nom. pl., 14: 197

machair, f. (but sometimes m.), level (usually grass-covered) plain, frequently extending inland from the shoreline, 35: 10

Mac Talla, m., the echo (‹ *mac*, son + *talla*, possibly from *a(i)l*, stone, rock, but assimilated to *talla*, f., hall), 12: 37; 13: 32; 30: 40

madadh, m., dog, hound; gen. pl. (older biblical form) *madraidh*, 15: 32; dat. pl. *madaibh*, 30: 52; *madadh-allaidh*, m., lit. 'wild dog', wolf, 2: 12

madraidh, see *madadh*

magail, adj., mocking, sneering, 34: 11

maighstir, see *tuath*

mair, vb, last, endure, 34: 47

maireann, adj., lasting, durable, 1: 123; 11: 19

mairg, in idiom, *is mairg (do)*, woe betide, pity help, 1: 82; 40: 21

maise, f., beauty, 8: 9, 43; 16: 95

maiseach, adj., beautiful, 15: 94; 30: 7

maisealachd, f., beauty, 14: 9

màl, m., rent, 1: 72; 11: 6, 28; 19: 19 etc.; *air mhàla*, on rent, 44: 35; pl. *màil*, 4: 15; 26: 7

mala, f., brow, 14: 36; of a hill, 43: 46

malairt, vb n., trading, selling, 15: 69

mallachd, f., curse, 3: 20; 28: 83; 38: 32

mallaich, vb, curse; past part., 14: 123

màm, m., breast-shaped hill; gen. pl., 8: 34

mang, f., fawn, one-year-old deer, 1: 20

maodal, f., paunch, stomach; gen. pl. *maoidlean*, 1: 84

maoin, f., wealth, 32: 65, 76

maoirneachd, f., office of being a *maor* (see below), 21: 20

maoisleach, f., roe deer, 1: 15

maol, adj., bald, 38: 10

maor, m., official; used of officers or agents who enforced the civil law at various levels, from the constable (probably intended in 13: 33; 17: 1) to the ground officer, 14: 248; pl., 19: 3

maorach, m., shellfish, 21: 19

map(a), m., map; pl., 23: 7

maraiche, m., sailor, mariner, 2: 44

marbhrann, m., elegy, 38: intro.

mart, m., cow, 1: 28

martar, m., martyr; *am Martar*, nickname of John MacPherson, one of the so-called Glendale Martyrs, 37: 78

martarach, m., martyr, 44: 40

màs, m., buttock; pl., 10: 10

masa, conj., if (it be), 1: 106

meachainn, f., discretionary power, 4: 28

meal, vb., enjoy; vb n. *mealtainn*, 15: 80

meall, vb, deceive, 28: 108

mealltair, m., deceiver; pl., 31: 23

mealltaireachd, f., deceit, 14: 55

meanbh-sprèidh, f., small cattle, 32: 56

meann, m., kid, 1: 15

mearachd, f., error, wrong; injustice, 33: 7

meàrsadh, m., marching, 13: 36

meas, vb, regard, value, 14: 95

meas, m., regard, esteem, 14: 177; 24: 35; 32: 28, 62

measail, adj., highly esteemed, 31: 13; 42: 3

meataich, vb, show cowardice, weaken, 37: 8

meidh-thomhais, f., weighing machine, scales, 12: 67

mèinn, f., disposition, 14: 218

meud, f., size, extent, 35: 32; *cuir am meud*, extend, extol, 34: 60; *rach am meud*, grow, increase, 25: 12; *le mheud*, with all that (there were), 31: 18

meudachd, f., size, extent, 36: 18

miann, f., wish, desire, 4: 6; 14: 106, 118; 16: 79 etc.

miaran, m., 9: 25; difficult to interpret with certainty, since there is a range of possible meanings, but probably to be equated with *meuran*, m., thimble, implying that the man's face is pock-marked like a thimble; see also *breac*

miath, adj., fat, plump, 14: 253

mì-cheartas, m., injustice, 18: 19

mì-dhìleas, adj., unfaithful, 27: 13

mì-fhallain, adj., unhealthy, 11: 35

mì-fhiùghail, adj., unworthy, valueless, 14: 95

mil, f., honey, 35: 15

mìle, m., one thousand; pl. *mìltean*, 12: 11; 15: 64; 16: 77

milis, adj. sweet, 32: 74

millsearachd, f., sweetness, confectionery, 12: 62

millteach, adj., destructive, 13: 58; 15: 43; 24: 28 etc.

milltear, m., spoiler; pl., 34: 50

min, f., meal, 1: 68; 33: 39

mì-nàdarrach, adj., unnatural, 14: 211

minig, adv., frequently, 33: 22

ministear, m., minister, 42: 7; pl., 42: 17

mìorbhaileach, adj., wonderful, miraculous, amazing; superl., 28: 1

mìorun, m., ill-will, dislike, spite, 8: 77; 14: 48; *luchd am mìoruin*, those who dislike them, 35: 35

mìothlachd, f., offence, unpleasantness, 43: 39

mì-riaghailt, f., disorder, 16: 73

misde (second compar. of *miosa*, of *dona*), the worse, 29: 33

misneach, f., courage, encouragement, 22: 41; 37: 63; 42: 13; in sense of 'audacity', 34: 1

moch, adv., early, 1: 57, 74

moch-thràth, adv., early in the morning, 41: 15

mòd, m., law court, 22: 22; *taigh-mòid*, m., court house, 22: 36

modhail, adj., polite, 37: 26

mòine, f., peat; gen. sg. *mòna*, 43: 4, 100

mòinteach, f., moorland, mossy ground, 13: 26; 16: 57; 36: 25 etc.

mol, vb, praise, 14: 249; vb n. *moladh*, 11: 34; 44: 37

molt, m., wedder; pl. *muilt*, 1: 63

monadh, m., high and rugged ground, moor, 6: 8

mòr, adj., great; used as prefix, *mòr-chuid*, f., lit. 'great portion', i.e. majority, 44: 48; *mòr-shluagh*, m., lit. 'great host, people', i.e. the mass of the people, 25: 25; *mòr-uaislean*, nobles, 14: 217

mòrachd, f., greatness, majesty, 8: 43 n.

mòralach, adj., noble, majestic, 31: 7

mòrchuis, f., self-esteem, ambition, 7: 36; 44: 45

mòrchuiseach, adj., proud, haughty, 14: 219

mothaich, vb, notice, observe, 12: 68

muc bhiorach (< *muc*, f., pig + *biorach*, adj., sharp-pointed), either the long-beaked porpoise or the bottle-nosed dolphin, 2: 16

mùch, vb, extinguish, 14: 33; 26: 27

muineal, m., neck, 21: 32

muinntir, f., people, 13: 1, 2; 15: 17, 19; 22: 35 etc.

mùirneach, adj., cheerful, joyful, 1: 47

mulad, m., sorrow, 23: 1

muladach, adj., sad, sorrowful, 11: 1; 15: 1; 21: 38; 40: 1

mullach, m., top, roof, 3: 9; hill top, pl. *mullaichean*, 44: 4; *air a mhullach*, on top of him, 38: intro.

muran, m., bent grass, marram grass, 35: 13

mu sgaoil, in idiom *leig mu sgaoil*, let loose, release, 31: 30

mùth, vb, change, alter, 19: 21

nàbaidh, m., neighbour, 1: 61; 40: 24; pl., 28: 53

nàdar, m., nature, 8: 43; 14: 8

nàdarrach, adj., natural, pertaining to one's nature, 14: 81

naimhdeas, m., enmity, hostility, 14: 33

nàire, f., sense of shame; *gun nàire*, shameless, 43: 89

nàireach, adj., shameful, 14: 209

nàmh, *nàmhaid*, m., enemy, 12: 26; 16: 20; 19: 8 etc.; pl. *naimhdean*, 14: 192; 37: 23

naoidhean, m., child, infant; gen. pl., 38: intro.

naomh, adj., holy, 43: 60

naomhair, m., holy person, minister;

pàirt, f., part, 18: 6
pàirtich, vb, impart, 14: 17
pàirtidh, f., party, 2: 31
pàisde, m., child, 39: 25; pl., 3: 11; 10: 11; 42: 29
paisgte, past part. of *pàisg*, vb, fold, wrap, 37: 58
Pàp(a), m., Pope, 32: 4, 51; papist, Roman Catholic, 14: 142
Pàrlamaid, f., Parliament, 28: 35, 47, 119; 34: 53
pasgadh, vb n., folding; in phrase *am pasgadh*, folded away, 23: 7
pathadh, m., thirst, 1: 30
peacach, adj., sinful, wicked, 4: 26
peanas, m., penalty, 15: 39; 28: 86
pian, vb, cause pain to, 33: 21
pian, m. or f., pain, 14: 86; gen. sg., *pèine*, 14: 99
pìob, f., pipe; pipes in stills, gen. pl., 15: 62
pìobaire, m., piper; pl., 30: 38
piseach, m., prosperity, good fortune, 32: 1
plàsda, m., plaster, daub, sticky substance, 21: 31
ploc, m., sod, turf, 43: 24
poca, m., bag, sack; pl., 42: 26
poiliosman, m., policeman; pl., 34: 9, 51
poit, f., pot; pl., chamber-pots, 39: 27
poll, m., mud, 38: 16
poll-mòna, m., peat bog, 21: 28
pong, m., musical note, 14: 71
pòr, m., seed, 8: 12; breed, 1: 124
pòsadh, m., marriage, 1: 41
prèisgeil, adj., preachy, loquacious, 14: 121
prìob, f., bribe, 38: 39
prionnsa, m., prince; pl., 14: 101
prìosan, m., prison, 2: 23; 22: 6, 37; 35: 36 etc.
prìosanach, m., prisoner; pl., 28: 93; 31: 30; 34: 63; gen. pl., 35: title
prìs, f., price, 1: 63; 26: 8
prìseil, adj., valuable, precious; used sarcastically, 39: 17
pronnadh, m., crushing, 13: 51
puinnsean, m., poison, 15: 72
punnd, m., pound (weight), 32: 80
rabhadh, m., warning, 36: 36

rachd, otherwise *reachd*, f., keen sorrow, 37: 80
ragaichean, pl. of *raga*, rag, in sense of 'newspaper', 29: 12
ragair, m., villain, rogue; pl. 34: 11
ràidhtinn, variant of *ràdh*, vb n., saying, 29: 4
ràmh, m., oar; pl., 18: 18
rànaich, vb, n., crying, shouting, 6: 13; 21: 37
raon, m., open field, plain, 2: 27; 12: 20; pl. *raointean*, 16: 14
ràp, 38: 24; cf. *ràpair*, m., noisy or worthless fellow
rath, m., luck, good fortune, 32: 54
ratreuta, f., retreat, 21: 21
reachd, f., law, rule, 8: 42; 18: 29; 19: 9 etc.
reachdmhor, adj., strong, robust, 34: 43
reic, vb, sell, 38: 40
rèidh, adj., smooth, 8: 2, 26; 14: 70; 28: 16 etc.; in agreement, 1: 90; *dèan rèidh*, make ready, 30: 11
rèir, dat. sg. of *riar*, m., pleasure, will, desire; *dar rèir*, according to our desire, 34: 54
rèis, f., race, 38: 15
rèisgneach, adj. (from *riasg*, *rèisg*, m., moor, fen; ley ground) sedgy, 23: 20
rèitich, vb, unravel, make smooth, 14: 35
reoth, vb., freeze, congeal; vb n. *reothadh*, 37: 30; past part. *reòt'*, frozen, frigid, cold-hearted, 14: 80
reub, vb, tear apart, tear off, 13: 16; 14: 63, 98; in the sense of ploughing, 4: 12
reubal, m., rebel, 25: 17; pl., 21: 43
reul, m., star; pl. *reultan*, 36: 28; *reuliùil*, m., a guiding star (‹ *reul* + *iùl*, f. guide, guidance), 27: 12
riab, variant form of *reub*, q.v.
riaghail, vb, rule; vb n. *riaghladh*, 14: 3; 15: 67; 24: 28; 28: 3, 38; 30: 6; 37: 2
riaghailt, f., rule, regulation, order, 18: 4
riaghladair, m., ruler; pl., 12: 25
rian, m., order, orderliness, 30: 5
rianail, adj., orderly, 44: 15, 23

riasladh, vb n. of *riasail*, vb, tear apart, 26: 32; harass, 44: 22

rìbhinn, f., maiden, girl, 41: 4; pl., 16: 87

Rìgh nan Dùl, m., King of the Elements, i.e. God, 3: 21; 7: 15

rìoghachd, f., kingdom, 1: 53, 125; 12: 1; 35: 18

rìoghaich, vb, rule; vb n. *rìoghachadh*, 43: 1, 17, 33 etc.

rìoghail, adj., royal, 16: 34; 24: 6; 35: 18

rìoghalachd, f., royal reign, 24: 27

rìomball, m., circle, crescent, 8: 45

rìomhach, adj., pretty, 35: 8, 25

robaireachd, f., robbery, 15: 75

ròd, variant of *rathad*, road; pl. *ròidean*, 43: 74

rògach, adj., roguish; superl., 14: 154

roghainn, f., choice; in phrase *gan roghainn*, lit. 'to their choice', i.e. just as they wanted, 32: 67

roghnaich, vb, choose, 15: 11

ròig, f., scowl, threatening look, 14: 248

roinn, vb, divide, apportion, 8: 57; vb n., perhaps in sense of 'discriminating', 28: 10

roinn, f., portion, lot, 8: 14

ròn, m., seal, 2: 17

rosg, f., eyelash, eye, 37: 37

ruadhan, m., red scum in water, 8: 35

ruadh-bhoc, m., red-deer buck, 1: 21

ruadh-chearc, f., grouse; pl., 14: 221; gen. pl., 15: 32

ruadh-mhadadh, m., lit. 'red dog', i.e. fox; pl., 44: 28

ruagarnach, 38: 24, possibly a variant of *ruaigear*, m., pursuer, chaser, hunter

ruaig, vb, chase away, put to flight; vb n. *ruagadh*, 5: 4; 6: 10; 12: 51 etc.

ruaig, f., rout, foray, 1: 52; 15: 28; 30: 32 etc.; a 'drive' (of deer), 42: title; *cuir ruaig*, to make a rout (of the enemy), 30: 28

ruamhar, vb n., digging, delving, 23: 20

rudha, m., headland, promontory; pl. *rudhachan*, 11: 27

rugaid, f., neck, 2: 19

ruigheach, m., probably in sense of

'handcuff'; pl., 37: 19

ruinnsear (< Eng. *rinser*), m., worthless person; pl., 15: 31

rùisg, vb, lay bare, strip (of sails); vb n. *rùsgadh*, 7: 31, etc.; past part. *rùisgte*, unsheathed, at the ready, 16: 5, 19

ruith, vb, run; used of wind, 8: 2

ruith-lùb, f., 'running loop', noose, 38: 33

rùm, m., room, space, 15: 8

rùn, m., wish, will, 43: 68

Sàbaid, f., Sabbath, 1: 57

sàbhailte, adj., safe, 18: 21; 24: 31; 30: 35

sac, m., burden, load, 1: 78

saighdear, m., soldier, 38: 25; pl., 34: 17, 34, 51; 35: 45; 38: 25; gen. pl., 34: title

saighdearachd, f., soldiering, 17: 15

saighead, f., arrow, 14: 64; pl. *saighdean*, 15: 43

sàil, f., heel or sole of shoe, 17: 11; pl. *sàiltean*, lower slopes of a hill, 37: 44

sàl, m., sea, salt water, brine, 8: 41; 10: 12; gen. sg., 7: 16; 43: 30

salach, adj., dirty, 13: 57

saltair, vb, trample; vb n. *saltairt*, 38: intro.

sàmhach, adj., quiet, silent, 14: 245, 252; 35: 1

samhladh, m., illustration, example, 28: 87

sanas, m., placard, notice, 43: 71

sanntach, adj., greedy, covetous, 3: 15

saoghal, m., world, 7: 8; 11: 17, 22; 14: 49, 65, 183; lifespan, 24: 5

saoibhir, adj., wealthy, 15: 77

saoibhreas, m., wealth, riches, 14: 39, 103, 230; 22: 85

saor, vb, free, liberate, save; in pass. constr., 15: 17

saorsa, saorsainn, f., freedom, deliverance, 16: 13, 59; salvation, 3: 27

saothair, f., labour, hard work, effort, 22: 87; 28: 51

sàr, adj. (preceding noun), excellent, 15: 5; 29: 32; 34: 61

sàradh, m., arrestment for debt, distraining; used as vb n., 2: 13

sàraich, vb, oppress; vb n. in pass.

constr., *sàrach*, 18: 20, more commonly *sàrachadh*, 13: 39, 55; 14: 183; 28: 43 etc.

sàr-mhaiseach, adj., truly beautiful, 14: 1

sàs, in phrase *an sàs*, caught, ensnared, 34: 8; in captivity, 14: 92; put in harness, 33: 26; get to grips with, set to (in fight), 34: 30

sàsaich, vb, satisfy, 44: 36

sàth, m., what fulfils or satisfies, 33: 28

seacaid, f., jacket, 2: 45

seach, prep., in comparison with, 28: 50; *ma seach*, adv., in turn, 35: 47

seachran, m., wandering; *air seachran*, 14: 108; 15: 41

sealbh, m., possession; *taighean seilbh*, houses possessed by (those who have left us), 8: 81; good fortune, 15: 68, but perhaps with the intention of pun on 'possession'

sealbhach, adj., fortunate, propitious, having a good outcome, 37: 34; 44: 7

sealgair, m., hunter; pl., 1: 13

seall, vb, look, show; vb n. *sealltainn*, in pass. constr., 17: 32

sealladh, m., view, prospect; 3: 6; 20: 13; 37: 29

seamair, f., shamrock, 8: 29

seamrag, f., shamrock, 35: 9

seanair, m., grandfather, 1: 38; pl., ancestors, 31: 28

seang, adj., slender, thin, 1: 22; 26: 14

searbh, adj., bitter, 16: 29

searg, vb, wither, cause to wither, 14: 21

searmonaiche, m., preacher, 14: 121

seas, vb, stand; stand up for, 5: 5; stand up to, 12: 45; *seas àite*, hold or represent a place, 28: 48

seasgair, adj., snug, weatherproof, 14: 166

seasmhach, adj., firm, steadfast, 16: 50; 24: 15

seicealair, m., possibly a variant of *seiclear*, m., flax-dresser, but here in sense of 'disturber', 10: 10 n.

seiche, f., skin, hide, 9: 29; 14: 61

sèid, vb, blow, fan (as flames), 5: 10; breathe out, 22: 75

seillean, m., bee, 35: 16

sèimh, adj., gentle, 8: 52; 20: 16

seinn, vb, sing, 1: 42; 11: 2

sèisd, f., chorus, 8: 90

seòid (pl. of *seud*, m., jewel), heroes, 8: 91

seòl, m., sail; pl. *siùil*, 18: 18

seòl, vb, sail, 11: 4

seòlta, adj., cunning, 22: 50, 60; 40: 16

seòrsa, m., type, kind, 13: 6; 28: 31; 39: 4

seudar, m., cider, 10: 7

seumarlan, m., chamberlain; pl. *seumarlain*, 44: 24

sgàil, f., shadow, 8: 53

sgairt, f., cry, shout, 1: 77; 14: 122

sgairteil, adj., vigorous, active, 37: 67

sgamhan, m., lungs, 2: 30

sgànraich, vb, send fleeing in terror; vb n. in pass. constr., 14: 174

sgaoil, vb, disperse, spread out, 15: 94; 31: 30; divide, separate, 16: 52; vb n., 1: 127; in sense of 'coming apart, disintegration', 4: 20

sgaoil, in phrase, *leig mu sgaoil*, release, 34: 63

sgap, vb, scatter, 8: 77

sgar, vb, separate; vb n. in pass. constr., 6: 6

sgarach, adj., capable of tearing apart, causing separation, 11: 17

sgàth, m., shelter, 14: 204

sgèimh, f., comeliness, beauty, 14: 20

sgeòil, see *sgeul*

sgeul, m., story, 7: 24; *an cuid sgeòil*, 'their pack of tales', 28: 8; account, 13: 54; news, 10: 1; *sgcula*, news, 1: 55; 7: 25; 20: 1

sgiamhach, adj., beautiful, splendid, 8: 5; 35: 11

sgiath, f., wing, 14: 138; wing of coat, pl., 13: 71; shield, 43: 32

sgiobalt(a), adj., neat; nimble, 15: 36

sgioladh, vb n., shelling, act of removing the husk from the corn; laying bare by stripping off the skin, 33: 18

sgìos, m., weariness, 7: 34; 8: 6, 98

sgìre, f., parish, district, 40: 37

sgiùrs, vb, scourge, deal harshly with someone, drive out, 10: 8; vb n. *sgiùrsadh*, 10: 12; 12: 31, 71; 13: 7 etc.

sgleò, m., idle talk, falsehood, 22: 94

sgòrnanach, adj., relating to the gullet, 38: 36 n.

sgreabag, f. small crust; used of land, pl., 26: 8

sgread, m. or f., screech, 1: 75

sgreamhaich, vb, disgust, sicken, 38: 30

sgriachail, f., screeching, 1: 16

sgrìobh, vb, write; vb n. *sgrìobhadh*, in pass. constr., 22: 65

sgrios, vb, destroy, 15: 72; vb n., 1: 4; 6: 7

sguab, vb, sweep, clean with a broom; pres./fut. pass. *sguabar*, 38: 19

sguairigeadh, vb n., from Eng. 'squaring', military term for a certain type of drill, 17: 14

sgùilleach, m., seaweed cast up on the shore, 14: 96

sguir, vb, stop, cease from, 13: 62, 73

sgùr, vb, scour clean; vb n. *sgùradh*, 39: 28

siabann, m., soap, 32: 80

siaman, variant of *sìoman*, m., straw rope, 2: 22

sian, m., particle, element, 26: 23; pl. *siantan*, the elements of the weather, 26: 31

siar, adv., in the west, 35: 7

sìn, vb, stretch out, lie; vb n. *sìneadh*, 10: 4; 21: 14; past part. *sìnte*, 10: 10 n.; 40: 39; *sìn air*, set about, start on, 1: 59

sinnsir, *sinnsre*, ancestors, 16: 33; 24: 24; 35: 17; *sinnsirean*, 16: 69

sìob, vb, make smooth; past part. *sìobte*, 8: 46

sìochail, adj., peaceful, 8: 3

sìochaire, m., contemptible fellow, 38: intro.

sìol, m., seed; descendants, 30: 27; dat. pl., 26: 9

sìolach, m., seed, progeny, 8: 21

sìor, adj. commonly used as adv. before vb n., continually, 25: 12

siorramachd, f., sheriffdom, shire, 29: 22

sìos, adv., down; in idiom *dol sìos*, lit. 'going down', i.e. charging down the slope in battle, advancing against the enemy, 8: 76

siorram, m., sheriff, 13: 33, 41

sir, vb, seek out, look for, 42: 28

siteag, f., dung-hill, muck-heap, 38: 27

sìth, f. peace, 16: 39, 83; 17: 3; 22: 52 etc.

sìthiche, m., fairy being; pl., 43: 37

siubhail, vb, travel, 22: 77

siùil-chinn, pl. of *seòl-cinn*, m., head-sail, probably jib-sail, of a ship, 7: 21

slabhraidh, f., chain, 2: 42

slacadh, m., act of beating, thrashing; used as vb n. in pass. constr., 16: 6

slacan, m., stick, club, baton; pl., 37: 31

slàn, adj., complete; in one piece, 44: 31

slànaich, vb, heal, restore, 14: 27

slaod, vb, drag, pull; vb n. *slaodadh*, 11: 22; 38: 16

slat mhara (‹ *slat*, f., rod + *mara*, gen. sg. of *muir*, m./f., sea), rod of tangle, i.e. stem or root of seaweed; dat. pl., 2: 22

sleamhainn, adj., slippery, smooth-surfaced, 8: 3

sliabh, m., moorland, high rough ground, 16: 80; 33: 29; 43: 56; *uachdar slèibh*, surface of a moorland, 14: 222

sliasaid, f., thigh, 2: 26; 13: 72

sliob, vb, stroke, rub, 14: 75

sliobadh, m., stroking, rubbing, smooth talking, 24: 26

sliochd, m., offspring, descendants, 15: 5; 16: 31; *fìor-shliochd*, true descendants, 14: 212

sliomair, m., flatterer, person who talks deceitfully; pl., 31: 24

slios, m., side, 1: 6

sloc, m., pit, 10: 9; 13: 64; 15: 100; 36: 12

slògh, m., 28: 22, variant of *sluagh*; see next entry

sluagh, m., people, population, 13: 9, 78; 14: 42; 15: 54 etc.; pl. *slòigh*, 14: 52, 234; 15: 72

sluic, gen. sg. of *sloc*, above

smachd, f., control, discipline, 1: 18; 19: 32; 14: 234

smachdaich, vb, subdue, discipline, 18: 32; 19: 10

smàl, m., ashes, embers; dat. pl., 2: 34

smalan, m., gloom, dejection, 1: 114; 11: 7

smaoint, f., thought; pl., 28: 98

smaointich, vb, think; vb n. *smaointinn*, 7: 3; see also *smuaintich*

smear, see *smior*, below

smearail, adj., vigorous, lively, 35: 45

smeòrach, m., thrush, 35: 14; pl., 30: 42

smig, f., chin, 38: 35

smior (also *smear*), m., marrow, essence, 32: 23; sometimes applied to the best of anything; perhaps 'good-quality animal', 17: 29

smiùradh, vb n. (< Scots *smuir*), smearing of sheep with tar (to prevent ticks etc.), 1: 96

smuaint, f., thought; pl., 3: 2

smuaintich, vb, think, 3: 21

smuairean, m., sorrow, dejection, 22: 4

smùid, vb, send flying, 19: 14

smùid, f., smoke, steam, 37: 38; see also *bàta*

smùr, m., dust, fragments, 21: 8; *gun smùr*, unspotted, 16: 24

snàigeach, adj., crawling, 14: 249

snaim, f., knot, 38: 8

snàmh, vb, swim; vb n., 12: 69

snasail, adj., handsome, beautiful, 40: 22

snàthainn, m., thread, 14: 177

snighe, f., drops of water through a roof; tears, 26: 2

snuadh, m., appearance, 43: 36

snuadhmhor, adj., of good appearance, 35: 5

socraich, vb, settle, lay down, 15: 89

sodal-cùirte, f., flattery in court, 24: 26

soilleir, adj., bright, clear, 8: 1; 14: 1; 44: 8

soillse, f., radiance, brightness (of a light or fire), 8: 67

soirbheachadh, see next entry

soirbhich, vb, prosper, 26: 26; vb n. *soirbheachadh*, used as n., m., progress, prosperity, 25: 6

soirbheas, m., fair wind at sea, 7: 13

soisgeul, m., gospel, 14: 43

soisgeulach, m., evangelist, 8: 99

sòlas, m., joy, 14: 193; 37: 53; 16: 59, 83; pl., 14: 15

sòlasach, adj., joyful, happy, 14: 51

sonas, m., happiness, joy, 6: 8; 18: 3

sonn, m., hero; pl., *suinn*, 16: 25

sònraichte, adj., particular, specific, 24: 15; 42: 22

soraidh, f., farewell greeting, parting salutation, 26: 25; *soraidh slàn*, a fond farewell, 11: 3; 24: 3

spaid, f., spade, spadeful, 9: 13

spàirn, f., struggle, 11: 38

sparr, vb, thrust, push in (with force); vb n. *sparradh*, 26: 12

spèis, f., esteem, regard, 30: 9; 32: 40

speur, m., sky; gen. pl., 8: 4, 58

spìd, f., spite, 14: 93

spìocach, adj., miserly, mean, 9: 23

spiorad, m., spirit, 14: title, 1, 2 etc.

spòrs, f., sport, 14: 102, 220; 15: title, 80, 86

spòrsail, adj., inclined to sport, 16: 61; 32: 38

spoth, vb, castrate, 1: 100

sprèidh, f., cattle, 1: 48; 5: 15; 8: 17 etc.

sprogan, m., crop of a bird, small tuft of hair under the chin of a deer, goat or ram; applied disparagingly to the gullet of a human, 38: intro.

spuaic, vb, break, splinter, knock on the head; vb n. *spuaiceadh*, 37: 27

spùill, f., plunder, pillage, 38: 41

spùinn, vb, plunder, rob; vb n. *spùinneadh*, 39: 8

spuirt, f., sport, 26: 19

srac, vb, tear; vb n. *sracadh*, 7: 21

srad, m., drop, 18: 28

sràic, otherwise *stràic*, f., pride, haughtiness, 34: 24; 36: 18

sràiceil, otherwise *stràiceil*, adj., proud, haughty 16: 11; 40: 7

sraid, f., street; pl., 37: 85

srath, m., strath, broad flat-bottomed valley, 1: 22; pl., 36: 13

sreath, m., row, drill (of potatoes), 28: 45

sreupa, see *streup*

sròl, f., satin, 22: 84; banner (originally one made of satin), 4: 22; 27: 19

sròn, f., nose, 2: 15; *mar sròin*, (thrust) before our noses, 26: 20

staid, f., state, condition, 14: 199; 22: 28; 34: 3

stàideil, adj., stately, well off, 29: 44

staillear, m., distiller; pl., 15: 62

stamh, m., stem of seeweed, kelp, 'tangle'; gen. pl., 9: 18

stèidh, f., foundation, 8: 49, 85

stiall, f., a small piece or slice, taken off a larger piece, 33: 35; pl., 32: 82

stiùir, f., helm, rudder, 12: 26; 18: 17

stiùir, vb, steer; vb n. *stiùireadh*, 12: 41

stob, vb, pierce, vb n. *stobadh*, 15: 76

stòiridh, f., story, 1: 59, 109

stòl, m., stool, seat, 43: 111

stòlda, adj., steady, well paced, 15: 84

stòras, m., wealth, substance, 7: 35; 11: 22; 14: 77 etc.

stràic, see *sràic*

stràiceil, see *sràiceil*

streup, f., struggle, strife, 26: 29; *sreupa*, 15: 18; *streupaid*, 12: 33

strì, vb n., striving, 24: 30; 43: 86; n., f., strife, contention, 34: 40; 37: 8, 56, 72; storm, 8: 4

strìochd, vb., submit, yield, 18: 24; 44: 42; bring into submission, vb n. *strìochdadh*, 36: 1; past part. *strìochdte*, 33: 33

stròdhaileach, m., prodigal person, waster; pl., 14: 216

stuagh, f., wave; gen. pl., 27: 10

stùc, m., hill, 22: 20; pl., 8: 19; gen. pl., 22: 20; dark cloud, 24: 20

suaicheantas, m., emblem, motto, 27: 5; 28: 79, 109

suaimhneach, adj., quiet, secure, enjoying luxury or ease, 14: 75; 22: 83

suain, vb, wrap; vb n. in passive constr., *suaineadh*, 37: 19; past part. *suainte*, wrapped, 1: 79

suairc, 15: 58, a reduced form of *suairceas*, q.v.

suairc(e), suairceil, adj., kindly, 14: 73, 172; 16: 10; 22: 5 etc.; with intensive *ro-*, exceedingly kind, 28: 69

suairceas, m., kindness, 32: 26

suarach, adj., mean, despicable, 15: 4; 22: 92; 28: 61, 68 etc.

suas, see under *cuir* and *thoir*

sùgan, m., straw rope, 38: 17

sùghadh, vb n., sucking, 1: 102

sùgradh, m., mirth, merriment, sport, 2: 6

suidhich, vb, settle, put in place, 15: 91

suilbhearra, adj., good-natured, hearty, 37: 84

suim, f., concern, care, 1: 26; 16: 64; 28: 114

suinn, see *sonn*

sumanadh, vb n. (< Engl. *summoning*), summonsing, serving with summons, 21: title, 1; pl. *sumanan*, 14: 243

sunndach, adj., joyful, spirited, cheery, 16: 26; 22: 19

tabaid, variant of *sabaid*, vb n., fighting, 32: 44

tàbhachdail, adj., efficient, effective, 13: 4

tachair, vb, meet, 1: 58

tagair, vb, plead a cause, claim (rights), 15: 98; 42: 32; *tagairt*, vb n., 27: 22

taigh-òsda, m., hostelry, 1: 90

taigh-seinnse, m., change-house, inn, public house, 20: 23; 21: 5

tàillear, m., tailor, 32: ascription

tainead, m., thinness; *cuir an tainead*, reduce numbers (of people), 11: 37-40 n.; *rach an tainead*, attenuate, 1: 29

tàir, f., shame, insult, disgrace, humiliation, 19: 30; 25: 11; 29: 47; *nach tàir*, who are not to be despised, 26: 30

tàirceach, adj., enticing, attractive, 14: 250

tàireil, adj., despicable, 36: 17

tairis, adj., compassionate, tender, kindly, 2: 20

talaich, vb, complain, murmur: vb n., 1: 65; 36: 13

tàlaidh, vb, entice; *a thàladh*, 28: 54

talamh, m. and f., land, 30: 56; ground, 42: 33; see also *aran*

tàmailt, f., humiliation, 35: 32

tàmailteach, adj., humiliated, 28: 55; humiliating, 28: 65

tàmailtich, vb, humiliate, 21: 40

tamall, m., short period; *car tamaill*,

for a little while, 7: 45

tàmh, m., rest, inactivity, 8: 6; 14: 26, 144; *am thàmh*, quiet, passive, 34: 1

tana, adj., thin, 2: 46; in number, 11: 39

taobh, m. or f., side, 3: 8; 13: 22

taod, f., halter, rope, 38: intro.

tapadh, m., strength, vigour, 42: 11, 35

tapaidh, adj., strong, vigorous, 14: 189; 27: 1; 42: 30

tàrlaidh, vb, happen, come about; pres./fut. rel. *thàrlas*, 22: 61

tàrr, m., ability, capability; *cha tàrr mi*, I am unable to, 14: 88

tarraing, vb n., pulling, attraction, 14: 24; 18: 22; dragging away, 38: 18

tatadh, vb n., enticing, 32: 85

teachd, vb n., coming, 1: 44; 14: 86; 24: 7

teachdaire, m., messenger; commissioner; gen. pl., 24: title, 1

teachdaireachd, f., message, report, 24: 33

teagaisg, vb., teach, 25: 17; 43: 83

teaghlach, m., family, 16: 51; pl., 12: 51

teanga, f. tongue; *cuideachd nan teang'*, people of the tongues, i.e., orators, 25: 24

teann, adj., tight, close, 14: 178; intense, hard-fought, 14: 118; used as adv., firmly, 1: 18; 16: 12

teann, vb, in idiom *teann ri*, set about, begin; vb n., 42: 5

teannaich, vb, tighten, 38: 8; vb n. *teannachadh*, tightening, 38: 36 n.; increasing, 11: 6

teàrainn, vb, save, convey safely; vb n. *teàrnadh*, 7: 15; 14: 198; 16: 68

teàrainn, vb, descend, come down (stair, hillside etc.); vb n. *teàrnadh*, 17: 29

tearb, vb, separate; vb n. in pass. constr. *tearbadh*, 16: 32

tearc, adj., scarce, 9: 32; 26: 29

teasairg, vb, save, rescue, 14: 214

teich, vb, flee, run away, 14: 58

teine, m., fire, 2: 7; 3: 11; 6: 12; pl. *teintean*, bonfires, 30: 37; *tein'-èibhinn*, lit. 'joyful fire', i.e. a bonfire, 10: 14

teinteach, adj., fiery, perhaps in sense

of 'inflamed', 14: 106

teis-mheadhoin, the very centre, 2: 8

teud, m., string (of musical instrument), 14: 70

teudach, adj., having musical strings; accompanied by stringed instruments, 1: 114

thairis, adv., across, overseas, 11: 35; 36: 15

thoir an àird, *thoir suas*, bring up; of a Parliamentary Bill or official report, bring forward, present, 24: 33; 33: 34; *thoir bharra chàich*, excel others, 17: 15

tì, m., person, individual, 15: 81; used of God, 15: 89

tiamhaidh, adj., sad, sorrowful, 8: 85

tig, vb, comes; in idiomatic phrases, *tig...air*, be concerned with, 1: 60; *tig...do*, befits, becomes, 40: 6

tighearna, m., lord, landlord; pl. *tighearnan*, 28: 4; gen. pl., 14: 163

tighearnas, m., lordship; *tighearnas fearainn*, landlordism, 38: intro.

tilg, vb, throw, 1: 94; 12: 67; be thrown down by a gun-shot, 13: 63

till, vb, return, 8: 70; repulse, repel, 33: 13; 34: 16; 35: 43; probably in sense of 'retreat', 20: 8; revert to, 28: 31

tìodhlaic, vb, bestow as a gift, 44: 38

tionail, vb, gather, 11: 14; 15: 70

tiormaich, vb, dry up, run dry, 31: 14

tiotal, m., title, 34: 25

tìr, f. land, 14: 198; 34: 35; 35: 4; *tìr chèin*, distant or foreign land, 25: 32; *tìr mòr*, mainland, solid ground, 7: 33

tiugh, adj., thick, 27: 4

tlàth, adj., gentle, 8: 22

tlus, m., genial warmth (of weather), 8: 58

tobar, m., well, 12: 54

tobhta, f., ruined wall of a house, 23: 14

todharail, adj., fit for dung or manure, 2: 37

tog, vb, raise, lift; *tog dàn*, raise a song, 11: 2

togradh, m., desire, inclination, 14: 105

toil, f. will, wish; *fhuair iad...an toil fhèin*, they got their own way, 25: 21

toill, vb, deserve, 14: 158; 15: 76; 20: 21

toillteanach, adj., deserving of; responsible for, 34: 33

tòir, f., pursuit, chase, 19: 3; 22: 76; 26: 19

toirm, f., loud noise, 14: 98

toiseach, m., front; *air thoiseach*, in the front line, 11: 34

toisg, f., perhaps 'hostile expedition, attack'; pl., 15: 19

tòisich, vb, begin, 13: 10; *tòisich air*, set about, 21: 22

toll, m., hole, 38: 5; applied to a prison-town, 35: 37

tolladh, vb n., holing, piercing, 13: 59

tom, m., hillock; gen. sg., *tuim*, 1: 32

tonn, m., wave; pl. *tuinn*, 18: 16, 44; pl., 35: 6; gen. pl., 7: 16; 30: 22

toradh. m., fruit, produce, 22: 87; 37: 91

torrach, adj, fertile, 35: 5

torrann, m., noise; applied to music, 38: 21

tòs, variant of *tùs*, q.v.

tosdach, adj., silent, quiet, 35: 1

tràigh, f., shore, beach, 6: 7; 8: 36; 9: 17

tràigh, vb, ebb, subside; vb n. *tràghadh*, 30: 55

tràill, m. or f., slave, thrall, 33: 22; in sense of rogue, rascal, 21: 16; pl., 16: 7; 18: 24; 35: 41 etc.; gen. pl., 14: 90

tràilleach, m., seaware of all kinds, 2: 50

tràth, adv., early, 3: 23; 28: 99

tràth, m., time, occasion; in phrase, *an tràth seo, an tràth-s'*, now, at this time, 12: 63, 66; 13: 74; 16: 71 etc.

tràth, m., meal, 28: 46; 43: 11; meal-time, 44: 32

treabh, vb, plough; fut. pass., 33: 27

trèig, vb, forsake, abandon, 1: 41; 14: 57, 66; 22: 73

treòraich, vb, lead, guide; vb n. *treòrachadh*, in pass. constr., 2: 40

treubh, m., kindred, 28: 59; pl., 22: 70

treud, m., herd, flock, 1: 62, 116; 6: 10; pl., 8: 10

treun, adj., brave, 28: 78; 32: 13; 34: 62 etc.; strong, 14: 24; used as subst, in *dùthaich nan treun*, 'the land of the brave', 15: 30; *treun-chath*, battle of strength, 15: 20; *treun-fhear*, m.,

strong man, warrior, gen. pl., 14: 191

trian, m., third part, 1: 71

triath, m., lord, leader, 43: 28; gen. pl., 24: 27

tric, adv., frequent, 13: 60; 35: 15

trìd, f., rag, piece of cloth, 10: 2

trì-fichead, sixty, 13: 77

tri-fillte, adv., threefold; at three times their value, 43: 87

triùbhsair, f., trousers, 2: 46

triùir, f., three people, 1: 89

tròcair, f., mercy, 3: 25; 15: 73; 16: 64 etc.

trod, m., quarrelling, reprimanding, 14: 247

truagh, adj., poor, 3: 18

truaghan, m., pitiful person, 9: 15; 42: 23; pl., 11: 20; gen. pl., 37: 31

truaigh(e), f., calamity, difficulty, poverty, perdition, 15: 79; pl. *truaighean*, 14: 112; 22: 100

truaill, vb, corrupt, pollute, 8: 20; abuse, 15: 8, 9

truailleachd, truaillidheachd, f., corruption, 14: 21, 109; 32: 24

truas, m., pity, 14: 198; 15: 6

truasail, adj., filled with pity, merciful, 32: 30

trusdair, m., rogue, worthless fellow, 38: intro.

tuaileas, m., defamation, slander, 35: 49

tuar, m., colour, appearance, 7: 20

tuarasdal, m., reward, payment, 28: 77, 82, 111

tuasaid, f., struggle, conflict, contention, 5: 10; 30: 30; 32: 25

tuath, f., tenantry, 1: 127; 8: 110; 12: 4; 32: 31; 38: 32; farm, 19: 16; *maigh-stirean tuatha*, lit. 'masters of the tenantry', feudal superiors, 4: 29; *tuath-cheathairn*, tenantry, rural people, 37: 46, 57

tuath, see *àird*

tuathach, adj., northerly, 36: 5

tuathail, adj., awkward, underhand, 19: 22; awry, out of joint, 14: 65

tuathanach, m., farmer, but loosely used of 'crofter', 19: title; pl., 37: 6

tuathanachas, m., farming, working

the land, 23: 19

tuig, vb, understand, 11: 2

tuigse, f., understanding, 25: 26

tuigseach, adj., comprehending, 16: 74

tuil, f., flood, 30: 55

tuilleadh, m., something or someone in addition; used as adv., further, any more, 11: 37; 17: 9; 21: 44

tuim, see *tom*

tùirn, f., turn, action, 4: 26; 17: 18

tulach, m. or f., hillock, 3: 10; 7: 1; pl. *tulaichean*, 11: 9

tulgadh, m., tossing about (on the sea), 18: 19

tur, adv., completely, 38: 42

tùrsa, f., sorrow, sadness, 7: 27

tùs, m., beginning, 16: 92; *air t(h)ùs*, at the outset, 28: 40; 29: 28; in the front line, 37: 7

uabhair, m., pomp, pride, vain-glory, 14: 116, 242

uachdar, m., top, surface, 3: 4; 9: 7; 42: 24

uachdaran, m., landlord, 14: 237; 19: title; 22: 90 etc.; pl., 16: 11, 34; 19: 2; 22: 81 etc.; gen. pl., 42: 21

uaibhreach, adj., proud; used as n., proud person; pl., 12: 50

uaigh, f., grave, 3: 24; 9: notes

uaigneach, adj., lonely, remote, 8: 11; 11: 9; 35: 14; 24: 7

uaigneas, m., solitude, 3: 30

uaill, f., pride, source of pride, 35: 26; *dèan uaill à*, boast about someone or something, 43: 112

uaimh-mheul, f., louse; pl., 1: 80

uaine, adj., green, 35: 13

uair, f., time, hour, 35: 40; *uairibh* (dat. pl. of *uair*), adv., sometimes, 22: 51

uaisle, f., nobility, noble status, 19: 30; 26: 16; noble-heartedness, generosity, 35: 39

uaisleachd, f., nobleness (of character), 14: 67

uallach, adj., cheerful, playful, 9: 5; 11: 29; 38: 13

uamhann, adj., terrifying, 14: 187

uamhar, m., pride, fear-inspiring arrogance, 15: 99

uamharrachd, f., horror, frightfulness,

14: 93, 134; 15: 82

uamhas, m., horror, 37: 29

uamhasach, adj., terrible; with intensive *ro-*, very terrible, 28: 81

uamh-bhiasd, f., terror-inducing beast, monster, 15: 81

uan, m., lamb, 13: 59; pl., 9: 32; gen. pl., 1: 112

uasal, adj. and n., noble, 24: 4; 26: 16; 31: 2, 7; superl. 37: 17; pl. *uaislean*, 1: 125; 22: 89; 28: 64; 29: 26; *duin'-uasal*, 28: 105, 107; *daoin' uaisle*, noble folk, aristocrats, 12: 35, 66; *uasal as*, proud of, 28: 57

uchd, m., chest, breast; *air uchd a' chuain*, on the breast of the ocean, 24: 8

ùghdarras, m., authority, 39: 8

uidheam, f., equipment; *uidheam ghiùlain*, means of conveyance, transport, 21: 6

uileann, f., elbow; *air m' uilinn*, resting on my elbow, 41: 9

ùilleadh, m., oil, 2: 47

ùine, f., period of time, 22: 26

ùir, f., earth, soil, 9: 13; 15: 93

uiread, as much; a certain amount, 31: 15; with negative, *cha deach uiread is*, not even (as much as), 36: 4

uisge-beatha, m., whisky, 10: 7

uireasbhaidh, f., poverty, lack, 25: 6; 44: 20, 32

ullaich, vb, prepare; vb n. in pass. constr., *ullachadh*, 34: 37

ullamh, adj., ready, prepared, 34: 30, 58

ùmaidh, m., dolt, blockhead; pl., 16: 4

umhalta, adj., obedient, 19: 9

ungte, past part. of *ung*, anoint, 38: intro.

ùrail, adj., flourishing, fresh, 8: 51

ùrlar, m., floor, 38: 20; pl., 8: 102

ùrnaigh, f., prayer, 37: 89

urram, m., honour, 11: 38; 17: 23; 29: 17 etc.

urramach, adj., honourable, 34: 61; 44: 40, 52; as n., m., reverend person, minister, 30: 48; 42: 2, 37

BIOGRAPHICAL AND GENERAL INDEXES

INDEX 1

BIOGRAPHICAL INDEX OF POETS

Bàillidh, Dòmhnall / Baillie, Donald: Nothing is known of this poet, except that he was connected with the county of Sutherland, and was alive in the second decade of the nineteenth century. Poem 2.

Dùghallach, Ailean / MacDougall, Allan (c.1750-1828): Born in Glencoe, **Ailean Dall** ('Blind Allan') became poet to Alasdair Ranaldson MacDonell of Glengarry c.1798. He composed panegyric and satiric verse and a couple of poems commemorating the arrival of steamships. See Dùghalach 1829. Poem 1.

Mac a' Ghobhainn, Iain / Smith, John (1848-81): A native of Iarsiadar, Uig, Lewis, Smith studied medicine at Edinburgh University, but his studies were terminated by illness around 1874. Some of his verse, of which a fair amount survives, is within the genre of the township bard, but his finest poems reflect wider perspectives. See MacLeòid 1916: 67-131. Poems 14, 15.

MacAoidh, Gilleasbaig / MacKay, Archibald: MacKay was apparently a crofter in the Easdale district of Argyll. He was imprisoned briefly in the Calton Jail, Edinburgh, for his part in local land agitation in the late 1880s. Poem 41.

MacCaluim, An t-Urramach Dòmhnall / MacCallum, Rev. Donald: See Index 2. Poem 43.

MacDhòmhnaill, Cailean / MacDonald, Colin (d. 1943): Known locally as **Cailean Fhearchair** ('Colin son of Farquhar'), MacDonald belonged to Balephuil, Tiree, and is regarded as the last of the many traditional Gaelic bards associated with that township. See Cregeen and MacKenzie 1978: 16. Poem 34.

MacDhòmhnaill, Dòmhnall / MacDonald, Donald: Apart from his link with Greenock, no other details of this poet are known. Poem 27.

MacDhunlèibhe, Uilleam / Livingston, William (1808-70): Born in Kilarrow, Islay, Livingston became a tailor, and worked mainly in Glasgow. Largely self-taught, he had a deep antiquarian interest in Scottish history and, beyond his native Gaelic, acquired a smattering of classical and modern languages. He composed long 'epic' poems and shorter pieces in which he hammered out his response to what he saw as the attrition and maltreatment of the Gaels. See Livingston 1882. Poem 8.

MacFhionghain, Dòmhnall / MacKinnon, Donald: Apart from his being resident in Glasgow in the 1880s, nothing further is known about MacKinnon. Poem 26.

MacFhionghain, Teàrlach / MacKinnon, Charles: MacKinnon was a native of Kilmuir, Skye, and evidently a crofter, but no more details about him are known. Poem 23.

MacIlleathain, Alasdair / MacLean, Alexander: A native of Glendale, Skye, MacLean (probably born c.1860) was known locally as **Alasdair Dhòmhnaill** ('Alasdair son of Donald'). He composed several songs on land agitation in Glendale in the 1880s, some of which have survived in newspapers and oral transmission. Poems 20, 22.

MacIlleathain, Iain / MacLean, John (1827-95): Born in Tiree, he lived in Balemartin in the south-west of the island, and was known as **Bàrd Bhaile Mhàrtainn** ('The Balemartin Bard'). He composed several songs on themes

connected with the local land agitation, and was in effect
the poet of the local branch of the Highland Land Law
Reform Association. His more popular love songs and his
timeless satire on his neighbour, Calum Beag, are still well
known. See Cameron 1932: 142-87; Cregeen and Mac-
Kenzie 1978: 19-22. Poems 11, 24, 30, 31, 35.

MacIlleathain, Iain / MacLean, John: A crofter from
Drynie Park, Mulbuie, near Muir of Ord in the Black Isle,
MacLean (born c.1850) was appointed poet to his local
branch of the Highland Land Law Reform Association in
1885. He was known locally as 'The Bard', and his family
(currently represented at Drynie Park by Tommy Mac-
Lean, to whom I am indebted for information) is still
'styled' in that way. Poem 29.

MacIlleathain, Murchadh / MacLean, Murdo: Mac-
Lean belonged to Waternish, Skye, but nothing further is
known about him. Poem 42.

MacLachlainn, Iain / MacLachlan, John (1804-74):
MacLachlan was from Rahoy, Ardnamurchan, although
his kindred, the MacLachlans of Dunadd, belonged to Mid
Argyll. He trained as a doctor at Glasgow University.
Despite his aristocratic connections, he had much sympathy for the ordinary people of his district; traditions
about his physical strength and great kindness survived in
Mull and Ardnamurchan into the twentieth century. He
composed a number of love songs and several poems
commenting on the Clearances. Poem 3.

MacLeòid, Murchadh / MacLeod, Murdo (1837-
1914): Known popularly as **Murchadh a' Cheisteir**
('Murdo, son of the Catechist'), MacLeod was born in
Leurbost, Lewis. He was a temperance agent and evangelist, based in Glasgow, and is best known as a composer of
hymns, some of which have remained popular. See Mac-
Leod 1962. Poem 13.

MacLeòid, Murchadh / MacLeod, Murdo: MacLeod belonged to Bru in Barvas, Lewis, but, apart from his keen interest in local politics, no more details have been recovered. Poem 28.

MacLeòid, Niall / MacLeod, Neil (1843-1913): A native of Pollosgain, Glendale, Skye, MacLeod was born into a family with some conspicuous bardic talent, his father, **Dòmhnall nan Oran** ('Donald of the Songs'), having published a booklet of songs in 1811. MacLeod went south to Edinburgh, where he became a traveller in the tea business owned by his cousin, Roderick MacLeod. His immensely popular poetry blended moral instruction with a sentimental attachment to his homeland. See MacLeòid 1975. Poem 16.

MacPhàil, Calum Caimbeul / MacPhail, Calum Campbell (1847-1913): Born in the parish of Muckairn, Argyll, he was apprenticed as a shoemaker in Inveraray. As a poet, MacPhail won initial acclaim for a piece on the marriage of the Marquis of Lorne and Princess Louise, but his later verse displays a more radical turn of mind. He worked as a shoemaker in Dalmally for most of his life. See MacPhàil 1947. Poems 12, 18, 19.

MacRatha, Iain / MacRae, John: MacRae belonged to the Lochcarron district, where he was evidently a crofter in the mid-1880s. No further details are known. Poem 33.

Niall Ceannaiche ('Neil the Merchant') / Neil MacPherson (c.1834-1924): Son of Angus MacPherson and Ann Stewart, Niall Ceannaiche was living in Scorr, at the mouth of Portree Loch, in 1861. By the 1880s he was resident in Gedintailor, Braes, Skye, where he composed popular local verse. See Nicolson 1994: 289. (I am very grateful to Dr Alasdair Maclean, Aird Bhearnasdail, Portree, for biographical details.) Poem 17.

Nic-a'-Phearsain, Màiri / MacPherson, Mary (1821-98): Popularly known as **Màiri Mhòr nan Oran** ('Big

Mary of the Songs'), Mary MacPherson was a native of Skye. Her verse, which was stimulated by a miscarriage of justice in 1872, combined her own personal sorrow with the suffering of her fellow Gaels, set against a realistic and hauntingly attractive portrayal of Skye. She removed from Inverness following the death of her husband and her allegedly unjust 'humiliation', and worked in Glasgow and Greenock in later life, retiring to Skye in 1882. See Nic-a-Phearsoin 1891 and Meek 1977b. Poems 37, 38.

Peuton, Uilleam / Beaton, William: A native of Kilmuir, Skye, Beaton was one of a group of crofters who served a prison sentence in the Calton Jail, Edinburgh, early in 1887. Poem 40.

Ròs, Uisdean / Rose (or Ross), Eugene: Rose (or Ross) was a crofter in Mull from the 1840s to the 1870s. Poem 10.

INDEX 2

BIOGRAPHICAL INDEX OF
POLITICAL AND OTHER MAJOR FIGURES

Camashron, Iain Dòmhnallach / Cameron, John MacDonald (1847-1912) (Poem 29: 28): Born at Ballantrae, Ayrshire, Cameron entered the Inland Revenue service in 1866, and having worked at Somerset House as an Assistant Chemist (1871-74), became an instructor in the Chemical Research Laboratory of the Royal School of Mines (1874-79). He travelled extensively, and wrote a series of papers on aspects of minerology. An advanced Liberal in favour of Irish Home Rule, Cameron held the seat of the Northern Burghs from 1885 until his defeat in 1892. Thereafter he went to Australia, where he became the Master of the Sydney Mint. Latterly he developed an interest in the Borneo oilfields (Stenton and Lees 1978: 55).

Clarc, An Dotair / Clark, Dr Gavin Brown (1846-1930), M.D., F.R.C.S. (Edin.), L.R.C.P. (Edin.) (Poem 29: 32): Born at Kilmarnock, Clark wrote a number of pamphlets on the land question, South Africa, India and some social issues. Prior to 1891 he was Consul-General of the South African Republic. A Radical Liberal in favour of federal Irish Home Rule, he held his seat in Caithness from 1885 to 1900, when he failed to gain readoption because of his allegedly pro-Boer sympathies. He unsuccessfully contested the Cathcart division of Glasgow as a Labour candidate in 1918 (Stenton and Lees 1978: 66).

Collings, Jesse (1831-1920) (Poem 29: 36): Collings was a native of Exmouth, Devon, who moved to Birmingham, where he was in business as a merchant until 1879. He was also active as a Common Councilman for the Edgbaston Ward (1868-75), and was Mayor of Birmingham from 1878 to 1879. He was a Unionist, and sat as a Radical Liberal for Ipswich from 1880 to 1886, when he was unseated on petition in April. He was elected as a Liberal Unionist for the Bordesley division of Birmingham in July 1886, and sat until he retired in 1918.

Collings was founder of the Allotments and Small Holdings Association, and President of the Rural Labourers' League. In Parliament he moved the Small Holdings Resolution, regretting the omission from the Speech from the Throne of measures benefiting the rural labourer. The carrying of the resolution caused the resignation of Lord Salisbury's administration on 21st January 1886 (Collings and Green 1920: 182-4; Stenton and Lees 1978: 71). Salisbury had held power after the General Election of November-December 1885 with the support of the Irish Party (the so-called "86 of '86", whose alliance with the Conservatives was critical to the delicate balance of power, the Conservatives having gained 249 seats and the Liberals 335 in the election). By January 1886 Salisbury had decided against handling the Home Rule issue, and, with the collapse of his caretaker government, the Irish Party switched their support to Gladstone (see Gladstone, William Ewart).

Collings was also a vice-president of the Highland Land Law Reform Association (Hunter 1974: 51). The reference to Collings in the same context as the main pro-crofter Highland M.P.s suggests that he was regarded as a strong supporter of the crofters' cause.

Dòmhnallach, An Dotair / MacDonald, Dr Roderick (1840-94), L.R.C.P. and S. (Edin. 1867), F.R.C.S. (Edin. 1883), M.D. (Durham 1883) (Poem 28: 17; 29: 4-27): Born at Fairy Bridge, Skye, MacDonald was the son of Angus MacDonald, joiner, and Elizabeth, daughter of R. Mac-Neil, merchant of Stein, Skye. His crofting connections are emphasised in 29: 4-7 because he and G. B. Clark were accused of being 'carpet-baggers' by the *Scotsman* newspaper. A physician and surgeon, MacDonald practised in

Millwall, and later became coroner for N.E. Middlesex. He was a vice-president of the Highland Land Law Reform Association, and treasurer to the London Crofters' Aid and Defence Fund. An advanced Liberal and anti-Parnellite Home Ruler, he held his seat until 1892 (Stenton and Lees 1978: 230-1; MacPhail 1979: 389-90).

Friseal Mac-an-Tòisich, Teàrlach / Fraser-Mackintosh, Charles, of Drummond (1828-1901) (Poems 27: 23; 29: 46): A native of Inverness and a solicitor in the town from 1853 to 1867, Fraser-Mackintosh was M.P. for Inverness Burghs from 1874 to 1885. Continuing as a Liberal Unionist, he held the county of Inverness from 1885 until his defeat by Dr Donald MacGregor in 1892, the latter being a Gladstonian Liberal and therefore in favour of Irish Home Rule. He was a member of the Napier Commission, and an early and very influential supporter of the crofters' cause (Stenton and Lees 1978: 128-9; Mac-Phail 1979: 385-6).

George, Henry: see **Seòras, Eanraig.**

Gladstone, William Ewart (1809-98): British Liberal Prime Minister during four Ministries (1868-74, 1880-85, 1886, 1892-94) (Poem 30: 58). Born in Liverpool, Gladstone entered politics as Tory M.P. for Newark in 1832, but became a Liberal, representing South Lancashire (1865-68), Greenwich (1870-80) and Midlothian (1880-95). The Third Reform Act of 1884, which enfranchised, among others, the male crofting population, was passed during his second Ministry. His third Ministry, which began late in January 1886, following the defeat of Salisbury's Tory government (see Collings, Jesse), produced the Crofters' Holdings (Scotland) Act of 1886. This ministry was insecure because of Gladstone's conversion (in December 1885) to Irish Home Rule, which he had previously opposed. This had the effect of splitting the Liberal party, and alienating the Radical Liberal, Joseph Chamberlain, later to become a member of Salisbury's Conservative-

Unionist government of 1895. Opposed by Chamberlain and his supporters, Gladstone's first Home Rule Bill was defeated in June 1886, and his government fell.

MacCaluim, an t-Urr. Dòmhnall / MacCallum, Rev. Donald (1849-1929) (Poems 27: 9; 30: 48; 42): Born in Barravulin, Craignish, Argyll, MacCallum was a Church of Scotland minister. He was the most prominent Presbyterian clergyman to support the crofters' cause. His 'calls' came strategically from parishes where there was strong anti-landlord resistance, and he gave himself fully to the crofters and cottars. He was minister successively in Morvern (as assistant), Arisaig and South Morar (1882-84), Waternish (Skye) (1884-87), Heylipol (Tiree) (1887-89) and Lochs (Lewis) (1889-1920). He was known for his preaching of the 'land gospel', a form of what would now be termed 'liberation theology'. Drawing the wrath of many of his clerical contemporaries, he was arraigned before the Presbytery of Skye in 1886 and censured. He was briefly imprisoned in Skye for 'inciting the lieges to violence and class hatred', precisely the same charge as has been levelled against certain Roman Catholic priests in some present-day, Third World countries. He was released without trial (Meek 1977a; 1987). Composer of Poem 43.

MacPhàrlain, Dòmhnall / MacFarlane, Donald Horne (1830-1904) (Poems 27: 19; 29: 45; 30; 31; 32; 34: 53): A native of Caithness, MacFarlane spent his early years in Australia, and then pursued a commercial career in Calcutta. On his return to Britain he became interested in Irish politics, allegedly through the influence of his wife. He became a Roman Catholic, and in 1880 he was elected as M.P. for Co. Carlow in Ireland, but, as a Liberal Home Ruler, he became uneasy with Parnell's hardening line in the British parliament, and relinquished the seat in 1885. (See Parnell, C.S.) As the Land Agitation developed in the Highlands, he took an interest in Highland affairs, and his speeches on behalf of the crofters earned him the nickname, 'the Member for Skye'. From 1878 to 1885 the Argyll constituency was held by Lord Colin Campbell, but, because of domestic difficulties, he decided not to contest the seat in the General Election of November-December 1885. MacFarlane, as the Radical Liberal candidate of the Highland Land Law Reform Association (known as the Land League after 1886), then won the seat by a margin of about 500 votes over William MacKinnon of Balinakill, an Independent.

Gladstone's short-lived third Ministry fell in June 1886. By an ironic twist, MacFarlane lost his seat in the following General Election of 15th July 1886, little more than a week before the Land Agitation reached its height in Tiree and troops were dispatched to quell the unrest. As Gladstone had refused to sanction further military intervention in the Highlands, the troops were sent under the authority of Lord Salisbury's new Conservative administration (see Gladstone, William Ewart).

MacFarlane's defeat was due to several factors. The Duke of Argyll, originally a Whig who had left the Liberal party because of its emerging Radical tendencies, regarded MacFarlane as 'a thorough blackguard', and strongly supported the Conservative candidate, Lieut.-Col. John W. Malcolm of Poltalloch (see below), who was successful; MacKinnon of Balinakill emphasised MacFarlane's Roman Catholic interests in his earlier campaign, and appears to have done so again in 1886; and the issue of Irish Home Rule, which led to the collapse of Gladstone's third Ministry and to a split in the Liberal party, undoubtedly played a significant part in MacFarlane's defeat. Mac-Farlane was in favour of Home Rule, and this led to further emphasis on his religious affiliations and Irish interests.

Other Radical Land League M.P.s who, in line with party policy, supported Irish Home Rule – but who were not directly linked with Ireland and were not Roman Catholics – were able to retain their seats in 1886, and another seat (see Sutherland, Angus) was won for the League. In 1892, however, MacFarlane regained the Argyll seat, holding it until 1895. By contrast, Charles Fraser-

Mackintosh, the Land League M.P. for Inverness from 1885 and an opponent of Home Rule, lost his seat in 1892. The winner was another Land League candidate and a Home Ruler, Dr Donald MacGregor. This demonstrates that Home Rule had again become an issue with some measure of popular support. Gladstone drew up his second Home Rule Bill, which passed through the Commons, but failed to go through the Lords, in 1893.

The contest between Fraser-Mackintosh and MacGregor for the Inverness seat shows that the Land League was itself rent by discord at this stage, largely on account of its increasing identification with Gladstonian Liberalism and the loss of its older Highland identity. As the pro-Gladstone wing emerged, a more radical element, which (despite his close allegiance to Gladstone) included MacFarlane, reconstituted the old Highland Land Law Reform Association. Yet MacFarlane's political career was soon to be at an end. Even though he retained a Radical interest, he accepted a knighthood in 1894, and his second tenure of the Argyll seat corresponded closely in time to Gladstone's fourth Ministry (1892-94), outlasting it by only the remaining year of Liberal government under Lord Rosebery (*Who Was Who* 1967: 451; Hunter 1974; Stenton and Lees 1978: 231, 239-40; MacPhail 1979; MacPhail 1985; Meek 1995).

MacRath, Dòmhnall / MacRae, Donald, 'The Alness Martyr', later known as 'Balallan' (1851-1924) (Poem 44: 37-44): A native of Plockton, MacRae was a schoolmaster who played a leading role in land agitation in Easter Ross and in Lewis. Having held a teaching post initially in Inverness High School, MacRae moved in 1879 to Bridgend School, Alness, Ross-shire, where he was Head Teacher. A series of moves by the School Board to dismiss him was initiated after he had given his school a day's holiday when the Land League held its annual conference at Bonar Bridge in 1886, since so many parents would be attending the meeting. The resulting dismissal became a *cause célèbre* in the district, with MacRae maintaining that the charges against him had been trumped up. His re-application for his job was unsuccessful, but he secured a post at Balallan School, Lewis, on 17th January 1887. There he provided the 'ideological stimulus' for the raid against Park Deer Forest in 1887 (Orr 1982: 139). Along with other local leaders, he stood trial in Edinburgh in January 1888 on charges of incitement to riot, but the charges were dismissed. Later MacRae contested Inverness after Dr Donald MacGregor relinquished the seat in 1895 in protest at the tardiness of the Liberal government in introducing legislation to abolish the deer forests. Mac-Rae's campaign (in which he chose the Gladstonian Liberal M.P. for Leith, none other than Munro-Ferguson of Novar, as his touring companion) was unsuccessful (Gibson 1986: 19 ff.).

Malcolm, John Wingfield, of Poltalloch (1833-1902) (Poems 31: 16; 32: 22): Born in London, Malcolm was a Lieutenant-Colonel in the Argyllshire Highland Rifle Volunteers and a Captain in the Kent Artillery Militia. A Conservative in politics and also a Unionist, he was M.P. for Boston from 1860 to 1878. He resigned his Boston seat in order to contest Argyll, but was unsuccessful in 1878 and in 1880. Winning Argyll from Donald H. MacFarlane in 1886, he held it until 1892. He was awarded the honour of C.B. in 1892, and became the 1st Baron Malcolm of Poltalloch in 1896. He owned over 85,000 acres (Stenton and Lees 1978: 239-40). See also Poem 5, notes.

Parnell, Charles Stewart (1846-91) (Poem 32: 6): A native of Co. Wicklow, Ireland, Parnell was elected as an M.P. for Co. Meath in 1875, and in 1877 became the leader of the Irish Home Rule movement. Using obstructionist tactics in the House of Commons in order to attract attention to the Irish situation, he was arrested and imprisoned in 1881 in Kilmainham Prison, Dublin, for inciting defiance among the Irish, but was later released by Gladstone. He was an ardent supporter of Gladstone's first

Home Rule Bill (see Collings, Jesse, and Gladstone, William Ewart). His political career was effectively terminated in 1890 as a result of a divorce case involving his mistress, Katherine O'Shea, the wife of one of his colleagues (Palmer 1986: 223-4).

Poltalloch: See **Malcolm, John Wingfield.**

Seòras, Eanraig / George, Henry (1839-97) (Poem 25): Known as the 'Prophet of San Francisco', George was an American economist and political thinker. From a humble background, he was largely self-educated, and worked as a land-prospector and newspaper man in San Francisco. He developed radical theories of taxation, and advocated the redistribution of wealth. His book, *Progress and Poverty*, published in 1879, became very influential, and contributed strongly to the growth of socialism in Britain (Palmer 1986: 128).

Sutharlanach, Aonghas / Sutherland, Angus (1848-1922) (Poem 29: 42): A native of Helmsdale, Sutherland studied at Glasgow University, and became a mathematics teacher at Glasgow Academy. A Liberal in favour of Irish Home Rule, he contested Sutherland in 1885, but was unable to defeat the so-called 'Radical Marquis', i.e. the Marquis of Stafford, eldest son and heir of the Duke of Sutherland. Stafford's conversion to Radicalism gained support from influential Free Church ministers, and he won by 1,701 votes to 1,085. Nevertheless, Sutherland gained the seat in the 1886 election, and held it until 1895, when he became Chairman of the Scotch Fishery Board (Stenton and Lees 1978: 344; MacPhail 1979: 386-9).

INDEX 3

GENERAL

The index gives a poem number and line reference, followed where relevant by *n.* = 'line note' or *notes* = 'introductory notes to the poem', usually the 'Date and Context' section following each poem.